HIDDEN SHADOWS

An Opening to the Windows of the Mind

By

Leonard A. Sharkey

Shimmer in the Moments
Then Search the Shadows

Leonard A. Sharkey

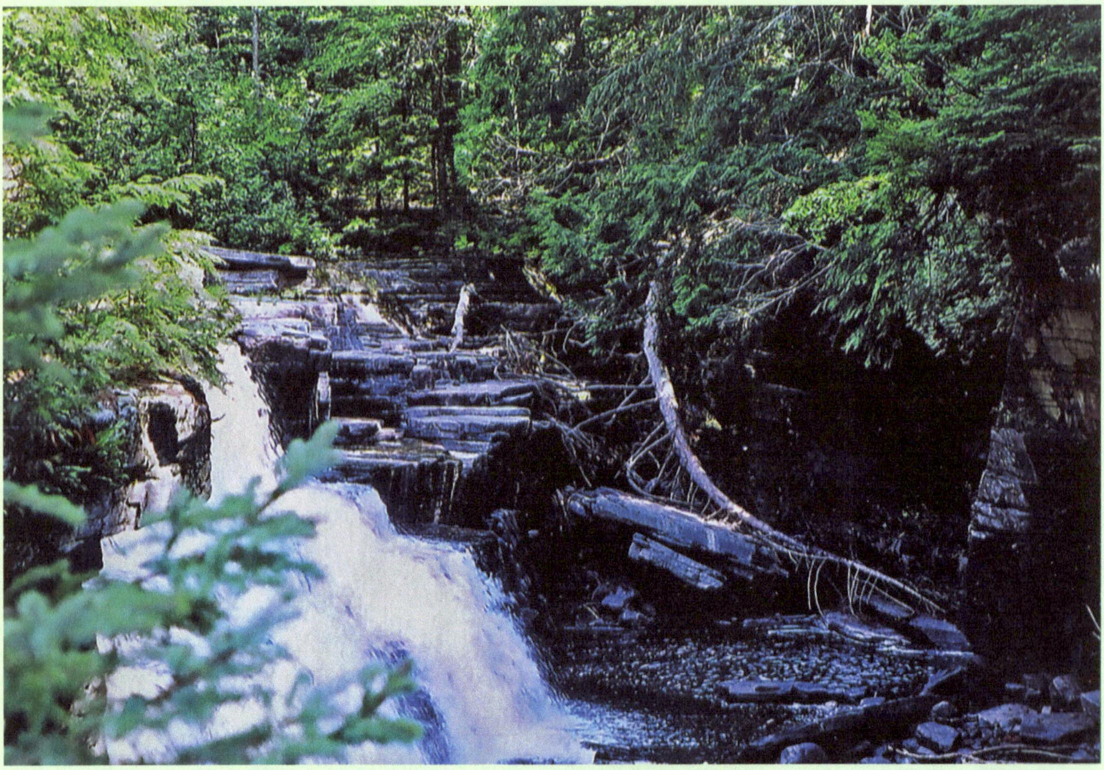

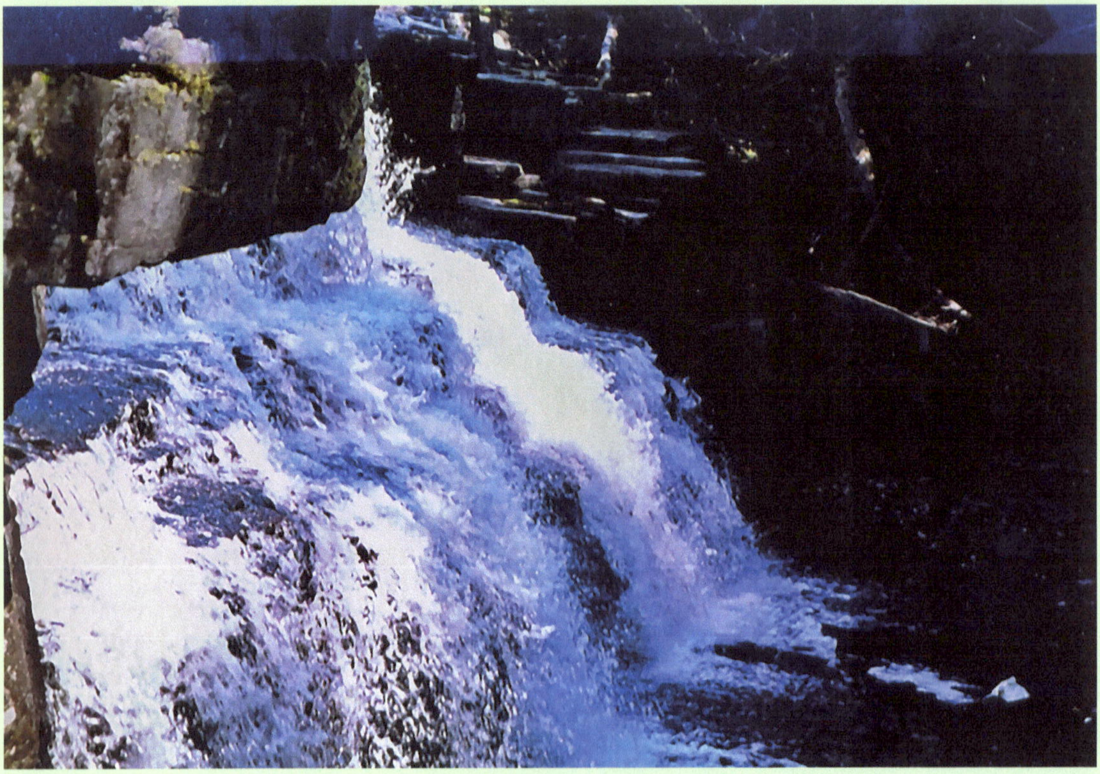

A SPARKLING CASCADE
LIKE A CRYSTALS SHIMMER,
WE ENTER LIFE
WITH MORE THAN A GLIMMER

FROM THE DEPTHS OF UNKNOWN
A NEW PLACE WE FIND HOME,
AND TRAVEL OUR TIME
TO FIND REASON AND RHYME

FIRST TO BLOSSOM
A PATH TO FIND,
THE WORLD BEGINS TO COMBINE

PLEASURED MOMENTS ALONG THE PATH
THE SCENT OF WONDER,
BECKONS SWEET WANDER

SAND AND WATER
WE'RE BOTH SON AND DAUGHTER

FARTHER WE TRAVEL
SEEKING THE ANSWERS,
AS WANDERING DANCERS

THE VOYAGE WE TAKE
WE TAKE FOR OUR SAKE

WISDOM IS BROUGHT
OR MAYBE IT COMES,
AS WE SAIL TO OUR OWN DISTANT DRUMS

THE RETURN TO THE SHORE
CAN BE RUGGED IN STORE,
SHOULD WE LOOK FOR MORE

LIKE A GOLDEN EAGLE
WE REST IN COOL AND WARY REPOSE
WAITING THE MOMENTS
TO THE KNOWING THAT HEAVEN KNOWS

THEN TO VENTURE AGAIN
WE TAKE TO FLIGHT

THIS TIME TO SOAR
TO LOFTY HEIGHT

HOPING TO FIND
CLEAR VISION IN SIGHT

BUT FROM THIS NEW VANTAGE
THE TRUTH CAN BE SEEN

THE CRYSTALS THAT SHIMMERED
FROM DEPTHS OF UNKNOWN

BLOSSOMED THE PATH
IN LIFE'S QUEST TO BE KNOWN

DANCED THE WAVES OF THE VOYAGE,
JOURNEYED IN WISDOM BE SOUGHT

TO RETURN TO THE SHORE,
HOPING PEACE BE MORE

RESTING AND WEARY,
WAITING THE MOMENT

WE FIND IN THE GLIMMER,
THE CASCADE
HAS BECOME A PROMENADE

PEACE IS THE HORIZON
AND LOVE IS THE BRIDGE,
TO THE MOMENT WE SIGH

MOMENTS
a poem of Life

A sparkling cascade
Like a crystals shimmer,
We enter Life
With more than a glimmer.

From depths of unknown
A new place we find home,
And travel our time
To find reason and rhyme.

First to blossom
A path to find,
The world begins to combine.

Pleasured moments along the path
The scent of wonder,
Beckons sweet wander.

Sand and water
We're both son and daughter.

Farther we travel
Seeking the answers,
As wandering dancers.

The voyage we take
We take for our sake.

Wisdom is brought
Or maybe it comes,
As we sail to our own
Distant drums.

The return to the shore
Can be rugged in store,
Should we look for more?

Like a Golden Eagle
We rest in cool and wary repose.

Waiting the moments
To the knowing that
Heaven knows.

Then to venture again
We take to flight.

This time to soar
To Lofty height.

Hoping to find
Clear vision in sight.

But from this new vantage
The truth can be seen.

The crystals that shimmered
From depths of unknown.

Danced the waves of the voyage,
Journeyed in wisdom
Be sought.

To return to the shore,
Hoping peace be more.

Resting and weary,
Waiting the moment.

We find in the glimmer,
The cascade
Has become a promenade.

Peace is the horizon
And love is the bridge,
To the moment we sigh..

by: *Leonard A. Sharkey*

Leonard A. Sharkey

HIDDEN SHADOWS

An Opening to the Windows of the Mind

By

Leonard A. Sharkey

ISBN: 1-4196-6908-7
ISBN-13: 9781419669088
Library of Congress Control Number: 2007903899

Visit www.booksurge.com to order additional copies.

CREDITS

Portraits and Sketches
By
Miriam Marcus
Fine Artist

Calligraphy
By
Rose Marie Muno
Calligraphy Artist

Photography
By
Leonard A. Sharkey

Word Processing and Editing
By
Advantage Services
Ann Stewart
Roanoke, Texas

Period Photographs
And Engraving of
Andrew Jackson Davis

Courtesy of
Dutchess County Historical Society
Poughkeepsie, New York

Photographs of the
Edgar Cayce Foundation
By
Leonard A. Sharkey

Courtesy of
The Edgar Cayce Foundation
Virginia Beach, Virginia

Photographs Involving
Thomas Edison
By
Leonard A. Sharkey

Courtesy of
Henry Ford Museum and
Greenfield Village
Dearborn, Michigan

Photographs of Sailing Ships
By
Leonard A. Sharkey

Courtesy of
Tall Ships
Traverse City, Michigan

Scanning – Photo Copy – Electronic Support
By
Business Imaging Group
Brighton, Michigan

DEDICATION

This book is dedicated to that which is not seen but is known and to those who are able to contemplate the meanings, presence and influences that envelope us, and of that which follows!

Ponder the more, for this opens the door.

PREFACE

Hidden Shadows is an achievement in understanding the human composition of physical and spiritual being that we continuously live and ponder, and is the result of seven years of intense effort.

The effort in research and experience has brought forth a commentary to the extraordinary aspects of life that are normal to life, yet are an obscurity within it. The expanse of text is presented as a comparative analytic criticism of the works and lives of the multitude of men and women addressed within its pages.

All of these men and women have publicly stepped forward of the line that many consider to be the containment of "normal life"! Their associations, precepts, and presentations to the societies of their time, and thus ours, form basis to expansion of knowledge offered within the pages of revelation that follow.

While the text holds strongly to the subject of the unseen realities of the physical and spiritual confederacy that's shown uniquely in each individual, this main topic allows sharing of personal thoughts and experiences that form a sub-topic to the stream and depth of presented knowledge.

The personal sharing is intended to allow you, the reader, the opportunity to open yourself in comparison to your own inner feelings, beliefs, and experiences. By combining the concept of triplicity to the process of reading, I believe that the reader will find a place in the midst of the prominent presented, the personal presented, and the personal invited.

You are personally invited to be part of the triplicity of heart, mind, and spirit that we all are.

TABLE OF CONTENTS

- "The Black Virgin"

- Mt. Athos

- The Khlisti

- Kama Sutra

- Nicholas II - Tsar

- Alexandra - Tsarista

- Alexis - Tsarevitch

- Seances

- M. Philippe

- Collective Unconscious

- Transference

- Alexander III

- Prince Felix Yusupov

CHAPTER 4 - EMANUAL SWEDENBORG

Topics and People

- Angels

- Order of Angels

- Queen Ulrika Eleonora

- King Charles XII

- Swedenborgianism

- Thomas Edison

- Phenomenology

- Ralph Waldo Emerson

- Ernest Hemingway

- Johann Wolfgang Van Goethe

- John Wesley

- William Blake

- Dr. Carl Jung

CHAPTER 5 - ANDREW JACKSON DAVIS

Topics and People

- Salpetriere Hospital - France

- Nancy School - France

- Dr. Charcot

- Dr. Bernheim

- Frederick Anton Mesmer

- Benjamin Franklin

- Academy of Science - Paris

- Marquis De Puysegur

- "Victor" Race

- Hypnosis

- Father Gassner

- Dr. Carl Jung

- Dr. Sigmund Freud

- Dr. Silas Smith Lyon

- Mr. William Fishbough

- Thomas Edison

- Edgar Cayce

- Melchisedec

- Emanual Swedenborg

- Aristotle

- Somnambulism

- Magnetism

- Transference

CHAPTER 6 - EDGAR CAYCE

Topics and People

- Spiritual Encounter

- Spelling Book Miracle

- Voice Affliction

  "Hart the Laugh King"

  Professor Giaro

  Dr. Quackenbos

  Self-Induced Cure

- Sanskrit - Kundalini - Chakras

  Kama Sutra

  Taoist and Tantric Forces

- Virginia Beach Hospital

- Description of Frederica

- Dark Spirits

  Cayce and Hauffe

- Comparison Between Sensitive and Intuitive Somnambulism

  Cayce and Hauffe

- Throes of Death

- Dr. Justinus Andreas Christian Kerner

- Four Levels of Sensitive Somnambulism

- A Different Language

- A Machine to Save Her Life

- Galen the Great Greek Physician

  Gladiators

  A Shrine

  A Hospital

  Dreams

- Socrates and the Demon

- The Name of Jesus

- The "Nerve Spirit"

  Auras

  Connecting Mind and Soul

  Ghosts

  Retention to Conscious Mind

- *Memories, Dreams and Reflections*

- Psychic Disclosure and Risk of Condemnation

- His Life's Work

- Discoveries

    Extroversion and Introversion

    Mental Function

    Arch Types

    Cultural Differences

    #1 and #2 Personalities

- Association of Somnambulic States with Frau Frederica Hauffe

- Identified: Collective Unconscious

- "The Sympathy of All Things"

- Dream Importance

- Anima & Animus

- Alchemy

- Transference

- Perception of Spiritual Contact

- Dr. Jung's Near Death Experience

CHAPTER 11 - "FINALITY"

Topics and People

- Prelude

    Allusion to Cayce, Richie, Jung and Rasputin

    The State of Being

PORTRAITS AND ILLUSTRATIONS

CHAPTER 2

- Thomas Alva Edison

- Thomas Edison's Secret Knowledge

- Photographs of Edison's Menlo Park Laboratory at Greenfield Village

CHAPTER 3

- Grigorii Rasputin

- Tsar Nicholas II

- Tsarina Alexandra

- Tsarevitch Alexis

- Friendly Persuasion

- The Black Madonna

- Makarii

- Rasputin, Bathing His Spirit

- The "Khlisti"

- Prime Minister Stolypin

- Death is Following Him

- Alexander Protopopov

- Prince Felix Yusupov

- Princess Irina

- Grand Duke Dmitri Pavlovich

- Vladimir M. Purishkevich

- Cherished Memories of Rasputin

CHAPTER 4

- Emanuel Swedenborg

- Vision of Stockholm Burning

- The Queen's Secret

- Pope Gregory the Great

CHAPTER 5

- Period Photographs of Poughkeepsie, New York

- Andrew Jackson Davis

- Benjamin Franklin

- Dr. Jean Martin Charcot

- Frederick Anton Mesmer

- Ben Franklin with Mesmer's Baquet

- Davis Practiced "Psychometry"

- Aristotle

- Isis - Egyptian goddess of Fertility

- Photograph from Engraving of Andrew Jackson Davis

CHAPTER 6

- Edgar Cayce

- Gertrude Cayce

- Gladys Davis

- A Spirit Visits Dr. Jung

- A Spelling Miracle

- Dr. Ketchum

- Cayce's Near Miss with Death

- Nikola Tesla

- A Childs Nature Revealed to Cayce

- Neath the Tree Cures Were Known

- August Kekule

- Hippocrates

- Marquis de LaFayette

- Photographs of the Edgar Cayce Foundation in Virginia Beach, Virginia

CHAPTER 7

- Dr. Justinus Andreas Christian Kerner

- Galen

- Asclepius - Greco-Roman god of Medicine

CHAPTER 8

- Upton Beale Sinclair

- Mary Craig Sinclair

- Spirit Revealed in 100 Books

- Jack London

CHAPTER 9

- Madame Gullfina

- Madame Gulfina's Healing Passes

- Gulfina Transferring Healing Energy to Herbs and Water

CHAPTER 10

- Dr. Carl Gustav Jung

- Dr. Sigmond Freud

- Drs. Jung and Freud Interpreting Dreams

INTRODUCTION

Hidden Shadows - An Opening to the Windows of the Mind is a revealing, enlightening entertainment that shares both knowledge and experience as it addresses life's mysterious journey.

Written by the author of *Split Decision,* which also addresses reality in life in open and honest exposition, **Hidden Shadows** views reality from a totally different perspective. This book walks the reader into expansions of understanding life's spiritual mysteries by revealing the experiences of prominent or noted people. In their travel to eternity, these individuals left legacies of recorded personal experience and experiment in the phenomenon of inner perception and deception that in many ways touch and include all of us.

The revealing pages also hold allusion to personal experiences by the author that are shared as a subtopic, enhancing the reader's ability to open to his or her own inner person. This personal sharing integrates itself to the flow of discovery, joining one chapter to the next. Each chapter is a building block of revelation to the knowledge that the medical profession harbors in the realm of what society has labeled the "Psyche," and an exposition of the duality of physical and spiritual life that we live.

The presence of spirit and flesh in common, yet separate existence, are plural in topic and tonic to the revealing of both, in both the book and the mind of the adventuring reader.

Prominent doctors of influence such as Dr. Carl Jung of our time and the ancient Greek Physician Galen flavor the pages and reveal life's inner perceptions as known through thousands of years.

Some thirty-five doctors are mentioned or addressed, as are prominent people in the fields of hypnosis and scientific discovery from this country and abroad.

Written as a comparative analytic criticism spanning institutions, individuals, objective and subjective experiences and experiments, and soundly-based research conclusions, *Hidden Shadows* is an extraordinary venture and investment in personal discovery to universal understanding.

Addressed is the realm of the mind from a vantage to which few have had exposure. The correlation of experience that builds from one chapter to the next results in an eventual revelation that a deep spiritual influence in our "normal" everyday lives actually underpins our thoughts and activities in ways we little realize or understand.

In the moment, the book lives in the reader's life. Life becomes an expansion that without it may remain a constriction to question and assumption!

Hidden Shadows - An Opening to the Windows of the Mind questions much, assumes little, reveals greatly, and shares deeply.

You are invited to share in its depths and grow in the experiences of others.

I believe it impossible to look into the shadows and not see yourself!!!

CHAPTER 1
MODERN SOCIETY AND THE PSYCHE

CHAPTER 1

MODERN SOCIETY AND THE PSYCHE

Increasingly within our modern society we seem to be looking to the future in wonder to what it holds for mankind and the world we all live on. The common occurrence of our looking to prophecies and visions as recorded or related by known visionaries of the past is drawing ever increasing interest.

Those who are biblical scholars, whether they are laymen or the clergy, are predicting the soon-to-be-seen culmination of this age and Christ's physical kingdom being established.

Others who are of differing persuasions in life are looking to men and women who have evidenced extraordinary psychic gifts of insight into the mysteries of the sources of such revelations and are studying the people, the predictions, and their relationships to the lives that we live.

Many people of note have experienced phenomenon associated with the spiritual depths of the inner person and the little seen realm of the spirit.

Without question many who choose to read this book will find evidence within it, and as a result of its reading, in themselves, that will bond them to a deeper understanding of the spiritual and physical interaction that life is and will grow with the knowledge that's offered.

Those in our society who have grown with such books as *I'm OK, You're OK* or with such people as Dr. Wayne Dyer or Dr. Carl Jung will find distinct relationships evidenced throughout the many pages of discovery.

Dr. Dyer's philosophy suggests that we look within ourselves and follow an inner direction. He does this with a convincing conviction and to my belief he is not wrong. I have lived many years of my life being mindful of that which is within us, allowing it to influence, guide or even direct me. I fully believe that being "that which you are" is far more fascinating than being that which you are "supposed to be."

Perception of such nature is not without risk. Dr. Dyer, in my knowledge of his tenant to approach to be inner directed, did not allude to the aspect of risk. To listen, to think, to watch others who have ventured to seeking an understanding of themselves, is in our society, a different realm than that of deliberately involving one's self in the gaseous volatility of being different. Being different means drawing attention, and attention brings with it not only the good but also the bad and the ugly. Notice that there is stated one part good to two parts bad. Such seems to be our world.

In attempting to understand the influences upon and within us, those who are students of the Bible know that it says that if you have a candle, its light should be shown, not hidden under a basket. This is considered to be an obligation because the candle and the light are a gift of spiritual brilliance.

Showing belief that we are living a spiritually influenced life is not always easy, but many find themselves seeking admission to it. One circumstance that is now a continuously occurring event is the appearance of the Virgin Mary in various places, and at times to masses of people. Such recognized events bear with them massive evidence that we see very little of the total world we live in and are a part of.

Recently such an event occurred at a Catholic Church in Cold Springs, Kentucky, and it is vivid testimony to our belief in the spirit and our longing to touch and understand it.

The continuing appearances there are not secret but are being revealed to many people. On the first occasion of the event, after a startling display of visual phenomena had occurred both inside and outside of the Church, in the hours after midnight the Priest of the Church is credited with saying that the Chief of Police, along with what appeared to be the entire Police Force—the entire parking lot was filled with patrol cars—asked permission to enter the Church and pray. Following this, the Priest claimed, another request was made in similar manner by the news media that was there to cover the anticipated event that had occurred.

Such testimonies to our belief in God and our recognition to the world of spirit are moving moments to consider, and the fact that literally hundreds of thousands of people around the globe are bearing witness to similar encounters, lends great validity to our searching and wondering.

Yet with all of this, it is still too easily accepted in our society that individuals who claim experience or belief to the realm of the spirit are playing with less than a full deck. We live hypocrisy within ourselves if we automatically associate spiritual claims to origins of demonic depth. Though both are real, labels are too easily placed in our society.

To this labeling, this book is addressed in search of understanding the subject of the total human person.

The distinct and absolute involvement of the medical profession in revealing spiritual encounters through the centuries that are highlighted through this progressing presentation offer great insight. This insight lends basis to the validity of presentation, and with all of the aspects combined, an understanding of the human person tries to peek through to our bewildered selves.

This critical analysis and commentary to the presentations of evidence and associations recorded for history by people, whose prolific contact to spiritual experiences, gifted individuals, and extraordinary events transcends the normal knowledge of society, brings a depth of offering to the venturing reader in recognition that the realm of the spirit is not a great distance away. Our objective society would certainly lead us to believe that it is, but people like Emmanuel Swedenborg of Sweden, Anton Mesmer of France, Edgar Cayce of the United States, and Dr. Carl Jung of Switzerland ventured within these spiritual worlds of wonder to our objectivity, and they did so in a matter-of-fact manner that lends all the more reality to the interaction of an objective world of physical being, and a subjective world of spiritual being.

It is easy to see that addressing such subjects requires uncommon presentation, written in a fashion to provide understanding of the uncommon to those of us who are the common people. Dr. Dyer's address to the common people is that inner confidence and inner directedness should be importantly manifested in a person's dreams and desires. The dreams and desires have to be connected to sincere effort and desire to succeed.

He lives and believes that if you listen to and follow the inner urgings of meaningful awareness that exists within, and look for the objective events that go hand in hand with our ever present inner perception, success and achievement will follow in abundance.

The Bible indicates that we are made up of heart, mind, and spirit. Dr. Dyer in essence says to be heart, mind, and spirit in conscious life, recognizing and being our *total self*, allowing for the infusion of that which is not seen to be real. To his thinking, I have the thought, "Are we captured within ourselves?" I think we are.

How long have you, the reading venturing person, known and been silent to intuition, or premonition, or actual lived unexplainable spiritual event? We're bombarded with books, T.V. programs, and movies galore, all of which clamor with knowing, but how long have you known that spirits are real, to see and feel, both within and without? Count the years, count the days, and count the ways.

Knowing that the reality of our accepted senses are the lesser of the essence of life is to know that another dimension to the human existence is a reality. It is a small step to a continuing recognition in daily encounter with what a materialistic society denies, and can be a personal reality to you, the open-minded venturing person.

Thinking again to the aspect of biblical comment to the triplicity of being heart, aind, and spirit, it's found that a person is charged with loving the Lord your God with all your heart, with all your mind, and with all your spirit, three distinct aspects of a human being. Years ago the best-selling book *I'm O.K.; You're O.K.* espoused three aspects of human behavioral make-up, the parent, the child, and the adult. God is presented in the Bible as God the Father, God the Son, and God the Holy Ghost, each capable of separate function and yet one with the other. Edgar Cayce while in his sleeping state described three separate yet inter-functional minds to the human make-up, the normal or conscious mind, the imaginative mind, and the subconscious mind that abides in the same area of the body to which the soul is located and which is connected to the universal truths of creation, the superconscious. Again, these are three separate and yet interrelated facets to being the human being. This allows us to look at ourselves in the light of being three distinctions within ourselves, and three distinctions of possible relationship to and with others.

To these thoughts of relationships, add your thoughtful curiosity and read on.

CHAPTER 2

THOMAS EDISON

<u>Born February 11, 1847 - Died October 18, 1931</u>

"A Meld of Spirit and Flesh"

Thomas Alva Edison

CHAPTER 2

THOMAS EDISON

Born February 11, 1847 - Died October 18, 1931

"A Meld of Spirit and Flesh"

Few of us are strangers to the name Thomas Edison, but it is the few who know that he harbored awareness that the physical and spiritual worlds of inner perception relate openly with one another.

In thinking about Edison, we have a well-founded tendency to relate the term inventor to his person and invention to his accomplishments in life. He accomplished something else, however, that is deeply important to understanding this book and growing with it. Recognizing that the infusion of unseen influence to thought can manifest itself to conscious levels, he made deliberate effort to cultivate the repetition of such events.

In accounts that I have read, it's not indicated as to how Edison came to understand that he could touch, or be touched, by a knowledge that revealed itself to him in the twilight moments just before he would fall asleep. It is indicated that he did and was.

Our society seems to want to allow us to be that which is homogenous to the flow of the mass. If all societies were of a like persuasion, then Edison certainly stood out from his, and in doing so he reaped personal fame, wealth, and influence to the directing forces of civilization's growth.

Edison, in his inventive research and practical experiment, would at times be troubled by the need of an answer to a difficult question or problem. Being unable to, by logic or experiment or assimilation of someone else's awareness, answer the question or solve the problem, he would turn to his awareness that the answer would possibly come to him if he allowed inner perception to manifest itself.

Edison devised a process that would help him to retain the information that the twilight sleep would bring and depth of sleep would steal from him. He settled on a practice in his problem-solving effort of seating himself in a comfortable chair and allowing sleep to creep upon him in hopes of answers. He would allow his hands and arms to dangle over the sides of the chair. In each of his hands he would grasp a metal ball, and below this odd arrangement, resting on the floor beneath his arms and hands and clasped balls, would be two metal pans. If the answers came and sleep with it, he would drop the metal balls in the pans and thus retain the message as the sound would rouse him.

There is no real way to say where the information would come from, but Thomas Edison's contributions to science are certainly beyond question; and it is possible that Dr. Dyer's philosophy is linked with Edison and possibly other people and beliefs that are yet to be discussed as these pages proceed.

Edison may well have been the greatest inventor in recorded history. He is credited with having patents on one thousand and ninety-three inventions, and Henry Ford I had said that Edison's lifetime could be called "The Age of Edison."

Thomas Edison's secret knowledge

He worked so hard that, when in the final stages of a project, he would labor for days without stopping, save for a short nap. Oft times he would crawl into a small enclosed space under the stairs in his Menlo Park laboratory to steal a few moments of rest. One could almost say that he was driven in his quest to complete a task and in thinking to Ernest Hemingway when he was in similar effort to writing, he too would work feverishly on a project when he claimed to have "The Juice"!

Edison's work style left little time for the women in his life, and it's possible they may have felt like widows. He married Mary Stillwell in 1871, and they had three children, quite possibly by osmosis, before she died in 1884.

He married a second time to the daughter of another inventor, manufacturer, and philanthropist, Lewis Miller. By this marriage to Mina Miller, three more children were born to the lady's complaints of far too little attention to her and such great amounts to his laboratory. Edison's view of women is said to have been stated by him as being in like company with mathematics; he understood neither.

Being massively independent and self-motivated to his own ideas, he had virtually no close friends but occasionally found time to visit with people such as Harvey Firestone, Henry Ford, and John Burroughs. With this list of acquaintances whose contributions to society are also outstanding, one might wonder if he shared his awareness with them that life's dimensions are more expansive than just that which we see.

Another facet associated with Edison that may well have contributed to his inward perception was his deafness. He could not hear well, but he claimed to be able to hear "through the skull." An example would be that he would lay his head against a phonograph and could instantly detect a misplaced note. It is interesting that Beethoven, who was also deaf, would lay his head upon a piano to "hear" the music. Deafness certainly promotes inner directedness and inner perception, and by its nature, secludes a part of the person, to the person.

Edison did not espouse a religious nature but believed that a supreme intelligence was a reality; giving no venting of ego that he might create even the simplest of life forms. He was a man of reality, but within that reality, in his later years he is quoted as saying many times over to the press that he was working on the development of a device "so sensitive that if there is life after death, it will pick up the evidence of it." To this statement, however, no one has ever found such a device in any of his laboratories.

I can't say that I have ever experienced the occurrence of Edison's sleeping discovery, but I have encountered such things in the course of waking. There can be a twilight then as well, and it can be consciously noted before a person's body awakens fully.

The awakening of the inner self, or maybe better stated, the awakening of that which is within, can be revealing in many ways. It can open a person to another person. It can manifest itself in dreams, as is commented to in Dr. Carl Jung's beliefs and practices. It can also be revealed in ways that became known to Andrew Jackson Davis, "the Poughkeepsie Seer," that are addressed in depth as the commentary continues, but most important of all, is that acceptance that we all are more than we seem to be and that this world is far more than the visible, open doors to understanding our persons and our natures that God allows in His good time and place.

Open-minded faith quickens the spirit and stirs the soul!

**THOMAS EDISON'S MENLO PARK LABORATORY IS PRESERVED
AT GREENFIELD VILLAGE IN DEARBORN, MICHIGAN.**

**THE BUILDING AT THE LEFT HOUSED HIS MAIN LABORATORY AND
IS AN ASTONISHING PRESENTATION OF EDISON'S GENIUS.**

THE SECOND FLOOR OF THE MAIN LABORATORY EVIDENCES
THE INTEGRATION OF HIS MECHANICAL, ELECTRICAL,
AND CHEMICAL KNOWLEDGE. ITS COMPLEXITY PROJECTS
THE MAGNITUDE OF EDISON'S DIVERSITY.
WHAT IT DOES NOT SHOW, IS HIS HIDDEN ATTACHMENTS
TO THE SPIRITUAL REALM THAT HE ACCESSED TO HELP
CREATE THE COMPLEXITY AND THE DIVERSITY.

EDISON'S RECOGNIZED CONNECTION OF THE SPIRITUAL INFLUENCE
IN HIS WORK WAS NOT UNIQUE TO HIM. IN THE FIELD'S OF MEDICINE
AND ADVANCED CHEMISTRY, OTHERS ARE SPOKEN OF IN THIS TEXT.
MANY ARE EQUALLY AMAZING, AND SOME MORE SO, AND THE
SPAN OF TIME ARE THE CENTURIES OF MAN'S DEVELOPMENT.

BENEATH THE STAIRS IN THE MAIN BUILDING, EDISON WOULD CRAWL INTO A CUBBY HOLE BEHIND THE SMALL DOOR TO NAP IN THE MIDST OF A PROJECT.

THIS BUILDING HOUSED EDISON'S EXPERIMENTAL AND PRACTICAL MACHINE SHOP.

EDISON'S OFFICES AND DESIGN FACILITIES WERE ESTABLISHED IN THIS BUILDING.

CHAPTER 3

GRIGORII RASPUTIN

<u>Born January 10, 1869 - Died December 16, 1916</u>

"The Mad Monk"

Successor of Nizier-Vachod Philippe,

a Savoyard peasant born in 1849,

in spiritual friendship to the aristocracy of the Russian Empire

Grigorii Rasputin

CHAPTER 3

GRIGORII RASPUTIN

<u>Born January 10, 1869 - Died December 16, 1916</u>

"The Mad Monk"

Successor of Nizier-Vachod Philippe,

a Savoyard peasant born in 1849,

in spiritual friendship to the aristocracy of the Russian Empire

Grigorii Rasputin was a man about whom many books have been written. Within these books, he has been presented to be many things. He was definitely a Russian peasant whose origins have been established in a Siberian village named Pokrovskoe. His parents were uneducated, and his father was considered to be unimaginative as well as intolerant of Grigorii's spiritual gifts.

His daughter, Maria, has related stories that as a child he had a special way with animals. He was uncanny in his ability to calm and even heal the farm animals he was surrounded by.

He seemed to also have a sensitive ability for judging character and motivation in people he would encounter. Andrew Jackson Davis as well as Edgar Cayce also displayed this ability and, as such, a linking aspect of the extraordinary can be seen.

In childhood, Rasputin had actually thought that his ability was universal to all and had lived accordingly restrained in conduct. One oft quoted commentary by Rasputin reads, "I used to play with the children of Pokrovskoe and quarreled with them, but I never dared to steal or pilfer the smallest thing. I used to believe that everybody would at once see that I had stolen something, since I myself was aware of it as soon as one of my comrades had stolen. Even when he had stolen in a distant place and hidden the objects he had taken, I could always see the object behind him."

At the time in his life that he was twelve years old, an event occurred that is said to have deeply affected him and changed his behavior, temperament, and abilities. It was in the summer of 1883, when he and his brother Misha were intending to go swimming in a river near their home. The river Tura was fast flowing, and his brother had gone in first, but to no sound footing. As he was going under, Rasputin reached for him and was pulled in himself. They were swept along in the current, and a farmer heard them crying out and managed to rescue them. Both boys developed an inflammation in the chest, and Misha eventually died from what was possibly pneumonia.

A Siberian shaman is a person who has experienced an overwhelming psychological event in his life. The event turns the person inward and brings movement to his life in seeking life-long enlightenment. Rasputin became such a person. Following the death of his brother, his mother said he went into a deep depression. His behavior became strange as well as unpredictable. He would be reclusive and distant, seeking solitude in the woods one day, and the next he would be pretentiously overactive, shouting and swearing and being bothersome to his mother. Some have suggested that a form of mental illness may well have taken him at that time.

It's not an impossibility that such was the case and that his gifts of mystic natures, along with his religious and aristocratic associations, shielded him from a true revealing of his person to the society of the era.

Drunkenness was also a part of Russian cultural expression in Rasputin's time. It was so acceptable that it was the universally acknowledged precept that a person was not held accountable for his actions if he was drunk. Vodka was the preferred drink, and the aspect of public inebriation was not at all confined to the men. The environment could easily be seen as contributing to blatant protection within the society of the social and criminal misconduct that existed. If a person was drunk and even killed another person, he was treated in a less severe manner than if he were sober. Because of this acceptance of drunkenness within the society, a person's oddity of behavior in a sober state would seem to be less odd, and thus Rasputin's behavior, which was odd at times, was possibly less noticed.

Most people had little education, as over ninety percent of the population could have been considered serfs. Serfs in the cities were little more than slaves, while those who lived in rural areas were less controlled and had more abundant food. Rasputin came from a rural background, and it probably contributed to his true nature of addressing the aristocracy as though he were equal; he did this casually and naturally. Many marveled at this aspect of the man, but one thing they ignored was that Rasputin ascribed to the belief that God could be found within you, and if a person finds that inner aspect of life and cultivates it, he changes both inside and out. I believe Rasputin, in quite a number of ways, evidenced that by the very way he lived.

A noted event that occurred in Rasputin's childhood that evidenced mystic portents involved the theft of a horse. Horse stealing in Siberia was a regular event, and punishment if caught was generally to find one's self beaten nearly to death.

On this occasion, Rasputin was confined to his bed ill with fever. A horse in the village had been stolen, and a number of men had come to the Rasputin home to talk of it with Rasputin's father, who was the Headman of the village. No one knew the thief or the whereabouts of the horse. As they spoke, Rasputin, suddenly rising from his bed, pointed to and accused one of the most well-to-do villagers of being the thief. Rasputin's dad was angered at him, and much discussion ensued about his brashness. Some of the men present did, however, think seriously about the intensity of the boy's statement.

They took it upon themselves to follow the accused man home. As they watched, the man led the stolen horse from his barn. The men took the horse and left the beaten thief lying in the snow.

Rasputin's father was not much impressed with his unique abilities and was oft times frustrated by his daydreaming son and considered him lazy. Rasputin was not the brightest of people and I think could have been described as being a little slow. His dad would not hesitate to beat him on occasion.

Interesting to this aspect of not being brightly gifted and having difficulty with his father, so also did Edgar Cayce consider himself to be a slow person. He did not learn quickly and considered it to be the case all his life. Cayce's encounters with knowledge were based in his spiritual nature. His father was intolerant of him, just as Rasputin's father was, and he too was physically punished.

As Rasputin had grown beyond boyhood, his nature was quite wild and his pursuit of the company of village women intense. It also came to be that his fear of stealing had subsided, and with it another life-changing event occurred.

On a certain occasion, he was caught stealing part of a neighbor's wooden fence. When the neighbor ordered him to come with him to the village elder, he refused and attempted to hit the man with his ax. Unsuccessful, the man then smashed Rasputin in the face with his pitchfork—it was a friendly neighborhood—knocking him out cold. When he came to, he still refused to go and was hit at least once more in the face with the pitchfork. This gentle act persuaded him to comply.

The general consensus of this encounter's effect on Rasputin was that from this point on in his life and until his death, his speech was rapid and fragmented and at times incomprehensible. He also developed the strange stare in his eyes that, along with the physical scars of this encounter, he would bare to his grave.

One would consider that Rasputin at this point in his life had come quite a distance. He started out being afraid of wrongdoing, because of his then not recognized gift, and evolved to a woman-chasing thief who would actually make an effort to injure a fellow villager, not exactly a stellar citizen, I would say.

He was about to enter into an endeavor that was to direct his life from this point forward. Rasputin fled the village to avoid action by authority in larger settlements that might have brought severe legal chastisement.

The place that he fled to was a monastery at Verkhoturye. It was a place that he had visited before, so he had a pretty sound idea of where he was going. He gained what religious teaching he was to obtain, in majority of speaking, during this time of contact with the monks and starets who lived there, though his stay only lasted three months.

Though he never really became a monk or a legitimate staret, he did from this encounter eventually gain the titles of both. He was often called "the mad monk." It was from the starets that he learned the principles of inner contemplation and came to be aware of the values of seclusion. He would later in his life employ the practice of singular spiritual devotion and prayer, usually doing so in the underground chapels that were common to the Russian aspect of worship in rural areas.

A staret is a holy man who has gained great stature and respect within the faith that was Orthodox Christianity. Eastern monasticism is considered to be predominately contemplative and inward looking, seeking knowledge of God through prayer and contemplation.

For over a thousand years, the center of eastern monasticism was a rocky peninsula located in the north of Greece; it is called Athos. Rasputin was eventually to journey there. The peninsula ends in a six-thousand foot mountain that is considered the holy mountain. The entire peninsula is covered with monasteries and during its peak period contained over

Friendly Persuasion

forty thousand monks. By 1930, only about four thousand remained. The population was entirely male, even the animals, save for a few hens.

The staret or elder can be described as a monk whose function is outside of the monastic hierarchy; he is an unofficial spirit guide. His living is generally outside of the community, and he usually lives as a hermit.

At Verkhoturye they lived in the forest in huts outside of the monastery. Surrounded by a great variety of fowls, they supplied eggs to the monastery. Their diet was basic to black bread and water as well, and they would sleep directly on the ground.

The staret is considered to be specially graced by God and is said to have power to see into the hearts of men and be able to know their secret selves. At times he is said to have extraordinary powers such as precognition. These men came from no particular background to life, and their diversity became focused to the same intents in pursuing and living a faithful change in life.

Makarii was a staret of reputation who lived in the woods by the monastery at Verkhoturye. In his earlier years he had traveled greatly in Russia. It was common in the time for holy men to wander across the face of Russia and beyond, and it was part of accepted cultural life for people to invite and accept such pilgrims to their homes and tables. Rasputin would later do this extensively as a pilgrim and also would live with people of note in the cities when he eventually ventured beyond the rural settings that were his heritage. Makarii had been received by the Tsar and Tsarista of Russia. Rasputin was to later become deeply associated with the aristocracy, and eventually he made prophetic statements regarding the end of the lives of the Royal Family that became reality.

Rasputin had encountered and been deeply influenced by Makarii. A staret is considered a healer of the spirit. Rasputin eventually became known to have a comforting and reassuring capacity. He had also surges of intuition and healing power. His intuition even led him to predict his death, a circumstance somewhat shared in common with Nostradamus and Emanual Swedenborg, who predicted the actual day they would die.

When Rasputin returned to his village from this stay at the monastery, it is said that he experienced a visionary encounter with "The Black Virgin" or "Black Madonna." "The Black Virgin" is an icon symbolizing power, majesty, inspiration, and passion. Its presence is found in various religious settings in Russia. Rasputin's vision of her was moving to him and certainly not something that he would have shied from, given the struggle of his prolific sexual portents with his religious beliefs.

An icon of her was unearthed in the City of Kazan, and it became evident that prayer offered in its presence was often answered to the working of many miracles. A convent was actually built at the site of her discovery to house it and was named the Bogoroditski Convent. The icon became so valued that it was eventually moved to Moscow and then to St. Petersburg for safekeeping.

Such can be the case in this mystery of life that we live; that such influence to society as a whole can become deeply seated.

The Black Madonna

Makari

Rasputin, being of the part of believing society, added a part of the wonder to the influence and powers that belief and faith can somehow help impart to physical life, and by that faith direct and change the history of great nations.

In Rasputin's encounter, he was plowing in the fields, and at the end of a run he had looked to the sky. It was lit with an unusual radiance. Looking into the light, it amazed him to see the image of the Virgin veiling the sun. She was not stationary but was rather moving or gesturing her hands toward the distance, as though toward the horizon. Rasputin closed his eyes and opened them to find that he was still seeing the same image. She was clothed in a manner different than that which Rasputin had seen on icons at monasteries and at churches. Falling to his knees in prayer and then looking up, the vision was gone but not the effect on him.

Sharing the experience with his friend Pecherkin, who had been expressing thoughts of becoming a monk, they decided to journey to the monastery for advice and possible explanation from Makarii.

Makarii considered the experience to be a sign from God and concluded God had some great work for Rasputin's life to fulfill. He told Rasputin that he should prepare for a very long journey. The place that was to be Rasputin's destination was identified as Mount Atho's in Greece. There he was to pray for further guidance.

It was to be a long journey, indeed, because Greece was some two thousand miles distant from his village where he had lived some twenty years, and what he was to find was quite different than he had expected. It meant leaving his father and his wife. It meant traveling on foot with virtually no money and little more than the clothes he could wear or carry with him. It would be a religious pilgrimage of the rawest nature, but it would bring again added change to Rasputin's life.

He would be gone for two years; and when he returned, his wife would not know him until he spoke. He would actually be extended the hospitality of a stranger and be sitting in his own home without recognition.

To our thinking today, such a thing would not be considered very feasible, but at that time there were literally thousands of Russians wandering the country. It must be remembered that poverty in the peasant class was the way of life and that wealth was distributed to the wealthy. It was a total class-oriented society; and as such, Rasputin's eventual friendship and active involvement with the Tsar and his family was an extraordinary occurrence.

Rasputin did not embark on this journey alone; his friend Pecherkin was his traveling companion, and together they eventually attained their destination, the peninsula Atho's.

Pecherkin immediately endeavored to fulfill his dream of becoming a monk. Rasputin, however, observed, prayed, and sought spiritual enlightenment. What he found was not exactly the purest of circumstances, and he tried to no avail to persuade Pecherkin to leave with him. His friend would not, and Rasputin departed on his own and did for the rest of his life denounce the place as being a hot bed of homosexuality.

When he left, some say he continued his pilgrimage to the Holy Land and Jerusalem and found great comfort and enlightenment there. In returning to Russia, he spent considerable time wandering about western Russia, and did so in much contact with a religious sect that he had joined. It was a forbidden and denounced sect that practiced its worship and carnal fulfillment in the secrecy of underground or sequestered places. The Khlisti, as it was named to be, was Rasputin's license to be himself and yet fulfill both his spiritual and sexual needs in pursuit of holy ambition and God and women, and not necessarily in that order.

His introduction to this sect, which he had heard about while at the monastery at Verkhoturye, is said to have come during one of his wanderings. His daughter relates the story that Rasputin had sought food at a peasant's home and had found a family in distress. It seems that their daughter was ill and not recovering. Rasputin sat with the child and continually prayed over her until the crisis had passed and the child stirred.

Over a joyful meal, Rasputin was eventually asked if he practiced a chaste life, as often is expected of holy men, indicating that he had not, eventually brought invitation to attend a session of worship with a local sect group. The leader of each group within this sect was the only one permitted to break a vow of silence. So the mother of the daughter that recovered had taken a chance in opening the invitation to Rasputin.

The Khlisti, as the sect was called, was condemned by the established church but yet flourished through the rural areas of Russia. The leader of this group impressed Rasputin with his prolific justification that through the expression of man's carnal nature without guilt, he drew closer to God. Such thinking was most acceptable to Rasputin, given his prolific indulgence, but yet being possessed with religious fervor as well. He eventually espoused that it was necessary to sin to be forgiven for it, and thus that it was perfectly correct to participate in the promiscuous aspects of life.

This practicing sect combined the religious with the erotic, the aspects of excitement with that of danger. For Grigorii Rasputin, nothing could have fit better in his life.

The door opened to a coded knock, and Rasputin found himself in an underground cellar under an old barn. The cellar was lit by candles. Ten people were present, three of whom were men.

As the proceeding started, everything seemed to follow the straightforward aspect of the normal Orthodox service and prayers. However, as the service progressed, the leader began to allude to "the highest worship of God" and talked of each person being an incarnation of God. This led to the aspects of love and worship of one another.

At this sign, the people present formed a circle around the leader and dropped their robes to the ground. They were totally naked, as part of participation was to know beforehand what was to ensue and special robes had been worn to the occasion.

The group began to dance in a circle holding hands and becoming wild in abandon until a frenzy of ecstasy led to a sweating exhaustion. At the peak of this dancing frenzy, one woman abandoned the ring to wildly cast herself on the leader, bringing immediate copulation to the scene. Things continued from this point to the group collapsing to the ground and indulging in a communal orgy of orgasmic note.

Rasputin found this to be a happiness of impulses within him fulfilled. The nature within him to be his sexual person and his religious person came together without guilt and with release to the spirit and the flesh. This was for him the finding of a self that would dictate

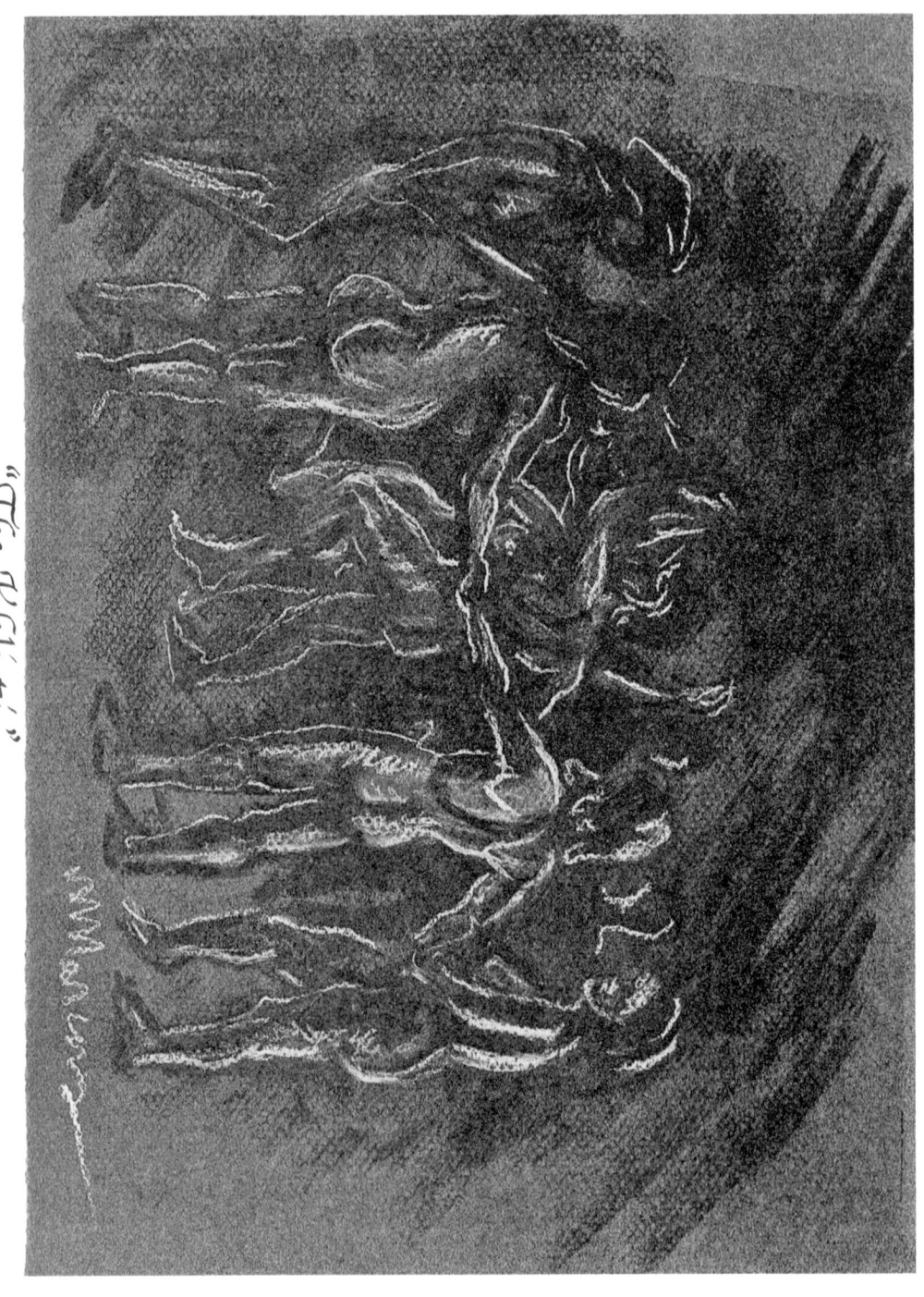

"The Kālistí"

the remaining years of his life's attitude. This would draw women to him from all levels of society to share in his abandon. It was a friendly neighborhood indeed!!

Human sexual nature is continually a part of us, and many think it to be the primary motivator to thought and action. Drifting away from Rasputin for a moment, a short group of comments to circumstances and people that accentuate the depth of influence to both physical and spiritual life that sex plays a role in is important to this moment and to further comments as the text continues.

The advertising industry gives great consideration to sexual motivation. I believe the depth to which that consideration goes is not something to take lightly.

It was rather poignantly illustrated to me many years ago. The incident at the time brought recollection of standing in a B. Dalton Bookseller in a mall and browsing and leafing as I do occasionally. I had stumbled on several books that dealt with the aspects of printed subliminal imagery of sexual nature being inserted in various forms into pictures, illustrations, or packaging formats. One book was written by a person who claimed to have been involved with contriving the efforts.

I leafed casually and to most extent dismissed the material as being something I couldn't do anything about, even if a person could prove existence or wrongdoing in its existence. The thoughts lingered, however, and the day I was browsing the menswear area of a major department store brought recollection at perception.

I was in the underwear section but not looking to buy, merely casually browsing one area after another. At that time the multi-colored tight fit and cut briefs had not long been on the market and were as much a curiosity as practicality. My eye happened to catch something unusual in the glare of fluorescent lights, and I stopped to take a close second look. What I saw surprised me, as the display of one name brand brief in the color of white, evidenced a distinct bare and erect penis placed vertically and superimposed on the picture of the man wearing the briefs, being located just to the right of where a strategically placed sock might enhance the imagination. The image was on all of the packages that were white and were easily evident. It could not be seen with the naked eye on any of the other packages that contained different colors.

The aspect of sexual reality is recognized in other areas also. Sigmund Freud, M.D., the noted psychiatrist, formed his basic theories about human behavior, inhibitions, and motivations around the aspects of sexuality. He was so adamant in these beliefs that Carl Jung, M.D., another noted psychiatrist who founded modern psychology, actually and distinctly broke philosophies with him on the matter.

Another noted European psychiatrist who had survived a Nazi concentration camp, Viktor E. Frankl, took a different view of human motivation. He considered "will to meaning" to be an area of deep searching. Carl Jung looked deeply to dream interpretations and relationships to reality.

A fourth psychiatrist, Dr. George Richie, presents another thought worthy aspect of the sexual human. Dr. Richie in his book *Return from Tomorrow* claims to have experienced death and returned. In his journey to that which is beyond and recalled by him is an encounter with the sexual aspect of humans extending in desire and activity to another world. In that world's depiction he encountered a plain or huge flat area upon which people who had died were in some way detained.

The people were in constant conflict with those close to them, arguing, fighting and striking blows. Also, great attempt was being made in all manner of sexual activity. It sounded like an area of desperate action to events, desires, or circumstances unfulfilled in this life but directly relating there to this world.

The difference to that world from this was that the blows struck did not meet their mark. They merely passed through the person they were meant to strike without any effect at all. Likewise, the acts of sexual endeavor were bringing no physical presence to note, just attempt after attempt. A place where emotion is known but not felt physically. A place where the ugliness or passion of this world continues, but without physical resolve. *I wonder if it is part of this physical journey's goal to fulfill the physical resolve?*

Dr. Richie's experience is that which set Dr. Raymond Moody on his quest to research and write many books on death's experience, some of which have been bestsellers. If one looks to the medical sector, one finds many revealing theories, accounts, and beliefs surrounding the mystery that we all are.

If we look to the Eastern cultures, we find within *The Tibetan Book of the Dead*, a description of sexual temptation to encounter. Within the process, or maybe better stated, journey of death, the book says that a spiritual state called Nirvana is the goal of attainment that each is seeking, and that in death that state is offered in the vision of being a clear colorless light of the void.

If chosen by the person that died, it breaks the cycle of reincarnation that is believed to be the fate of those who do not attain Nirvana. If they do not choose it, then a very definite sexual activity becomes part of the process to eventual reinvolvement in this physical world. A state of Nirvana is the ultimate spiritual state of being and is an extension of the culture and religion of Buddhism.

If we look again at the aspect of sexual encounter in ceremony of worship, the practice of Satan worship involves the aspect of gathering in congregation or coven and being nude for the activity. A circle can also be involved, being formed by the participants.

The person performing the rites is nude and can be a man or a woman depending on certain circumstances within their practice. It is not an uncommon involvement in their rites to either simulate intercourse or for the male or female witch within the group performing the rites to have intercourse with another witch of the opposite sex as part of the celebration.

Sexual motivation in any society is unquestionably an intricate influence to both the society as a whole and the individual enveloped in it. It spans religions, borders, and cultures and holds massive sway over the individual as life's journey continues.

Returning to Rasputin, we find that though he was married, it did not prevent him from expressing his sexual nature with other women, and his wife was well aware of it. She accepted it and even made comment that he had enough to go around. His approach was very direct; he would approach a woman, pull her closely to him, fondle her or even start to undress her or suggest an encounter. If the woman declined, he would merely let it pass; such was his nature, spiritual and carnal.

All of Rasputin's religious tenets did not entail sexual involvement. In fact, when he returned to his village he had dug an underground chapel that would allow him meditation and prayer in seclusion, which he did extensively. He also established a religious following of mostly women and would have gatherings to worship.

The Orthodox Church was afraid of the breakaway religious sects, and because of that, Rasputin was actually investigated by policemen sent to his village. They found nothing so disturbing as to elicit any action against him, and in fact, one policeman was so impressed by his interpretation of the Scriptures and his zeal in expressing them that he actually joined the group.

Though religious wandering was to continue with Grigorii, he had yet to journey to any of the large cities. In the return from his pilgrimage to Athos, Grigorii had journeyed to Kazan. There he was overcome with joy at seeing for the first time a representation of "The Black Virgin" as he had seen it in his vision in the field. She was depicted in a painting arrayed in the same dark raiment that was different from any icons or paintings he had seen before. Such events were to instill in him faith and purpose that sustained his later involvements in the cities.

When Rasputin eventually approached the city environment, he did so with fears. One of the most noted was that he would lose his powers, meaning the spiritual powers that had been cultivated from childhood. The possibility of losing the powers of healing, discernment, comforting, and clairvoyance was of no small matter to him.

The stability of belief regarding the relationship of his sexual nature to his spiritual was also of great importance to him. That stability was enhanced when on one of his wanderings he had been in the woods attempting prayer and meditation.

He was finding it impossible to concentrate, with no clarity to his prayers and no fervor. His sexual desires were overwhelming his conscious person and exhausting him. In despair and without understanding, he gazed into the trees above him where a male songbird was singing to its mate in the song of love. Rasputin suddenly saw truth in the bird's song. He thought it a sign from nature, from God. He realized that the song of such desire could not be evil.

It was a revelation to him, and he wandered on through the woods uplifted. Hearing laughter, he followed it to a clearing by a small lake. To his arousing delight, he found three young women bathing in the beauty of nature in nature's clothing. Without restraint or reservation, he joined them in revealing bliss. As one might believe, there was abounding playful encounter in the waters of the lake, and the delights of arousal overtook them all. Rasputin eventually joined each in turn on the grassy shore in passion's release, as the two in turn looked on to the moment's abandon.

As his daughter related to the encounter, the fervor of three young women carried away the clouds of despair and cleared Rasputin's senses to allow him to pray with clarity and zeal and without regret or repentance. It was a friendly encounter!!

This was one of the shaping incidents in building a philosophy of spiritual awakening through sexual fulfillment that was to follow Rasputin and impregnate his following through his life. Rasputin came to believe that without sex the universe that God created would hold no animal life and that humanity and religion could not exist.

Rasputin, bathing his spirit

Rasputin's struggle to understand himself and his nature was one between the need of God and the need to fulfill that which God created. For him and many with him, acceptance that both are possibly the "one self" that Dr. Carl Jung alludes to in his writings; and the will and meaning that Viktor Frankl struggles for in his beliefs of human quest; and the sexually-driven man that Dr. Sigmund Freud would have the world believe is this life's mentored existence, is manifest in Rasputin's strange stare into the persons he would influence to the perception of his revelations.

Rasputin is enveloped in accounts of his extensive powers in what we call the paranormal. In the end, he was credited with healing or helping the recovery many times over of the young heir to the Throne of Russia. In the beginning, he was said to heal the animals on his family's farm. If this is not a journey of wonder in life, I know none.

As a young child, a horse had gone lame on the farm. Rasputin, without any urging, had gone to the horse without being told which leg was ailing and placed his hand upon it. With his eyes closed in concentration and his head tipped back, he stood with the horse. After a while he stirred himself to pat the horse and say to it, "You're all better." It was a side to Rasputin that was not of this world; a horse that was lame was no longer lame.

Rasputin distressed his father when, on another occasion, he warned him of a horse trader representing an animal in excess of the animal's being.

His daughter claimed that he could dilate and contract his pupils at will. Rasputin's eyes were a matter of note always. In his youth, he would have a distant stare. After the pitchfork beating, they became even more estranged to the normal and his hold and influence to woman was definitely associated with his piercing blue gaze.

That gaze, along with many other factors, brought Rasputin to have the most intimate contact with literally hundreds of women as he became a spiritual and sexual legend. Through all of this, he was said to have not been emotionally attracted to any woman save his wife.

There is an account given to Rasputin's ability to affect medical cures that is notable. It's been recorded that a woman of prominence had been bedridden for years with neurasthenia. She was married to an engineer who worked for the government. The doctors of the time could not help her. Rasputin affected a cure that freed Mme. O. V. Lokhtina from her bed.

The story continues by saying that though her body was healed, she became deranged and would fall to her knees and worship Grigorii in front of him. The behavior continued and became even more exaggerated as time passed.

If one looks and reads deep enough, it can be found that Rasputin is attributed with mystic abilities beyond clairvoyance and healing. One account gives it to be that he was capable of separating spiritually from his body.

Spiritual separation from one's body is something that is said to be practiced by avatars of the Buddhist and Hindu faiths, and it is claimed that in India and Tibet it is a prevalent practice. Some claim an absolute physical detachment. It is said that complete mental detachment allowed Rasputin to wander beyond the confines of the fleshly bounds. With this, a person might wonder if the distant stare that came to be a part of his person did not claim more to his reality and relationship to the spirits of others than might be expected.

This might explain the magnetism of women to him. Women are the human creation of feeling; their spirit is close to the surface, and part of that which they are is the premonition of spirit's contact with the flesh.

A woman who realizes and allows her inner spirit to direct and show in her is a delightful attraction to a man who has grown within himself to recognize both his and her real beings. A man who can open himself in honest spiritual projection can also receive the same natural presence from an openly beautiful woman. It is such that each woman seeks when she searches the eyes of those men she's attracted to. It is a secret thing, so she thinks, but the quickness, the rush of a woman's inner spirit, is a delight not just for her to know within herself. An open man can feel it with her, just as if it were his. She will know and he will know, and together each will glow. Such may well be what Rasputin knew about women and women knew about him. A lady's secrets are not really as secret as she thinks.

Rasputin would at times test his spiritual resolve with women by lying naked with several at a time, they all being clothed in the sensual beauty of mere being.

His resolve was not as strong as it could have been, and he would oft not be successful in his effort, and neither would be the women in their efforts of mental restraint to the physical.

As accounts would have it be, Rasputin and the ladies in nude temptation would first bathe together, with the feminine nature allowed to thoroughly soap and cleanse his physical parts of desire without restraint. They would then lay together, Rasputin in the middle, each sharing the bare pressures of touch, while the ladies were told to refrain from passion's rise while he too would do the same, or at least they would try to. One can imagine the results of such effort's failure; it was a friendly place, this Rasputin's Russia!!!

It should probably be noted at this point that Rasputin's propensity for lovemaking was a circumstance renowned. Some claimed he could exert a great control to the duration of love's union, and also exposed is said to be the length of his penis. It is common knowledge that in his erect state it measured some thirteen inches, and also it's said that he had a wart that somehow was in just the right place upon it. One account gives it to be that he had made love to one woman, and the intensity of her fulfillment caused her to faint. Keep in mind that his wife said he had enough to go around.

Such stories may well be true; and if Rasputin actually was able to separate his spirit from his physical being, then the union of a woman's so highly felt and known spiritual being could find attraction, excitement, and solace with such a man. This, combined with the curiosity and desire that such physical propensity presents, could also build an intensity of want to know and associate. Rasputin also gave forth with beliefs that such things were natural and acceptable to God because of man's carnal nature being linked to and part of his spiritual nature, thus stepping to the freeing of feminine restraint and hesitation. I believe that Rasputin looked at a woman in total and joined with her in spirit, in mind, and flesh. It would be very hard for some women to resist such a man. Even if she thought him mad, she might venture to experience his company at least once.

Many did just that in the physical sense, having one encounter and then no more, but sometimes still seeking his presence. Rasputin's attraction seemed to be a rawness of the total human person that was somehow laced with, and linked with, the supernatural. This combining has made him a man that we are drawn to read about, and write about, and wonder about!

One fascinating aspect to the stories of the feminine following that was always found present, and that pertain to the sexual aspects of life, can be found not in the writings surrounding him and Russia, but rather in the writings of the Kama Sutra, the text of origin from India that is devoted to the art of love and had been banned for so many years in America.

Our society has come to dwell all too heavily on the aspects of prodigious male endowment. One would think that that which Rasputin was evidenced to be in this area is the ultimate, all that is desired to be. We see so very many aspects of socially open allusion and directedness to it, that even in one of the Superman movies dear Lois Lane wonders openly to Superman's. There was a slight chuckle in the audience; it was a friendly audience!!!

Most know also that this aspect of social dwelling found its way to a nationally televised spectacle, the Clarence Thomas confirmation hearings to the Supreme Court, which withered on no less than another source of erotica, Capitol Hill in Washington, D.C.

Looking to the wisdom of knowledge of the Kama Sutra, one finds that within its pages both the physical aspects of the man and woman are expounded upon; and that by the descriptions given, no less than three forms of union can be joined between a man and a woman. The unions are described as relating to the identified three variations in size and accommodation in the male and female organs.

As described, it states three circumstances exist in both male and female—small, medium, and the much publicized large. Quite adamantly stated, the joining of a man with a large endowment with a woman of like configuration brings the greatest satisfaction and comfort in union. Likewise, a medium with a medium, and a small with a small, will bring the greatest of pleasures. Crossing the lines of perfect matching brings less compatibility.

If we allude to Rasputin, he being around the upper limits of large, consider that it states that a woman of like being will gain little satisfaction in joining with a small man. The aspect of fulfillments with Rasputin that may well have been known, that were not known before, would certainly influence the situation, especially in a society where sexual involvement was no small part of a flamboyant culture.

Also in looking from this direction, if a woman being small but adventuresome or a virgin were to venture to his influence, the result would probably be a painfully revealing disappointment in the physical sense. The Kama Sutra specifically mentions pain in such an encounter. Rasputin's nature of not forcing a woman physically would allow for the fact that many women after one encounter had access to him, and he to her, but never joined again in the physical sense. They remained, however, in company or association without friction.

I have never seen this alluded to before in regard to Rasputin, and I ponder the circumstance, especially so when I recall an incident of tragedy in real life that was related to my wife shortly after we were married in 1969.

My wife was a registered nurse and was working at the time in a nursing home. She had a friend who was a nurse's aid and who was a very beautiful woman and pleasant in company.

Hidden Shadows

The lady had known a young man who was twenty years old or maybe a little less (it's been a long time to recall). She told my wife that this fellow had a penis that was twelve inches in length when erect—Rasputin's was thirteen—and that he had been traumatically distressed by it. She said that he was unable to find a woman who could have relations with him, and that those that had tried found it too painful to continue the encounter. She was very hurt in saying that the man had committed suicide and thought that it was a direct result of his travail.

The parameters of life can be measured in many ways. Rasputin's society was promiscuous and he possibly mad. Our society is promiscuous and certainly mad. For him in his society, pleasure. For the young man in our society, travail and an end in horror. I wonder if our world has become so hardened and pragmatic that we are ignoring conscious reason and conscience. Have we put on a false face so we can have one?

Rasputin held fear within himself that by being in the city he would see his powers diminish or that they would be lost. Since his life had been centered in the country, he had grown to be a man in a setting that allowed seclusion not only of the flesh but also of the spirit. Keep in mind that the starets adhered to a reclusive life.

The compressive life in the city lends itself to very little of either form of seclusion, as a person's life is bombarded by the actions and interests of other people almost constantly. Many years ago, I came to recognize that when feeling pressed within the city circumstance, a sojourn to the country will oft times lift the internal burdens that others place upon you. You become one with yourself again; your identity can be yours again. A man such as Rasputin, who looked within to his inner person, would have known this.

His vices were magnified while in the city, and his powers were reduced but not eliminated. It was Rasputin's religious and spiritual prominence that brought him to be in contact with both the established structure of religion and the upper class of people in the Russian Dynasty. He eventually made enemies in both sectors, and this along with his promiscuous nature with the women, resulted in his assassination.

Before that fateful event occurred, he was to become closely associated with the Tsar and Tsarista of the vast Russian Empire. The son and heir to the Empire of Nicholas II was to be the tie that linked a Siberian peasant to the power of Russia itself.

In this environment, he still kept to his peasant attire of baggy pants and shirt. He did at times, however, wear the fancy silk embroidered shirts that the ladies might give to him.

Rasputin's introduction to the Tsar and Tsarista Alexandra was by a letter of introduction from a St. Petersburg Priest with whom Rasputin was lodging. It was made as a request that Grigorii might present them with an icon of St. Simon, patron saint of the monastery at Verkhoturye.

At least this was the formal introduction, as by chance Rasputin had encountered them two days prior as they called on the Grand Duchess Militsa at her home. Rasputin had been visiting at the time.

These events began the odyssey that was to envelop the very seat of the power of Russia, with the Siberian peasant whose name would become even more revered and more hated. Revered by those he helped to console and heal, hated by those who were jealous of his closeness to the Empress and Emperor and his favor with the ladies.

Rasputin ultimately was living in St. Petersburg and was to make one or two trips home to his village a year. His daughter eventually lived with him in St. Petersburg and was there when he was assassinated.

Grigorii's acceptance with the Tsar and his family can be illustrated by the fact that he would call the Tsar "papa" and the Tsarista "mama." This acceptance centered itself in Rasputin's acclaimed ability to influence the travail of the heir to the Empire. The only son of the Tsar was afflicted with hemophilia. Hemophilia was to become known as the disease that brought down the royal houses of Europe. Once it had gained its foothold, it took but two generations to drastically affect the royal families in England, Russia, and Spain. Each lost sons as babies or young boys. The disease originated with the royalty of England in Queen Victoria; and through intermarriage it was carried from family to family.

The heir to Russia, the Tsarevitch Alexis, and Rasputin were to know their first moments in duress together as a result of a fall that brought internal bleeding in his leg at the age of three.

The Tsarevitch lay in agony for three days with Alexandra, his mother, by his bedside constantly. His leg was immensely swollen and the doctors could do nothing to affect the plight of the child.

The Grand Duchess Anastasia heard of the travail and went to the palace in an effort to speak to Alexandra. She expounded that Rasputin should be sought and asked to help, claiming him to be "more than a holy man; he is also a healer, one of the greatest of all time!"

Alexandra's belief in God was fervent, and she believed in His ability to work miracles. Taking the grand duchess's suggestion, she charged Anastasia to find him.

Anastasia's return ride to her palace is said to have equaled the hell to the wind dash that was the Pony Express. At her palace she dispatched searchers in all directions to find Rasputin with haste, as a young life was hanging in the balance.

Rasputin was found in the midst of a frenzied dance—he loved to dance—on the banks of the nearby river in the camp of the gypsies whose company he enjoyed, and he was drunk— he loved to drink. He had quit drinking for a long time but had returned with gusto.

At first summon he did not respond, but realizing that it was the Palace that called him and that a member of Tsar's family was in distress, he became focused to something distant. On his knees, he began to pray as the gypsies quaked at the power that seemed to rise to this peasant who never claimed anything to himself of the things wrought by him. Always he claimed it was not he that did things but rather God who extended his power.

One thing that Rasputin was reputed to be able to overcome swiftly was being drunk. It's said that he could, in times appropriate, transpose his condition of inebriation to sobriety almost at will. This was one of those occasions.

Rasputin's arrival and actions in the sick room were deliberate and composed. Blessing the room and everyone there, he greeted the Tsar and Tsarista with the traditional three kisses. He hugged them also before going to the side of the stricken child.

Tsar Nicholas II

Tsarina Alexandra

Tsarevitch Alexis

Kneeling, he began to pray, and all kneeled with him in hope to God's answer. After ten minutes of prayer, Grigorii stood and gazed with his piercing but friendly eyes at the young child and said, "Open your eyes, my son." It was said gently with God's care in it, and gently the eyes fluttered to see the smiling peasant above him.

Rasputin had affected the circumstance in apparent manner that began recovery where the doctors had stood helpless. The boy's mother, the Empress of all Russia, believed that it was Rasputin's efforts that saved her son. That belief was to be a bond between them to the end.

Rasputin also at this time prophesied correctly that Alexis would not die from the disease. The family would, as history proves, die from the wounds of revolution. He did not say this, but enough was said and done to spread the fame of the moment riding the winds of awareness to the event.

It should be noted here that in the cities of Russia at the time, it was much in fashion with the upper class to indulge in seances and soothsaying. It was common practice to attend an evening in companied gathering to talk to the dead or hear of the future. In this atmosphere, the presence of a man such as Rasputin found a favorable repose.

Rasputin was not the first man of unusual renown to have access to the Royal Family. Before Rasputin a French man, who was also of lowly origins, became massively influential with both the Tsar and Tsarista. He was a butcher from Lyons, France. Having been born in 1849, he became an apprentice butcher at the age of thirteen. As time passed, he began to discover that he had unusual powers. By the age of twenty-three, he was establishing himself as something of a doctor and faith healer. His powers of the paranormal extended themselves in healing and clairvoyance, and it is stated that he eventually predicted the actual day of his death.

In the waning days of his influence, he was to be declared a charlatan in his native France and had also made many enemies in Russia as well. However, the Tsar and Tsarista were to remain loyal in belief that he was a man touched by the power of God.

Just as Russia during the time of Nicholas II was a place where being carried away with spiritualism was in vogue, so also was this the case in the Royal Palace. Both the Tsar and his wife were devout Christians, and both shared a belief in the power of God being manifest in the saints and men of God. It did not matter to them if these gifted men were of the Orthodox faith or something diverse from it.

What mattered was whether, in their perception, such people were perceived to have prayers answered or if they could induce spiritual events that were considered real. If such a person was accepted in such stead, then influence to the Emperor and his wife was strongly present. Nicholas and Alexandra believed that the age of miracles was still ever present.

Possibly here is seen part of the reason that Russia lost touch with itself. It became a division of the upper class, diverse in its pursuit of opulence and spiritual entertainment from the oppressed peasants and a lower class guided by needs of the most basic survival, primitive in education, and with both classes influenced by the religious power of the Church.

The lower class sought relief in the religious sects of hidden passions released, and the upper class dawdled and dabbled in boredom's valleys of flippant pursuits to the fashionable unknown, as the aristocracy walked a path to continuing seclusion from the reality that surrounded them.

They were rulers and guides to one hundred and fifty million people; and they themselves were influenced by guides such as Rasputin and Philippe, both of whom were ultimately denounced by the advising majority to the Tsar and both of whom were held even then in the highest regard.

Philippe and Rasputin were both termed "friend" by the Royal Family. Both spoke with the ease of authority, had a quiet smile and remarkable eyes. M. Philippe, along with his power of clairvoyance, was said to also possess the distinct ability to "read" people and to assess their character. Philippe is said to have been able to tell a person in just a few words what was troubling him, and also he would know inner secrets that no one could possibly know.

This not-so-unique aspect of assessing and knowing the character of people encountered is something to ponder upon, and I should think that many a lady is pausing in recollection right now. Rasputin knew character, Philippe knew character, Edgar Cayce perceived it as well, and Andrew Jackson Davis, "the Poughkeepsie Seer," could determine it in seconds.

This is not some unique thing to me; this is one of the most basic occurrences that falls in the realm of Dr. Wayne Dyer's "inner directedness." It is an extension of one's own perception to one's self. To know yourself is to know others. To touch your inner self is to touch others. Carl Jung, M.D. mentions the "collective unconscious" and talks of "transference." All this is perception and feeling made conscious to the mind of normal perception.

A woman's intuition is an extension of this knowing of character. Don't ever look into the eyes of a mature woman for whom you have feelings, and she for you, and lie to her. She will know; she may ignore it or not believe it, but she will know. The spirit of a woman is far closer to the surface in her than in a man. He has it hidden and is afraid of it. A woman cherishes it and cultivates it and loves it.

A person who looks inside can have revealed to himself that he is more than one, more than just flesh; and when the recognition of spirit within is as real as the flesh without, then growth begins; and the more mature the growth, the greater the perception to others and to the other's inner person, and thus the knowing of character can become a normal occurrence to a feeling person.

I cannot ever remember not having the feelings within that reveal others I encounter, not all are known but many. I know also that until I consciously began to tie the feelings to the encounters in physical life, they were just odd feelings.

The feelings are those that can be consciously ignored or consciously perceived. Perceiving, recognizing, openly accepting their presence then leads to further revelation.

Be careful, they'll call you crazy; but you will know that you are not, and they have yet to grow or may never grow. There is nothing new about this, it's all happened before and may happen again. What is important is for the willing person to recognize, as did Rasputin and Philippe, that the power of God is all, and that from that power the human being lives, grows, and dies.

The Bible says that man perishes for lack of knowledge. Knowledge is not just that which is fleshly; it is spiritual as well, and the spirit is within and without. Christ says he stands at the door and knocks. It is for us to allow the entry, to open the door to ourselves. You have to look inside and perceive yourself and recognize that the self is more than the surface of being. *Carl Jung talks of the development of "one self," and also says that he who experiences the extraordinary is as much in knowledge to the experience as he who observes and comments.*

It is open intelligence that recognizes that allowing one's self to be is intelligent, and it is suppressive intelligence that recognizes that by your denial and their denial of that which they know, the bounds of control to understanding are maintained as mystery. Mystery then maintains control of the person that you know you are inside and allows society to promote its own physical circus that suppresses the growth of the inquisitive person and thus the growth in knowledge by each person. It is by knowledge that a person does not perish, and all knowledge of good is of God.

Rasputin, Cayce, and Philippe were just simple men. None claimed to themselves credit for that which is credited to them. It is part of the key; love is part of the key (Cayce alludes to love). Looking within is part of the key; opening to being is part as well. Fear to being closes the mind and maintains the socially acceptable. Be careful now, don't allow yourself to ponder this out loud; you want to be socially acceptable, and things can get out of hand.

Pilot asked Christ, "What is truth?" and Edgar Cayce wondered all his life and died wondering if that which came from within him from without was of God. There is within that which is from without.

It is said that Philippe was for a time the spiritual advisor to Tsar Nicholas II, ruler of one hundred and fifty million people. He was the most powerful absolute ruler in the world. It is also said that, at every decision, Philippe was consulted.

Philippe is believed to have been responsible for unexplained healings within the Imperial Court. The Tsar was so taken by this circumstance that he actually petitioned the Government of France to present a medical diploma to him; I don't know that they ever did.

Maurice Paleologue, the final French Ambassador to the Tsar, claimed that Philippe held regular seances to raise the ghost of Nicholas's father, Alexander III, to give him advice. To this, however, has to be added that some accounts say that Philippe was an astounding magician. Nonetheless, the influence was real.

The influence and the influencer were viewed in France as being hoax and coming from a charlatan. This fact began to discredit the Tsar and Tsarista. He also managed, as did Rasputin eventually, to bring powers of the Orthodox Church against him in resentment to his closeness to the Royal Family.

When the Tsar finally let him go and he returned to France, it was in the face of reports less than flattering having been received from the French Secret Police. In the latter part of 1902, M. Philippe returned to France but not in disgrace.

It was a reluctant parting for the Tsar, and he bestowed honors upon him. He gave him the title of Inspector of Port Sanitary Services. This made him a general and automatically made him a Doctor of Medicine. He was given a magnificent automobile; it was called a Serpollet and was described as "A Presidential Landau."

M. Philippe did not return to France without bestowing a gift on the Tsar and Tsarista. He gave them a gift of prophecy to comfort them, assuring them that one day he would be replaced. As quoted, he said, "Some day you will have another Friend who will, like me, speak to you of God." Friend was capitalized.

He maintained his contact by correspondence until his death in 1905; recall that was the day of his death he prophesied.

From the bedside of the stricken Aleksei, Rasputin's influence and involvement with the Royal Family expanded, and the depth of his affection with the Tsarista, which was to become widely known, can be illustrated quite warmly in quoting one of many letters that were written to Grigorii from her.

> My beloved, unforgettable teacher, redeemer and mentor! How tiresome it is without you. My soul is quiet and I relax only when you, my teacher, are sitting beside me. I kiss your hands and lean my head on your blessed shoulders. Oh how light, how light do I feel then! I only wish one thing: to fall asleep, to fall asleep, forever on your shoulders and in your arms. What happiness to feel your presence near me. Where are you? Where have you gone? Oh, I am so sad and my heart is longing—come quickly, I am waiting for you and I am tormenting myself for you. I am asking for your blessing and I am kissing your blessed hands. I love you forever—
>
> Yours M.

At first reading this, I felt I had invaded some sanctity of privacy that one human should respect of another, and I still do. There was never any evidence that the Empress and Rasputin were involved in a manner that would bring scandal to the palace, but some accounts allow for the presence of much rumor to that effect. It was a common and continuing thing for the Tsarista and her daughters to write to Rasputin, and one would think that a great trust existed toward Grigorii.

Though Rasputin is at times considered to have been mentally afflicted, as might be defined by our assumed identification of illness, an entry from his diary brings wonder at just who is really mad.

The entry was made while onboard a ship that was going to the Holy Land on a pilgrim's journey; it might well have been his second trip, with the first being associated with his journey to Athos in Greece. Rasputin was leaving St. Petersburg as the result of a growing resentment and hostility to him from within the circle of influence and power that surrounded the palace, and keeping in mind that Grigorii had approached the cities in fear of losing a part of himself to the shallow and corrupt society of class separation and dominance, the words in the diary have a special depth to them that may well be the revealing of his soul.

Oh, what a calm sets in. There is not even the sound of a bird, and man is left to his meditations as he walks the deck, per chance recalling his childhood and the futility of the world's ways. He compares his present calm to the vanities of the world, and he longs to dispel the wearisome torments brought upon him by iniquitous fellow-men.

Then, today, tomorrow, these are not the words of a mad man but rather the conscience of man's travail.

To Rasputin, there are attributed moments of clairvoyance. Two of note involved people close to the Tsar and his wife. Anna Vyrubova, who was the lady-in-waiting to Alexandra, was prophesied to suffer a disastrous marriage, and in fact did when it subsequently ended only weeks after the ceremony was consummated. The second involved a man who was Rasputin's enemy and had been in no small part responsible for Rasputin's ultimately leaving aboard the ship on pilgrimage. He was the Prime Minister and a very powerful man.

When Rasputin had returned to Russia from his journey to the Holy Land, he was at one point in Kiev when the Tsar and Tsarista were visiting the city. Rasputin had seen the Royal procession; and as the first carriage carrying the Emperor and his wife had passed, a second carrying the Prime Minister Stolypin did, also.

At the passing of the second carriage, Rasputin is said to have been suddenly moved to very loudly cry out, "Death is after him. Death is driving behind him."

If Rasputin felt or saw death following his carriage, then the event that followed would confirm it. For as the Royal party were viewing an opera, the Tsar himself gives this account of Prime Minister Stolypin's moment of injury that brought death.

> During the second interval we heard two sounds, as if something had been dropped. I thought an opera glass had been dropped on somebody's head. Directly in front of me in the stalls, Stolypin was standing; he slowly turned his face towards us and made the sign of the cross. Only then did I notice that his right hand and uniform were blood stained. He slowly sank into his chair and began to unbutton his tunic.

I ponder Rasputin's awareness to events. It would seem that he was taken from within to shout out the statement in the crowd. Such can be the spirit's voice, strong, loud, sure, and correct. To any who have known it, it is a mystery from within but known to the person with whom the mystery resides.

It's not known if he saw or felt the presence of death behind the carriage or if it was just the spirits release that occurred, but the man did die and in unusual circumstances for sure.

With this moment of thought to death's revealing, I'm going to venture to say that if it was the feeling of "the power of the presence of death" that brought voice to Rasputin, then I understand and believe that I know the feeling myself. Do you know the feeling, also?

Prime Minister Stolypin

"Death is following him"

Hidden Shadows

It at times is not a good thing to reveal the experiences of life, for it opens a person to ridicule; but if after living forty-eight years in this travel through time, one has to hide from reality to conform to normality, then why make the journey at all. If you cannot grow and let it show, wherein lays the purpose in the experience? To this thought maybe you will read with recognition or with curiosity, or maybe with disbelief—it is up to you.

On four occasions in my life I fully believe that I have felt and been in the presence of an entity, a being that is or somehow projects the power of death.

The incidents span many years and started in occurrence just prior to my great aunt's death. On this first occasion, I was not aware of the meaning of the feeling of encounter. I merely noted that something had occurred that I had never experienced before, and I marveled at having felt something so indescribably strong but not seen. I did note that the death had occurred just following the encounter and recalled that a sort of feeling of scrutiny had occurred with the presence.

On the second occurrence, I recognized the presence immediately and knew it to be identical in feeling of power to the first encounter. This time, however, it was not quickly passing; it lingered, and the full awareness of the immensity of authority present was nothing short of absolute.

The combining of the projection of power with the authority somehow brought awareness that death was associated with the encounter.

This is a living being that is finality itself, yet the feeling is that it is charged with its motives.

When it passed I felt somehow moved to pray for everyone I could think of that was close and did so in haste and concentration. Hoping that I had missed none, I felt shaken. Within several days of this event my wife's aunt died. Though she was well advanced in years, it was not expected.

Years later, again unexpectedly, this knowing happened again. The feeling is so singular in nature that it is instantly identifiable once encountered; and for me the awareness is that there is no possible way that a mere man could exert resistance to the will of this being. The strongest man is nothing to this. Arrogance or ego is not even a morbid joke to the emanating power of this being. Armies could not stand for a moment in opposition to the will that is felt to be so discerning, so deeply probing to the person of its encounter. It is frightening in its power but not in its being; it is not evil in feeling, just strong, oh, terrifyingly strong!!!

This occasion again brought the feeling of death with it, and again when it passed I prayed with intensity to all that I could think of. One does not know if events are coincidence or not, who is to say, but a young woman related by marriage within my family was stricken with leukemia almost immediately to the week of this encounter. She was just a young woman and tragedy to such a thing is mildly put. I had not prayed for her, but that is not to say that meaning could be put one way or the other; but her travail was real.

Many people prayed for this young woman for a long time after she was stricken, believing in God's continuing intervention in life's events. Today, to the doctor's wonder, she is not in a state of affliction.

Years passed again before the fourth and most recent event to date occurred. This encounter I consider to be very special indeed and may well have involved my wife prior to the presence revealing itself to me.

I will carry the night of my wife's experience with me forever, and the encounter has been related by both her and me to others on occasion. I, however, have never revealed before this, my experience in possible connection to hers.

This involvement may well be stated as revealing to more than speculation. We had moved from our home of twenty years to a place distant from the city and to a house sitting on ten beautiful acres which had never been finished completely, but had been lived in for many years before we bought it.

The man who sold it to us had lost his wife during the process of construction and had fallen in life. We were living in it, repairing and completing various things, and had not been there more than a couple of months. It was in the summer of 1990, and it was in the middle of the night. My wife was sound asleep in a bedroom at the far end of what was a very large ranch home. A long hall led from the bedrooms to the living room at the other end of the house.

I was asleep on the couch in the living room, when without warning my wife had awakened from a deep sleep with a primal ear-piercing scream that echoed through the entire house. We had not carpeted yet, and with the ten-foot ceiling in the living room it was an echo of chambers and, at this moment, of horror.

I have never heard such a scream before or after, not from any source. It was the depth of a soul screaming in startled response. Not thought about or put on or restrained in any way, it was a lingering piercing horrible release that charged the moment in terror.

I was asleep, and as it occurred, I actually believe that my body went straight up in the air horizontally off the couch and to the side in a movement not understood, as I crashed down full length to the floor without touching the couch in any way before slamming into the floor.

I leapt to my feet and ran at full speed down the hall; she turned the corner in the hall coming from the room, and we stopped, facing each other. She was terrified and said that she had seen a man standing beside the bed in a long robe with a large sickle in his hand. He was seen just as a real person might have been seen.

There is no question within me that she saw the man. I lived in marriage with her for twenty years to that time, and never did such a thing occur. She wanted me to go into the room and sleep with her there, but I would not enter the room. I offered her the couch and she refused, sleeping the rest of the night in the room.

That is the part of the story that has been told; this that follows has not. Either the next night or two nights following, in the late evening, I was lying on the couch but not asleep. I was not facing the room but rather the cushions on the back of the couch. My wife had gone to bed and may have been asleep. She was in the same room that she had seen the robed man.

I was not in thought to anything in particular or in any form of concentration. Without warning, definitely leaving her bedroom for the hall, came the power. It moved swiftly, filling the hall and then the living room with its presence. It flowed; it did not walk. It moved without movement; there was no mistake to what it was doing and no mistaking the instant association with the past, and I wondered to the moment and future.

It had never come this close before; it was beside the couch, and I could feel its disconcerting, probing inquiry of me. It was evaluating me! I think I failed; I know I deserved to fail then and now.

I felt no emotion from this presence standing at my back. This is a being unlike human; a human feels and gives off feelings of emotion. I was afraid but not in terror. I had known this presence, this power, before; and I believe I know what it was doing. Again, I knew that I was in total subjugation to this being, and I wondered. Time was passing, but I couldn't begin to say how much; but I knew the moment, time did not stop.

I did not want to turn and look; I did not want to see. My wife had not stirred, and no sounds were in the house. It stayed there, and I stayed there feeling it right beside me. I was still me but I was nothing, I wondered.

Finally, I sort of curled up a little into a semi-fetal position with my back still to the room and the power, this awesome power. I was thinking of my wife maybe a little more than me but thinking of me as well. A thought came to mind and became a statement or request to God Almighty.

Curled as a child and feeling a child, knowing that I was no more than a child and feeling funny because of it, I said, "Not into Hell, Lord, not into Hell, it would be a terrible thing." I didn't say it strongly or quietly or out loud, I said it as a child.

I said no more; I did not repeat it and had absolutely no thought to any more; I was just waiting, waiting without moving.

Again without emotion, no change felt from the power, not human, it turned and moved away toward the far corner of the room, away from me and the hall, away to somewhere else.

I lay there, now in recollection to the man in the robe, the man with the sickle. Somehow when the power left, I felt ashamed within me for being as I had been in life, like I had fallen short of what I should be. It was a child-like knowing that I had failed and failed and failed, but yet I didn't feel that the power was judging, only discerning, only evaluating.

I said nothing to anyone, but I can obviously relive the moment at will—it's May 13, 1994; it's Friday the 13th—in eight days I will be forty-eight years old.

This time I did not pray for everyone I could think of. I did not pray for anyone, not myself or my wife or anyone; the statement was enough. I believe the power was there for one or both of us. She has not died.

If Rasputin, being a man of feeling, knew this same presence, he could easily have shouted out as he did that "death is driving behind him." It would have been impossible for him not to know, and if you have known as well, then you know I have spoken the truth. Careful now, they'll call you crazy!!!

Rasputin had fallen from grace with those that surrounded the Tsar, and he no longer could stay at length close to the royal setting as long as Stolypin was alive. His death changed that, and Rasputin returned to the turmoil of the city. Eventually his detractors won out, and in January of 1912 he returned to his village. Six years had passed since his first influence was felt in St. Petersburg. He didn't break contact with the Royal Family when he returned to his village, but rather maintained communication with them through many telegrams.

Some call it a miracle; one wonders. The travail of Alexis, the young heir to the throne, was not over and neither was the influence of Rasputin over his condition.

The Royal Family was vacationing at their Polish estates when Alexis was injured while riding in a carriage and developed a large tumor from internal bleeding in the groin. The situation could easily have been fatal. Alexis was eight years old and the small boy's strength was waning. He wanted to know if the pain would go away if he died, and his mother knew that death might be his relief. He was given the last rites. Desperate and without asking her husband's permission, Alexandra sent a telegram to Rasputin in Pokrovskoe informing him of her dying son.

Maria, Rasputin's daughter, gives an account to the events that happened in Pokrovskoe, and they did not start with the telegram. They started the day before Alexis would be injured.

It was October of 1912, and she and her father were walking the bank of the river when Rasputin had a pain in his heart that caused him to stumble and to grasp his chest. Maria, in fear that he was having a heart attack, was reassured by him that the pain was not his but that "it is the Tsarevitch—he is stricken." He was not stricken until the next day.

The telegram arrived and Rasputin immediately began praying before his favorite icon of The Black Virgin of Kazan, the vision of whom he had seen in the field while plowing so many years before. He prayed with a great intensity, and when finally rising from his knees, he was ashen and soaked with sweat.

Hurrying to the village to telegraph Alexandra, he sent this message, "Have no fear. God has seen your tears and heard your prayers. Do not grieve your son will live."

Before the arrival of the telegram, Alexis was recovering, as the tumor was dispersing. With this event Rasputin was able to return to St. Petersburg. He returned to great influence and to assassination.

It took two attempts to kill Rasputin. The first was a knifing by a fanatical woman follower of a monk named Illiodor. The monk had once been Rasputin's friend turned enemy. She ripped him open from the navel to the sternum, and some of his intestines had been ruptured. Rasputin recovered but to weakness and was never to be well again.

Another person of note was healed by Grigorii between the first and second attempts on his life. She was the best friend of Alexandra.

At the beginning of 1915, a train wreck had brought Anna Vyrubov near to death, trapped in the wreckage with hips and legs crushed and a blow to the head. Unconscious and considering her to be hopelessly injured, she was left trapped while others were rescued. Finally she was removed to the hospital and given the last rites. Grigorii was summoned and prayed over her; she did not die but remained a cripple for life.

The second attempt on his life brought success. It was an elaborate plot that was intended to see him die by poisoning. Cyanide was baked into small cakes and also put into wine that was given to Rasputin to eat. However, for reasons that can only be a matter of speculation, the poison that he ingested did not have the immediate affect that was anticipated. Because of this, he met a very violent end at the hands of his assassins.

Rasputin had been warned for quite some time that a possible attempt on his life might occur. A man named Protopopov, who was the Minister for Internal Affairs and a friend of Rasputin's, had warned him, saying that the Secret Police and other sources had collected significant evidence of a plot. Rasputin chose to ignore the warnings and, even on the night of the assassination, went against strong advice not to expose himself to possible danger.

Rasputin had been having strong feelings within himself of his pending death and had said, "I feel my end is near. They'll kill me, and then the throne won't last three months." The prophecy proved true.

Five men plotted together to kill Grigorii including an army officer, Captain Soukhotin, and a man named Purishkevich, who was a member of the Duma. (The Duma was a national political body that was comprised of elected representatives from all over Russia. It had come to exist as a concession made by the Tsar during a previous attempt to overthrow the absolute rule of the Royal Family. Eventually, a confrontation between the Duma and the Tsar forced the Tsar to abdicate and thus end the rule of the Romanov's.) The Grand Duke Dimitri Pavovich, who was cousin to the Tsar, was also a conspirator. A doctor was involved, Dr. Lazovert, along with the man who lured Rasputin to his home in the middle of the night, Prince Felix Yusupov.

Prince Yusupov was born in 1887 into one of the wealthiest families in Imperial Russia. Their fortune amounted to just less than five hundred million dollars as valued in monetary terms of 1910. Their fortune encompassed real estate, palaces, jewels, and art.

Felix was considered to be many things. He was socially educated as well as having some formal education at Oxford. He was also spoken of as possibly being a homosexual, and Rasputin's daughter gives account of his advances being violently rejected by Rasputin. This, coupled with the disdained influence of Rasputin with the Royal Family, which was in the process of leading Russia to the turning point that ended the term "Empire," and thus the demise of fortune, may well have led to Rasputin's demise as well.

This key figure in Grigorii's final moments, in years later, made interesting comments to forays of influence to the revolution. He, being more than open-minded, considered the possibility that Russia had fallen victim to a satanic conspiracy, the thought being that it involved bankers and Jews with the unwitting Masons playing the role of instruments to the event. He considered further that M. Philippe had been sent to attack holy Russia's spiritual strength.

It has not been proven that Philippe was so involved, but consider that Rasputin followed closely in his footsteps, and more impetus to hatred and suspicion can easily be placed.

One of the mansions that were owned by Yusupov had been built for Ivan the Terrible. It was a hunting lodge. When Felix was young, hidden cells that lay below the cellar of this home were opened. They revealed rows of skeletons hanging in grim testimony from chains bolted to the walls, testimony to the reign of terror that impressed itself on a young mind.

It was such a person who was the primary instigator in the plot to assassinate a peasant who had spanned the gap between the aristocracy and the netherworld of the struggling masses.

As the plot unfolded, Grigorii was invited by Prince Felix to meet his wife, Princess Irina, at their palace. The invitation was to meet her in the middle of the night following a party that she was supposedly giving. In reality, she was not even in St. Petersburg.

The prince and the doctor picked up Rasputin near midnight and drove him to the palace. Invited to a lower room and with the other three conspirators hiding, Rasputin's introduction was delayed. Eventually, he was offered the cakes and wine, which he finally partook of in abundance.

Two of the cakes contained enough cyanide to kill six men, but Rasputin did not lie down and die. He did begin to become ill and bode the prince to play and sing with his guitar. To the growing dismay of the assailants, Grigorii kept him playing until 2:30 in the morning. The prince was in greater distress than was Rasputin. Felix at this point excused himself on the pretense that he was going to see about his wife's appearance. Ascending to the other conspirators, as he had been alone with Rasputin, he found them in great distress as well. The doctor had succumbed to the stress and had at one point fainted, being now barely sensible. The grand duke, being a delicate sort, wanted to abandon the plot; and Purishkevich, the politician, sought safety in numbers, as politicians oft do, and opted for a joint attack. They began the descent to the room, but the prince stopped them short; and taking the grand duke's pistol, returned to Rasputin alone.

Rasputin was sick now, and it was 3:00 in the morning. Shortly to Yusupov's return to the room, Prince Yusupov shot Grigorii in the back. With Rasputin on the floor, the others entered the room, and after a short time the doctor pronounced him dead. They took him off the bearskin rug he had fallen on and laid him in a corner.

Grigorii was not dead, and after a short absence of everyone from the room, Felix returned. Bending over Rasputin and possibly shaking him, much to his horror, Rasputin grabbed the prince by the throat. Struggling, the prince escaped to the courtyard with Rasputin in pursuit. The others had heard the commotion and followed.

Purishkevich fired several more shots at Rasputin and felled him in the courtyard. This allowed the prince the opportunity, again thinking him dead, to kick and mutilate Rasputin, cutting off his penis and displacing one of his eyes with a vicious kick to the temple.

There followed this activity, the binding of his hands with rope and his being wrapped in a cloth. Then he was summarily dumped in the river. When the police recovered his body from the river and performed an autopsy, it was found that his lungs were filled with water. Rope burns on his wrists and one free hand also indicated that he had endured poisoning by cyanide, being shot numerous times, being brutalized and mutilated, to finally drown.

Alexander Protopopov

Prince Felix Yusupov

Princess Irina

Vladimir M. Purishkevich

Grand Duke Dmitri Pavlovich

The depth of concern to Rasputin's end that was evidenced in the Royal Palace can almost be felt in this letter from the Tsarista to the Tsar who was absent from St. Petersburg at the time.

Alexandra wrote:

December 17, 1916

We are sitting here together—can you imagine our feelings—thoughts—our Friend has disappeared. Yesterday A. (Anna Vyrubova) saw him and he said Felix asked him to come in the night, a motor would fetch him to see Irina—a motor fetched him (military one) with two civilians and he went away.

This night big scandal in Yusupov's house, big meeting. Dimitri, Purishkevich, etc. All drunk. Police heard shots, Purishkevich came out screaming to the Police that our Friend was killed. Police searching and Justice entered now in Yusupov's house . . .

Chief of Police has sent for Dimitri. Felix wished to leave tonight for Crimea. Begged (Protopopov) to stop him.

Our Friend was in good spirits but nervous these days . . . Felix pretends he never came to the house and never asked him . . .

I can't and won't believe he has been killed—God have mercy. Such utter anguish (am calm and can't believe it) . . . Felix came often to him lately.

If any single thing could illustrate the depth of involvement and friendship that Rasputin had established with the rulers of the Russian Empire, this letter of desperate feeling is surely it. It is important to note that the Tsarista called Rasputin Friend, and with a capital letter. Recall what M. Philippe had said when he departed for France. That another Friend would come to them. I believe that there can be little doubt that Rasputin was the Friend that filled the shoes of the Friend.

Rasputin was a Siberian peasant who gained influence of astounding depth to an aristocracy that was incredibly remote to the people they ruled.

In the end, that relationship and position of influence cost him his life, for it was not the common people who found him in distain but rather the well seated to influence and power.

In death, more of Rasputin's clairvoyance was fulfilled. He had predicted that before the Royal Family would meet its end, they would see the village that had been his home. This did happen during what was the final journey for them before they faced a firing squad that physically finalized the abdication of power.

The Royal Family was murdered on July 16, 1918, in a cellar in Ekaterinburg by the revolutionary committee, after viewing the Village of Pokrovskoe from the deck of a boat that carried them on their way to Ekaterinburg.

The aspect of Rasputin's lived experiences to life fully illustrates the struggle between spiritual pretense to propriety and the human sexual nature. Time and again the struggle with our nature overwhelms us in one way or another. Grigorii came to grips with his human nature and spiritual needs in a way that allowed the existence of both; and in doing so; he attracted the favor of many women who also were only human.

I recently attended a stage play in Ann Arbor, Michigan, near my home (Ann Arbor is the seat of the University of Michigan). The play was "Cat on a Hot Tin Roof." For those not familiar with the plot, it centers on a prominent southern family, the patriarch of which is going to die shortly. Through most of the play his affliction is unknown to him. He has a married son who has succumbed to alcohol and is struggling with the weight of life.

There is one scene where "Big Daddy" is being very vocal with his son, and he alluded to a possible sexual exploit of extracurricular nature that the son may have experienced. In his boisterous pronouncements of activity, "Big Daddy" quite took the audience, which was comprised of a large number of lower middle and middle class people with a doctor or two in couple here and there, also.

"Big Daddy" was alluding to sexual adventures that might have been, if not let pass, and to the regret to restraint at having let such encounter slip away. He projected the aspect of pursuing a little "pooh-tang" or a lot of "pooh-tang" as being and having been an important part of life, either missed or experienced too little. Regret was the theme, and the reality of life was the subject.

To my surprise, at his reverberating pronouncements, ripples of identifying acknowledgment waved through this rather, or at least somewhat, proper audience. It took me totally by surprise, and as I was sitting to the rear, my attention was easily diverted to these now taken participants in "Big Daddy's" "pooh-tang" reverie.

I gather in myself the feelings that we are all just people, driven or lured willingly by our own fantasies, desires, and needs to life's adventures and misadventures, and that most are feeling in want to the past, maybe recognizing the present and searching as to what to do with it.

From this very real experience, it is not hard to understand or even relate to Rasputin's society, where entertainment was not electronic, and where life was a repression of total class struggle.

Each class entertains itself in its own diverse ways. For Rasputin, the mysteries of life and life's sexual fulfillments spanned class and religious belief and surely affected the history of one of the great nations on earth.

* * *

I selected Rasputin to help lead this walk through the mysteries of life because he represents the human struggle within. He had the raw nature of a peasant whose home was the arduous environment of Siberia. His need of religion and the crediting of God with all that occurred through him led him in paths to acceptance with the established religious order, which in turn led him to the Royal Family. His relished sexual nature brought him to involvement in the forbidden sects of religion mixed with carnal release, which in turn expanded his sexual prowess to fame in social circles. The consideration that he may have been mad as well expands wonder to his influence to anything, and yet his life became a legend, and his influence with the ruler brought his death.

Healer, clairvoyant, advisor to the Tsar, friend of the Tsarista and her family, lover to women of all social levels, husband, father, and considered holy man would form the marquee of this man still today. He was truly a remarkable man, and in the finality of it all, was both revered and hated.

The hatred brought it to be that his remains were dug up and burned, being cast to the wind. He was revered in that it is said that his severed penis was gathered up by a servant in the courtyard where he lay and was given to a White Russian lady to be kept by a various circle of women in St. Petersburg. Eventually, it was known to have been shown by a very old White Russian lady living in exile in Paris, still kept in a velvet-lined polished wooden box and appearing as a black overripe banana about a foot in length.

By the foot, or by the inch, we are all just human.

Cherished memories of Rasputin

CHAPTER 4

EMANUAL SWEDENBORG

<u>Born in 1688 - Died in 1772</u>

"The Aristotle of the North"

Prominent and Revered Swedish

Statesman -Theologian - Engineer - Clairvoyant - Scientist - Psychic

Emanuel Swedenborg

CHAPTER 4

EMANUAL SWEDENBORG

<u>Born in 1688 - Died in 1772</u>

"The Aristotle of the North"

Prominent and Revered Swedish

Statesman -Theologian - Engineer - Clairvoyant - Scientist - Psychic

In examining these spiritual mysteries of life, it is important to always keep in mind several things. First in importance is the fact that the Bible is very specific in some areas concerning our beliefs, statements, and activities to life. Understanding our relationship to the Trinity and how our directedness to knowledge and belief in God affects and governs our lives is paramount in importance.

The most frightening comment of all such involvement to me is the final statement in the Bible. It gives God's warning that if you add to the Bible, He will add to you the plagues that are written in it; and if you take away from the Words of the Book of Prophesy, God shall take away your part from the Book of Life and out of the Holy City, and from the things written in the Book. It is an ominous warning and one I fear.

Secondly, and of major concern, is that there is a statement within the Bible that if once you have accepted and known Jesus Christ in your life, and you depart from the path laid open to you by your belief and the entering in of Christ into your life, you crucify Him twice. The horror of that statement literally chills me to the bone.

My personal belief in life is that the "Holy Shroud of Turin" truly is the burial cloth in which Jesus was laid to rest. If we, in inner contemplation, examine the incredible spectacle of man's brutality that is so clearly shown on the body whose image has been somehow transferred to the shroud and thus to our minds and person, the implications of a person being in some mysterious way responsible for doing such a thing again is shaking indeed.

With these two ample thoughts in mind, embarking on a commentary to Emanual Swedenborg is, to say the least, a risky endeavor. Swedenborg wrote many books; and from my contact with some of them, his presented experiences to life and life's encounters can easily be considered precarious.

For these reasons, and also the aspect that his writings can be extremely difficult to understand or relate to, I think a person could devote a lifetime to such effort. This effort is going to center on him as a person and on his experiences of extraordinary spiritual encounter in his travel through life.

Swedenborg is a total contrast when placed in the same world with Rasputin. Both, however, shared the common bond of belief in God, and this possibly identifies their common link to the realm of the little known, little understood, and often derided world of spirit.

Rasputin was raw and of lowly place in society. M. Philippe was of lowly or common stature to society, but Emanual Swedenborg was not.

Swedenborg was a man of stature in the Swedish society of his time, and his works remain published and available yet today. There are not many in history to whom such a claim can be made; and with it, the claim of openly-related contact with the angelic realm was a matter of fact presentation for him.

With Rasputin, the openly sensual and exposed human desires were appropriately part of the thoughts and commentary to him. With Swedenborg, sophistication to his person and conduct are in order.

He was born in the year of 1688 and lived to 1772, spending the last twenty-six years in what he claimed to be communication with angels. His special relationship to spiritual life far proceeded this time, however. Because of both his spiritual openness and his vast achievements in physical life, he has been referred to as the "Aristotle of the North."

This man's writings fill some thirty significant volumes that have been in print for over two hundred years and are in the largest part preserved in the Library of the Royal Swedish Academy of Science in Stockholm, addressing religious tenets of the entire spectrum. He has been attributed with living many facets of life which we will touch on, as gradual awareness of this man's place in Swedish history reveals itself. The term "theologian" most certainly applies to his religious devotions.

As with Rasputin, Swedenborg experienced an extraordinary spiritual event that placed him on the path to open representation of his contact with the spiritual realm.

In 1743 and 1744, he experienced a deluge of visions and dreams which moved him in profound manner. The circumstance of these two years was very disturbing to him, and he kept quiet about the experiences.

In April of 1745, Emanual had an experience while in London and dining alone at an inn. Without explanation, the room grew dark, or so it seemed. In the midst of the darkness, an apparition spoke to him, and a vision appeared to him.

After leaving the inn and late in the night, the vision manifested itself to him again. The spirit spoke to him and conveyed a message of need for a human being to serve God by allowing Him to further reveal Himself to mankind, as in similar manner to Old Testament biblical visions.

From this encounter, Swedenborg came to believe a new revelation to the world would be given through him. Until his death twenty-seven years later, he would spend the majority of his life devoted and in communication to the effort.

For two years following this event, he studied the Bible and indexed it intensely. Recall that Rasputin sought learned advice and went on pilgrimage to Athos. Both men searched but in their own ways.

During the early years of his theological effort, he wrote anonymously and often in great seclusion; starets sought seclusion. Swedenborg was unmarried, and he was much alone with his books. He had built a small summerhouse on his property, towards the rear, and spent much time in seclusion there. In the latter years of his writing, his theological anonymity passed by the wayside and this eventually brought good and bad to him.

In death, Swedenborg holds a stature that few men in Sweden have attained. His remains are in public view in the Cathedral of Uppsala, Sweden. He was laid to rest in a sarcophagus of impressive red granite.

In Sweden, resting in public view is generally not extended beyond kings, generals, archbishops, and intellectuals of prominent stature. This distinction has been reserved to only a score.

If you recall the contrast, Rasputin's remains were dug up, burned, and cast in the wind.

Swedenborg's life began in a family of influence and stature. His father was professor of theology at the University of Uppsala, and he was also the dean of the cathedral. Later in life, he became Bishop of Skara. The post of Bishop raised him to the rank of nobleman by Queen Ulrika Eleonora. Bishop Swedenborg was also chaplain to the Royal Family. This naturally gave contact to the highest society and to political circles as well.

On his mother's side, her family was well situated in the mining industry, and this may have had influence to Emanual's eventual appointment to the post of "Extraordinary Assessor in the Royal College of Mines." He was twenty-eight years old when King Charles XII appointed him, and he served for thirty-one years as a member of the Board of Mines.

Emanual had graduated from Uppsala University in 1709 and after further studies published Sweden's first scientific journal, *The Daedalus Hyperboreus,* which brought to him considerable fame.

He was later also asked to serve as engineering advisor by King Charles XII, and Swedenborg functioned as construction supervisor in public works projects.

To a man of such stature, the aspect of clairvoyance being a part of his person would bring thought that a repressing scrutiny by the dominant Lutheran Church would have followed his activities and writings. It eventually did but not until the very end of his life, and it was by the highest authority of the Church.

To his early years, we can consider confirmed accounts of clairvoyance as unquestioned. One such instance that occurred in July of 1759 while Emanual was dining with wealthy friends in their home in Gothenburg is widely known.

Gothenburg is some three hundred miles from Stockholm, which was Swedenborg's home, and communication between the two cities was by hand-carried message. As he dined, Swedenborg suddenly became pale and disturbed. At the occurrence, he withdrew to the garden for a time. When he returned, it was with news that a massive fire had broken out in Stockholm and that he was afraid that he would lose some of his manuscripts, as the fire was spreading rapidly.

Apprehensive into the evening, he finally announced at 8:00 p.m., with great relief, that the fire was extinguished. He is quoted as having said, "Thank God! The fire is extinguished the third door from my house!" The people present found themselves disturbed by the incident as some had homes and friends in Stockholm. Keep in mind that insurance is something that was not prevalent to the time.

Vision of Stockholm burning

Those present were so impressed by Swedenborg's clairvoyance, that the story was related later that evening to the Provincial Governor. The Governor was moved to ask Swedenborg for a full account; and the next day he willingly complied, giving account regarding the means by which it was extinguished and the circumstance and extent of the fire.

The news spread rapidly through the city that Stockholm may have suffered a major fire, and it was a topic of concern and conversation on that Sunday. Monday evening details of the fire arrived in Gothenburg. A messenger had arrived from the Stockholm Board of Trade. The much aroused city was in anxious waiting for news of the possible disaster.

Swedenborg's claims and descriptions were confirmed. There had been a fire, and every major detail of the actual conflagration had been described accurately by the now-to-be recognized clairvoyant.

The attention brought to him by this extraordinary event aroused curiosity and interest in a man who would eventually be recognized to, in a very matter of fact manner, claim to be in contact with angelic beings.

The curiosity brought with it elevation to being a publicly known figure. People of prominence desired to meet him and began to write accounts of him and his habits.

Shortly following the events of the fire, Swedenborg's writings of "Heaven and Hell" and the Arcana Coelestia became known. With this, as might be expected, those viewing circumstances without having met and talked with him began to conclude that he had indeed become insane.

Frequently, if they would have opportunity to see and visit with him, their encounter would end with them in a state of quandary. The claims that he was making were so controversial and sweeping that acceptance was more than difficult; difficult to the extent that eventually the seated Lutheran Church openly examined and renounced them, but at the same time, those questioning departed convinced of his sanity.

Before devoting himself to deep theological endeavor, Swedenborg made contribution to society in areas not discussed as yet. Though he was a philosophic thinker he could also be experimental and pragmatic in nature.

In the area of metallurgy, his efforts manifested conclusions that brought deeper understanding to the treatment of iron and copper, as well as brass. It's important to keep in mind that this was an age when the existence of oxygen was unknown, and thus the composition of the atmosphere was not known. Neither was electricity or photography a known science.

Within this infancy of understanding, Swedenborg also supplied the first knowledge of the importance of the cerebral cortex and respiratory movement of the brain tissues.

In biology, metallurgy, engineering, and theology, Swedenborg excelled. He influenced many other areas of note in exposure to life's journey.

In the field of engineering, his assignment as construction supervisor involved such things as devising a means to move large warships across land, the construction of a canal, and the creation of a new design for dry-docks.

Hidden Shadows

Swedenborg's extensive education and keen mind placed him in the forefront of the scientific people of the day. His education started at Uppsala University at the age of eleven. The University at the time offered four major studies: medicine, philosophy, law, and theology. He majored in philosophy and at the time of his instruction also included the areas of science and mathematics. He studied law and learned Latin as well during this time. Later in his life, he also learned Greek and Hebrew.

His reasons for learning Greek and Hebrew centered about his religious studies and writings. He had a desire to read and interpret the original writings of the scripture himself, and it is obvious that the expansion of language is essential to such studies. Eventually, as a result of his studies, he actually made translations of portions of the Bible that remain yet today.

By applying his gained knowledge and the expansion of his claimed contact with angels, he actually developed a theology of his own. During his lifetime, he had no organized following. There were no sects or societies to influence or promote or enhance his person or writings. After his death, a society was formed and followers of his beliefs spread all over the world in small groups, with some existing yet today.

A man named Robert Hindmarsh organized the first group in London. Another man named James Glen, who had occasional contact with the London group, was responsible for bringing some of Swedenborg's works to America. It was Glen who attempted to establish Swedenborgianism in Philadelphia in 1784.

In the spring of the year following Swedenborg's visions of the fire in Stockholm, he is noted to have revealed further evidence of his contact with the paranormal.

There lived in Stockholm at the time a widow. She had been the wife of the Dutch Ambassador. Mme. De Marteville had an earth-shaking difficulty with a silversmith, and hearing of Swedenborg's evidenced ability, she sought him out to possibly help her.

The silversmith was trying to charge her for a silver service set that she recalled was paid for but could find no receipt. In distress and dilemma, as the bill was large, she was much in hope to Swedenborg's help.

By this time, it was considered that Swedenborg was able to, in some way, make contact with and converse with the spirits of departed people. This is what Mme. was hoping would happen and that help could be obtained.

Swedenborg agreed that if he encountered her husband in the spirit world and could converse with him that he would ask of the circumstance. As the story goes, he did so encounter him, and Swedenborg told the widow that her husband would tell her where the receipt was hidden. The receipt, along with a missing diamond hairpin, was behind a drawer in the desk.

Some eight days later, Swedenborg was again in conversation with the departed ambassador. During the course of the encounter, the ambassador indicated that he would have to leave to tell his wife where the receipt was located.

The next day, Swedenborg told the widow of his encounter with her husband, and she told him of hers with her husband in a dream. The receipt and the hairpin were recovered from the desk just where the ambassador had related to her in the dream that they would be.

Swedenborg's renown was spreading, and it was not uncommon for people to seek him out to visit a man who would, in matter of fact and calm manner, claim that he could and did converse with angels.

Keep in mind that this particular "crazy man" was a member of what would be equivalent to our Legislature in Washington for fifty years. It is there called the "Riksdag" or Legislature, and it is composed of four parts or Estates. Swedenborg was a member of the "House of Nobles." He first took his seat in 1719 and remained there Until a few years prior to his death in 1772.

Isn't it interesting that in different times and different settings, people who experience the extraordinary live such a diversity of lives and circumstances? Our society today would be and is far less tolerant to the unusual in proprietous circles. I fully believe that there are far too many psychiatrists and psychologists running loose in this society, espousing their own views or theories from positions of authority that a society of foolish gentiles has bestowed upon them.

There are many "reals" to life, and one person's real can easily become the target of another person's reasoned suppositions. Edgar Cayce encountered difficulty from time to time; and, interestingly, one of the four identified sources of information that blossomed forth from him was from that of contact with the departed spirits of people.

A third notable event for Swedenborg involved the Queen of Sweden; and as word of the Queen's confirming statements became known, so much the more did Swedenborg's fame spread.

In the fall of 1761, the Count Ulric Scheffer, acting on the Queen's initiative, invited Swedenborg to attend the Queen's Court with him. The Queen had heard of the many and varied abilities of Swedenborg in the spiritual realm, and her desire of him was that he make effort to contact her departed brother, Augustus William.

Swedenborg agreed to make an effort to do so and, as several days passed, called at the Royal residence with news for Queen Luisa Ulrika.

He presented the Queen with several copies of a number of his books and retired with the Queen to the far end of the room for a private audience. Swedenborg indicated that he had indeed been in spiritual contact with her departed brother, and he conversed in eased manner about the event with Her Majesty. Some secret was conveyed that brought immediate surprise and great amazement to the Queen, and she was thoroughly convinced that Swedenborg was indeed gifted in a manner that evidenced a truth to her. She made it well known that only her brother could have known what Swedenborg had told her, and the incident became widely known and discussed in social circles, gaining the title of being, "The Queen's Secret!"

Swedenborg's writings espoused that divine force underlies all matter and settled on a belief that the soul was the link between God and man. In this viewing of the infinite and the finite, he believed that man could not see or measure the soul.

Focusing on the blood and applying his knowledge of anatomy, he developed a hypothesis that the soul was carried in the blood. Keep in mind here that the Bible states that, "the blood is the life." Swedenborg believed that creation or "the Kingdom of Life" was an

"The Queen's secret"

incredible tightly-bound unity and that it was consistent in design, grand design, with the concept of the soul of the individual and that the soul was the center of creation.

These views are published in his work, *The Economy of the Animal Kingdom,* and maybe you can see why I have stated that viewing his writings presents a dangerous relationship to the established Bible. Swedenborg associates animal as man.

Cayce indicated that the soul dwells within the body and in such a fashion as to say it dwells within a sponge, the soul permeating the body as though it were a sponge.

Swedenborg actually approached a correct prediction regarding the manner in which the lungs purify the blood. Keep in mind that the existence of oxygen was unknown and not discovered for fifty years; it is but one of many attempts to discovery. Having studied the brain, he drew the hypothesis that the body and the brain, by flow of the blood, and by the blood, were dependent on a "spirituous fluid." This was something that he believed could not be known by scientific discovery but that it must be the carrier of the soul.

Within the pages of *The Tibetan Book of the Dead,* one finds that the language in which it was written actually had no word for the soul and that one was invented that would allow the correlation or conveying of the meaning within the pages of understanding.

Diversity of culture and thought produce diversity of literature and religious belief, and thus societies are formed about them.

Swedenborg also believed that two types of minds predominate mankind and that both occasionally occur in the same person. He believed that both are gifted. The first has a naturally finer acumen or sharpness to perceive. The second has the ability to elicit or reason. I believe that people like Thomas Edison were gifted with both, or possibly Alexander Graham Bell and Benjamin Franklin could be identified as well.

If you think about it, discovery is a process of perception and reason and revelation. The gift of a mind of such dual ability and a belief in God opens doors to possibilities that are boundless. Emanual's father was well aware of God's influence to a man's direction in life and offered this advice to Emanual on one occasion. "I beg you most earnestly that you fear and love God above all else, for without this fear of God all other training, all study, all learning is of no account, indeed quite harmful."

It is sound advice to fear God, and in looking to the subjects of comment in this work and to the lives lived by those addressed, my belief in the interactive relationship between the spiritual and material worlds has found new heights of intensity to development, as I tuned to the awareness in some degrees, of both types of human achievers.

The combined facets of fear of God, insight to initial development or perception, and the ability to reason and apply known principles and facts are the foundations of society's advancement, and maybe with this perception, Swedenborg found the key to communication with the realm of spirit and opened the door a little to the realities that God keeps so carefully guarded from us.

Here we can ponder the aspect of penetrating inwardly to observe the operation of the psyche in a methodology that has been "labeled" phenomenology. That is if you choose to read the ten pages in the Encyclopedia Britannica that are devoted to this recognized science of comprehending investigations of every real existence. The existence can be of beyond this sphere, but immediately deduced by a person from feeling, principles, and faculties of the human soul. Is that which Dr. Dyer espouses in being inner directed new?

Swedenborg's personality might be revealed a little in a quoted comment by an associate. The quote expands upon a diverse person and reads:

> Someone might think that assessor Swedenborg was eccentric and whimsical; but the very reverse was the case. He was very easy and pleasant in company, talked on every subject that came up, accommodating himself to the ideas of the company; and never spoke on his own views unless he was asked about them.

It is an extremely interesting description, given that people who openly espouse to awareness of spiritual realms often find themselves singled out by an objective western culture to criticism of idiosyncrasies that are actually possessed by the "normal" mass of humanity. Swedenborg again transcended the scope of social propriety and acceptance in the area of conversational aplomb to contemporary grace. He was not exactly your average "nut case." It is important to keep in mind that to espouse contact with angels today could easily bring rise to concern for your social acceptances'.

One of the ways that Swedenborg claimed contact to spiritual revelation is something that you may well have experienced and ignored or maybe secretly pondered. I myself did just that for many years, until I finally decided that being myself, and recognizing myself, was more important than making an effort to conform within myself to this now personally recognized society of blinders. I'm not a horse; I'm a human being and have God's given right to be myself and as I am, not as someone thinks I should be. Such is the same for you, if you will open to your real person. Such was the same for Ralph Waldo Emerson, who found himself to be influenced by the visions and writings of Emanual Swedenborg. Being special seems to recognize special and grow from it, and adds to humanity's development from it.

There exists a fashion of encounter to the revealing of an occurrence or scene that is seen in the eye of the mind. It is of a total clarity, just as if one were, with ultra clear vision in proper lighting, seeing it to recognition and recollection with the physical eyes. It is, however, not an event of the five senses; it is an event of interrelating spiritual contact; and the perception is an inner event that manifests itself to consciousness.

The event to conscious awareness usually lasts for seconds or portions of seconds in this form and conveys a distinct visual projection that shows an event in motioned form with distinguishable people in activity to surroundings and other people.

The awareness of the knowing to personal occurrence is absolute; it's not something that one has to guess about. You don't say to yourself, "Did that happen?" You know it happened. You might not know the people, or the place, or the activity to recognition of past or present physical encounters, but you will know with certainty, as though seeing a movie scene flash within you, that you are being shown something.

The scene can focus your attention to its entire spectrum, or it can be to a separate aspect of the entirety. The wonder to each occurrence is often, "Will or did this, or does this represent objective reality?"

Sometimes it will bring with it understanding to a puzzled circumstance, or clarify or correct a thought train. As the case may be, you will not be left wanting to your own belief that you are encountering something that's not taught in a high school cooking class.

Swedenborg believed that his angels were with him always, and that they would communicate with him spiritually in many ways. One such way that he specifically identified was by means of thoughts that would flash in his mind and bring with them revelation or instruction.

One such noted event brought with it the understanding that angels consider that all occurrences proceed from God. Man considers that all things are to be his way, and this is as evil spirits do as well. If good exists as spirit then evil also exists in spirit. Swedenborg also claimed that the angels repeat over and over that man should trust in divine providence, which brings things desired if they are for our good, after they are desired, and in time when they are not thought of.

Emanual also stated quite clearly that his angelic acquaintances would communicate with him by means of whispers and singing. Interestingly, one might consider the aspect of inner song that is oft times associated with current conscious involvement and wonder to or accept the directedness. The more one opens to the world of spiritual directedness or communication, the more eased will be the relationship. It is one of trust, understanding, acceptance, and love.

God is love to all, but vengeance is His and woe be it to who His vengeance falls upon. The more open a person becomes to the influence of spirit's good, the more evident it becomes that overcoming the spirit's evil requires the intervention, power, and guidance of God.

In viewing God's vengeance, it is important to note that the Bible tells us that if one gloats to the wrath of God's actions, then His vengeance is withdrawn. The Bible tells us, also, that the struggle in life is not in the flesh but rather against spiritual wickedness. Ephesians Chapter 6 Verses 12 through 17 describes the struggle and reads:

> For we wrestle not against flesh and blood, but against principalities, against powers, against the rivers of the darkness of the world, against spiritual wickedness in high places.
>
> Wherefore take unto you the whole armor of God, that ye may be able to withstand in the evil day, and having done all, to stand.
>
> Stand therefore, having your loins girt about with truth, and having on the breastplate of righteousness;
>
> And your feet shod with the preparation of the gospel of peace;
>
> Above all, taking the shield of faith, wherewith ye shall be able to quench all the fiery darts of the wicked.
>
> And take the helmet of salvation, and the sword of the spirit, which is the word of God;

* * *

Pope Gregory the Great

I pondered for years this biblical presentation of life's struggle; and oddly, without intention, I came to have contact with that which is presented as being angelic order.

I had for the majority of my life heard and read of angels and archangels and considered that the known or presented existence of these special creations of God encompassed the total sphere of angelic service to God's will.

This, however, does not seem to be the case; as study and conversation has now revealed the acceptance by scholars of biblical presentation, that an actual tier of special beings is defined, with some variation to belief. Little exists in man's knowledge that variation does not apply to, and in this case the Catholic Church acknowledges within the pages of *The New Catholic Encyclopedia* that various angelic beings exist, but the Church does not recognize orders of angels officially.

We find in looking under the sub-heading of groupings of angels, that since the fourth century nine choirs of angels are identified. Within that which is named the "Pauline Epistles" are five groups, being Virtues, Powers, Principalities, Dominations, and Thrones. These are looked upon as good heavenly spirits, and they are placed with Archangels and Angels. There is with this grouping also Cherubim and Seraphim.

The encyclopedia continues to say that this series was developed under the influence of Neo-Platonic speculation, is not in accord with the Bible, and is influenced by Psuedo-Dionysius to form a hierarchical structure of three triads.

Thus elaborated, the doctrine of nine Choirs of Angels has been held in the west since the time of Gregory the Great, and the concept of a celestial hierarchy is derived from the order of Oriental monarchism. Through all of this, we arrive at the recognition, or maybe concept, that there are three choirs consisting of three equally numbered groupings of angelic beings.

The first order being:

Seraphim
Cherubim
Thrones

The second order being:

Dominations
Virtues
Powers

The third order being:

Principalities
Archangels
Angels

In these groupings, Gregory the Great is attributed with having reversed the order of Principalities and Virtues. This occurred in the sixth century and he drew much criticism for having done so.

The belief in angels by acknowledged dogma of the Catholic Church dates to the First Council of Nichea in A.D. 325.

The functions and placement in the spiritual realm of the angelic beings has been a matter of debate through the centuries. To me the importance lies in recognizing that they are very real and that they influence our lives and man's history. Denial of their presence would leave for me a sorrowful void in my life, an empty place that reason and ego cannot fill. Once in knowledge of their existence, then existence changes. Consider the biblical statement alluding to life's struggle against Powers and Principalities.

Consider that the names of Powers and Principalities are directly identified within the Bible as being a focus of human struggle in this life, and consider that they are spirits, angels of a group or order. Consider, also, that along with Satan, one third of all the angels in heaven revolted against God and fought in heaven to overcome God, and the other two-thirds of the angelic realm. Allow yourself also to ponder the confinement of that one-third of the angelic host to this planet.

Now, no longer considered angels but rather called demons and devils, these spirit beings are alive and well to their own mischief within their confinement. Consider that Christ spent much of his time during the three years of his ministry dealing with these spirit beings that can live within a person and torment that person and, through that person, others.

Recall that they recognized Christ and spoke to him from within people they were possessing. They knew there was a time limit to their freedom of action here and alluded to it in speaking to Christ. Recall, "Hast though come to torment us before the time"; it's pretty explicit.

With the propensity of encounter recorded within the Bible, should it be a wonder that people might encounter some of the numbers of the good two-thirds of the heavenly host in some way in this fleshly life. I don't believe that God has left us and is leaving us to the torn chaos that this world has become.

Swedenborg's claim to angelic contact when viewed within the terms of human development, development meaning spiritual growth, is not so far fetched if one has a mind open enough to feel one's being, rather than fondling one's life. Remember he spent the last twenty-six years of his life in deliberately imposed withdrawal to public service, and remember that he fully believed that angels communicated with him by means of their whispering and singing to him and by means of bursts of feeling that came upon him, and through visions.

His communication was also with the departed souls of humans, and it was matter of fact to its occurrence. Recall also that there was an interrelationship with the spirit realm and the fleshly realm. Keep in mind also that the man had visions while he was conscious that represented realities of events occurring at the very moment he was experiencing the vision, and consider that all of this is well documented and confirmed by the establishment of the time.

Not all was accepted by the establishment, as Swedenborg's theological writings eventually brought him censor by the Lutheran Church, but that censor did not prevent the formation of societies that follow his theology even today.

His censor came in the waning years of his life and was the result of a review by the authorities of the Lutheran faith in Sweden. As a result of the review of Swedenborg's written theology, the Church forbade the teaching of his doctrines. Ultimately there was a mixture of some teaching and some refraining from pronouncing what Swedenborg espoused as being "The New Christian Religion."

An interesting quote attributable to Emanual's contact with angels alludes to the delights of existence and goes as follows:

> It is allowed everyone to be in his delight, whether spirits or angels, even the most unclean who delight in adultery, stealing, blasphemy, lying— these are the delights of our nostrils . . . Everyone whether good or evil is in his own delight—delight of his good, delight of his evil . . . And since that (evil) is our delight we are cast back, and are in torment!

Swedenborg made some interesting comments about angels. He says they not only speak but that they write. Ernest Hemingway often alluded to "having the juice" when he wrote. He meant writing with a uncontested inspired flow. If you have experienced such moments, then you know the meaning of Hemingway's "juice." I have experienced it many times and wonder to Swedenborg's descriptions and a possible relationship.

Swedenborg said, also, that angels breathe an atmosphere that is special to them. They are empowered by God and have no power of their own, and they are agents of God. Instantaneous weakness would come to them if they doubted the source of their power, and they would not be capable of resisting evil.

Holy men often believe they are attacked by evil spirits, and Swedenborg was no exception to this belief. He believed that evil spirits were real and alive and active to influence within this world of flesh.

All things that angels do are ascribed to the power of God working through them, and all praise to their actions is to the Lord and not accepted by them. They are instruments of God's will.

Swedenborg believed that his angels were with him always. He claimed that they have no language that allows the human traits of consternation. They can only speak or express love in perfect sincerity, as it is in them, as God is acting through them.

Swedenborg is attributed with influencing prominent people even after his death. Three such people are the poet, William Blake, following him, Johann Wolfgang Van Goethe, and also most importantly, Dr. Carl Jung.

Dr. Carl Jung is said to have read seven of Swedenborg's books. This is no small feat in itself and may well explain some of his concepts and stated experiences in the realm of the spirit. Jung also opened himself to the seclusion of his inner person, and we will eventually talk of him, as he is the father of modern psychology.

Swedenborg's beliefs and writings are founded upon the basis that divine force, emanating from God, underlies all matter, and that the soul is the link between God and man. "You must love the Lord your God with all of your heart, with all of your mind, and with all of your spirit," so says the Bible. This is a description of the triplicity of man, a triplicity of individuals within the individual that are the individual, linked to God through the soul. Is there little wonder that we gather ourselves in churches to listen to a greater wisdom, or visit stadiums to hear the message of salvation from evangelists, or cling to the T.V. as the pulpit comes to us, and wonder to what we are and where we are going?

A few days ago, I had occasion to watch an extraordinary presentation on T.V. It involved an explosion that occurred in an elementary school. The bomb was attached to a man who was in company with a woman who entered the school and took hostage well over one hundred people, the great majority children of elementary school age.

The man had declared himself to be in a state of revolution and threatened to detonate the bomb if his instructions were not followed. The people were gathered in a large classroom; and in the center, a square was either existent or drawn on the floor. It appeared to be six or eight feet square. The room was very open and filled with the normal furnishings of a classroom, and the building was of modern brick construction. The walking bomb claimed that the explosives that adorned his body would be sufficient to destroy a major portion of the building.

Claims were being made to the significance of the "magic square." I don't recall the exactness of the claims, but I do recall that the only two people inside the square were the man with the bomb and the woman.

With evident unintention, the explosives detonated. Photographs of the room after the explosion revealed that, indeed, a massive blast had occurred, but that it had been almost totally contained within the square.

The detonation caused total blackness within the room as smoke enveloped everything and everyone. One adult unsuccessfully attempted to push one child out a window. The windows in the room had not been blown out. A police officer interviewed following the incident was standing by a brick wall that was the exterior to the room and indicated that a major portion of it should have been blown out by the force of the blast.

Before the bomb exploded, killing the man and the woman in the square, some of the children in the room indicated that they saw white ghosts or angel-like forms descend through the ceiling into the room. One such being was recognized by one of the children and spoke to the child before the blast.

It was the face of a woman that the child recognized, and the woman had said to the child that what the man was doing was not right. This child had strangely misnamed the woman as being a grandmother that it could not have been. This puzzled the child's parents until some time later, while looking through a picture album; they encountered a page that contained two large photos of the child's grandmothers. Pointing to the one picture, the child indicated with absolute certainty that that was the person in the form of a white ghost-like being that had descended through the ceiling and had spoken the words. The child's deceased great-grandmother was identified. The other grandmother whose picture faced toward the deceased woman bore the name that the child had applied to the form in the room.

The documentation on the program was from an adult who worked in the school and was one of the hostages in the room when the bomb went off, and from uniformed police involved in the event. Photos of the room taken afterwards amazingly revealed, in two of them, the visible form of a ghost-like presence standing in the midst of the blast area in one photo; and toward or against the wall in the other photo, there was another similar presence.

Statements of police officers as to the event and intensity of the blast, statements of children as having seen the descending figures enter the room, photographs of some unexplainable figures in the room after the blast, two terrifying individuals dead, and of over one hundred children and a few adults in the room, none seriously injured, give in my estimation an account of angelic intervention in our world of objective suppositions.

> And they brought young children to Him, that He should touch them: And His disciples rebuked those that brought them.
>
> But when Jesus saw it, he was much displeased, and said unto them. "Suffer the little children to come unto me, and forbid them not: For of such is the Kingdom of God.
>
> Verily I say unto you whosoever shall not receive the Kingdom of God as a little child, he shall not enter therein."
>
> And He took them up in His arms, put His hands upon them, and blessed them.
>
> Mark 10:13-16

* * *

Swedenborg was one of those astonishing people in history who actually predicted the day he would die—March 29, 1772.

Emanual traveled to London in September of 1771. He rented quarters there and continued to work on his books. In December, he was stricken with a stroke that placed him in a coma that lasted three weeks. His ability to speak was destroyed as a result. January and February saw some recovery, and he was again able to converse with visitors.

At this time, Swedenborg did another extraordinary thing. He took it upon himself to write to a renowned English Minister, John Wesley. Swedenborg informed him that he would be very happy to discuss and exchange views on religion with him. In making this invitation, Emanual made mention to Wesley that he had become aware of Wesley's desire to discuss such matters with him from contact in the world of spirits.

John Wesley made known to his friends the surprise that took him at these remarks. He had an interest in such discussions but to his recollection had made mention of it to no one.

Wesley was just starting on a journey that was to encompass some six months and subsequently returned a letter to Swedenborg expressing a desire to acceptance of his invitation at journey's end.

Swedenborg, upon receiving the letter, knew and remarked that it would be too long a time, and that he would enter the spirit world on the 29th day of March 1772. His maid, Elizabeth Reynolds, confirmed his prediction along with a Mrs. Shearsmith, who had rented him his quarters, and both were with him when he died.

He had been in a long sleep on Sunday, March 29, 1772 when at five o'clock he awoke and inquired as to the time of day. He was told it was five o'clock. Responding, Swedenborg said, "That is good, I thank you. God bless you." He then was given to a gentle sigh, and he died.

CHAPTER 5

ANDREW JACKSON DAVIS

Born on August 11, 1826 - Died in 1910

"The Poughkeepsie Seer"

Healer - Clairvoyant - Philosopher -

Author of Twenty-Six Books

Andrew Jackson Davis

CHAPTER 5

ANDREW JACKSON DAVIS

Born on August 11, 1826 - Died in 1910

"The Poughkeepsie Seer"

Healer - Clairvoyant - Philosopher -

Author of Twenty-Six Books

In February of 1845, Dr. S. S. Lyon formed an acquaintance with Andrew Jackson Davis in the town of Bridgeport, Connecticut. Previous to their encounter the good doctor, being a successful medical practitioner in Bridgeport, had no belief in clairvoyance; but the overwhelming evidence that young Davis represented brought transformation to his beliefs and were too powerful in weighted manifestation for him to resist. He developed deep convictions to the importance of what he was encountering and did not hesitate to state open encouragement to the wisdom of the spiritual unknown. He availed himself in his medical practice of the clairvoyant's medical advice to aid treatment in difficult cases of disease.

What Dr. Lyon encountered in Mr. Davis, later to become Dr. Andrew Jackson Davis, manifested itself as a facet to the extraordinary that has evidenced itself as spanning time and distance in several cases and diverse circumstances. This facet is associated with the aspect of good being accomplished by direct application of the knowledge that is presented to this material and physical sphere of life from the spiritual realm.

Oft times this knowledge is involved with the diagnosis and treatments of ailments to people, or to the direct healing by divine intervention at the involvement of people who somehow have been chosen or made special by God to His will being worked through them.

Interestingly, this strangeness of occurrence often has happened to people who are doctors, or become doctors, or just somehow envelop themselves in the healing or helping of others in distress.

We've looked at Rasputin from many perspectives and seen that the Royal Family of Russia believed that God heard and answered his prayers. Though Rasputin was never considered a doctor, M. Philippe was made a doctor by the same Royal authority; and he was made such with apparent reason to the good he had done in influencing the divine to the healing of affliction. Both Rasputin and M. Philippe functioned to the good of those distressed. Both were simple men.

Emanual Swedenborg believed himself to be in contact with angels and wrote his many works to the intent of providing mankind with a guiding light and revelation to life as we live it and spirit as it surrounds us. His intent, also, was to the good of man's progression to Christ's return. Though he did not embrace the development of man's medical understanding, his focus to depiction and presentation was intense and had apparent influence on Dr. Carl Jung, who has had massive influence on our society and medical practices.

M. Scott Peck, M.D. also has had influence to our society by his writings and medical practice. His acceptance of the existence and influence of evil as a spiritual entity that can and does afflict the human race is testimony to modern medicine's subservience to God's created world of both flesh and spirit. Dr. Peck's bold and courageous rendering of his medical encounter with the evil that can be exhibited within people, envelop the understandings of Carl Jung. The existence of the human as being a continuously multifaceted life form, that is interactive to the material and spiritual realm in some manner of homogeneous creation, is revealingly evident in his writing; and they are recognizably a step to change in modern medicine.

Jung and Peck have uncovered to a great extent the mystery in the midst of which Rasputin, Philippe, Davis, Cayce and others lived their lives; and as we are able, we'll continue this journey toward understanding within these pages of discovery, the discovery of spirit— good and bad.

Andrew Jackson Davis was an American of simple roots and parentage who lived the greatest extent of his life in the simplicity of an almost non-existent education, having a mere five months of formal instruction in the basics that we are still trying to make basic.

In his teenage years and while working as an apprentice shoemaker, his life's path changed direction with sudden and unusual perspectives. By chance, this young man encountered what we today identify as the realm of the hypnotic trance.

At the time, being in the 1800's, the terms associated with hypnosis that were used stemmed from the process of revelation to man's awareness that the human psyche can be manifested in ways different than our conscious and normally sleeping selves.

The process was not something that was without trepidation to discovery and even our own Benjamin Franklin's name found its way into the way of questions and denials. The names "magnetism," "somnambulism," and "mesmerizing" are words of extraction and in some ways distraction to the modern experience of hypnotism.

Hypnotism is a recognized tool in our society and is used by such establishment agencies as the Michigan State Police. Their usage is applied in fashion to help individuals recall events or experiences that might aid in investigation and the hypnosis can be performed by psychologists that are part of their organization. One such entity is their State Police Behavior Science Unit.

Andrew, by encounter with a traveling "magnetizer" that visited his village and performed feats of hypnotic demonstration on his fellow citizens, was introduced to the phenomenon by an attempt to use him as a subject. The effort failed; he was not hypnotized by the traveling magnetizer.

Later, however, a tailor in his village, who was experimenting with the process after the traveler's had left, invited and induced Andrew to allow him to once again attempt to magnetize him. Mr. William Livingston, the tailor, was successful but in an astonishing fashion. The event was the beginning of a remarkable adventure through life for Andrew Jackson Davis.

Davis eventually dictated Tomes of "Revelation" while in a hypnotic state and diagnosed diseases and treatment for the ailing. His medical dissertations were later acknowledged by Edgar Cayce as being incredibly similar to his. Further, too, were similarities we'll talk about later. These men lived in different centuries, both were Americans, and both were simple men. They were in no way part of the upper structure of society as to the way they lived their lives, though Davis actually became a doctor when he was in his sixties and practiced as such until his death, being in his eighties.

Magnetism, as the word is used in hypnosis, is descriptive to one of two approaches to the establishment of a hypnotic state in a person. Dr. Bernard C. Gindes, M.D. and hypnotherapist, describes in considerable detail the aspects of both processes in his book, *New Concepts of Hypnosis.*

Magnetism is that which Andrew Jackson Davis was exposed to in the hypnotic process and it is such that manifested the unusual revelations of the man. Eventually as years passed and experience grew, he was able to, by merely touching the hand of a person while he was completely conscious, read that person. Cayce described this as psychometry.

In the process of scientific understanding, one thing stands head and shoulders above all else, and that is that before knowledge manifests itself to acceptance; superstition has to have its day and its say.

Magic and superstition preceded hypnotic procedure. Chemistry is rooted in alchemy; Nostradamous was an alchemist. The science of astrology was the forerunner of astronomy; Chinese astrology is today influential in the Orient and its revelations to person and personality is a wonder to its study. God's condemnation of it is a frightening wonder, also.

The practice of hypnosis was said to have existed in ancient Egypt and was involved with the worship of Isis, Nature Goddess of the Nile. The Greeks in the years 900 before Christ were aware of it, and it was used by a Greek physician of the time named Chiron, who was most renowned. As I'm saying this, I hope that you are contemplating the thought that if Andrew Jackson Davis and Edgar Cayce found contact with the realm and knowledge of the spirit through the psyche of the little understood forms of hypnotic states, then might possibly did ancient civilizations gain knowledge in the same manner?

Nostradamus used a crystal ball in his revealings, which also involve a tranced state in which diversion of conscious predominance is relegated to the depths of the crystal through scrying.

Hypnotism was lost in man's struggles for many centuries until in the 1800's people of medicine began to experiment with it. Past the turn of the century, physicians such as Dr. Carl Jung and Dr. Sigmund Freud exposed themselves to its mysteries.

Dr. Jung eventually rejected its use because he could not understand it. Dr. Freud found it to be of importance and even went to the Salpetriere Hospital in France in 1885 to observe and study the experiments and practice of Dr. Charcot, who was a neurologist of esteem. Freud altered his "theories" to assimilate those of the Salpetriere and Charcot, as the successful application of hypnosis was a recognized reality of assistance in treating patients there. It was noted that bodily changes could be both produced and eliminated in this hospital of over four thousand patients.

Freud was impressed to such an extent that he went to the Nancy Clinic, which was also experimenting with hypnosis and was itself in France. Dr. Bernheim was the director there, and Freud became involved with the study of post-hypnotic suggestion and was very impressed by the evident effects that could be wrought in patients in travail.

Dr. Freud, however, was not a very proficient hypnotist himself; and thus his studies and efforts were hampered and they did not manifest the results that some consider would have changed the direction that modern psychology and psychiatry have followed.

Dr. Jung is considered by the *Encyclopedia Britannica* to be the Father of Modern Analytic Psychology, and Dr. Freud is the man to whom psychiatry is rooted. Jung's rejection because he could not understand; and Freud's failure to advance in the science of hypnosis to a level of exemplary proficiency left hypnosis out in the cold, so to speak. If you don't understand something even though it exists, the thing to do is ignore it, right? If you're not good at something and might be upstaged in your field and might lose control of the direction which that knowledge might lead your profession, then let the exploration of the mystery pass by the wayside and in turn promote "other theories," right? This is actually what happened; and as a result, today a science of the psyche that claims it can produce a condition through suggestion in a person, that can allow the physical amputation of part of that person's body to occur without anesthetic, and also without pain, is not explored to wide and practical application.

It is to such scientific mystery that men like Andrew Jackson Davis somehow stumbled into and tapped knowledge and communication with a realm that we do not see, but that may well have provided knowledge to the ancients that we know existed but cannot explain the existence.

Paranormal in medical terms means abnormal. If medical knowledge ignores the known existence of the objectively unexplainable, because they can't explain it, rather than espousing its existence and opening the door to the pursuit of the understandings that were pursued in the 1800's, but today stands in subjugation to the chemistry that sprang from alchemy, are we not being deprived of the knowledge of the unknown because we are choosing to keep it so?

It is an interesting thought, and later we will discuss the best kept secret in modern medicine. It is the recognition of the phenomenon of the unknown, tagged by the very men who rejected its study in favor of "theory." Dr. Carl Jung wrote *The Psychology of the Transference,* and the *Transference* is modern medicine's recognition of the unknown. In my forty-eight years of distinct involvement with life, and much of it involving necessary contact with the medical community of the mind, it was never mentioned. When we talk of Dr. Jung and his associate for a time, Dr. Freud, we will talk of known that is not. I was amazed at the hiding of a feared phenomenon. You may well be, too!

Frederick Anton Mesmer of the late 1700's was the man who might have "mesmerized" you. It is to him that we will look to the hypnotic process of magnetism. It is he, who in examination of his work was branded a fraud by Benjamin Franklin and two others appointed with him to make official inquiry to his work. Mesmer fought the law and the law won, so to speak. The examination lacked the important element of "belief."

Hypnosis requires several elements to be effective. They are the following:

A. Heightened Suggestibility

This is an involvement of a person's own suggestibility being heightened by the person who is the hypnotist. The hypnotist's actions spur an increased potential in that which is already existent within the individual being hypnotized.

B. Impulse

A person who is impulsive is more readily hypnotized than a pragmatic reasoner.

C. Voluntary Submission

The person being hypnotized must trust or accept the hypnotist with the confidence that what is suggested to him is feasible, even if it is not true.

Both schools of hypnosis, "the physical and the mental," adhere to these necessary components within the individual for success.

The physical is associated with magnetism and can be associated with the use of objects of distraction or optic fatiguing devices such as bright lights or mirrors that rotate.

The mental approach is adherent to the belief that mere suggestion can induce the hypnotic state, and that it alone is all that is necessary.

Magnetism as employed by Mesmer involved the use of magnetized objects and eventually water that he claimed was magnetized to effect cures for various ailments by way of a rather unusual circumstance. From that description, which follows, hypnosis as we know it evolved. Mesmer did not discover the calm hypnosis that we think of today. That followed as a discovery of one of his students.

If you have the allusion that being "Mesmerized" was some lilac-scented visage of delicate temptations of beauty, think again. At the time, however, if you were in Paris and had not been "Mesmerized," you were not part of what we would term the "in crowd." It was the "in" thing to do!

Mesmer's popularity had grown so great that he found it necessary to devise a method that would "treat" many people at once. To do this, he devised large bottles of water, which he claimed to magnetize, that were immersed in magnetized water in a tub that contained iron shavings, and from which extended metal rods which allowed him to affect contact to many people at once. The following description of his activities bears reading and was recorded by one F. Deleuze in Paris in 1819. He was of the Royal Botanical and Zoological Gardens and was a librarian there. Hold tight, if you have enough imagination and allow yourself, you are about to be "Mesmerized."

In one room, under the influence of rods issuing from tubs filled with large bottles—the said rods applied upon different parts of the subjects' bodies—the most extraordinary scenes took place daily. Sardonic laughter, piteous moans and torrents of tears burst forth on all sides. The subjects were thrown back in spasmodic jerks, the respirations sounded like death rattles, and terrifying symptoms were exhibited. Suddenly, the actors of these strange performances would frantically or rapturously rush toward each other, either rejoicing and embracing, or thrusting away their neighbors with every appearance of horror.

Another room was padded and presented a different spectacle. There, women beat their heads against the padded walls or rolled on the cushion-covered floor in fits of suffocation. In the midst of the panting, quivering throng, Mesmer dressed in a lilac coat, moved about, halting in front of the most violently excited, and gazing steadily into their eyes, while he held both their hands in his, bringing the middle fingers into immediate contact to establish communication. At another moment, he would, by a motion of open hands and extended fingers, operate with great current, crossing and uncrossing his arms with wonderful rapidity to make the final passes.

I don't know about you, but I feel great!!! I've been on the floor a few times in my life, and I don't have too much trouble relating to some of this. Dean Martin has always been an interest and at times curiosity to me, in that he has such an eased manner. I have for years marveled at one quoted statement of his, it being so prolifically profound and maybe applicable here. Quoting from the inside of the cabinet door where I keep my ingestible alcohol, "If you can lie on the floor without holding on, then you're not drunk!" are the words that Crown the Royal of wisdom that beaker forth.

It's no wonder that Mesmer eventually fell into ill repute. As the curing of ills fell to the wayside of the social spectacle, his work became completely rejected, and in desperation, he made an appeal to the Academy of Science in Paris. He requested that a review be given his discoveries; and the Academy, in 1784, named three renowned scientists to a commission to evaluate his claims.

One of the distinguished three was none other than our renowned statesmen and scientist Benjamin Franklin. He and the other two noted gentlemen were to examine Mesmer's process and did so by dipping their hands in his magnetized water. To this experiment, each indicated that there was experienced no effect upon them. With their report to the Academy, Mesmer was totally discredited and fell into ill repute.

One of his students, the Marquis De Puysegur, revived some of Mesmer's ideas that had fallen from the public eye. The Marquis was living lavishly on his estate and providing diversion for himself by magnetizing peasants from the villages near his estate who were ill, effecting cure to some. The Marquis's experiments were haphazard, but he noted an unusual occurrence in a very sick young peasant named Victor Race. This young man was afflicted with a serious lung condition and had intense pains in the lumbar and thorax areas.

When the Marquis magnetized him, rather than reacting in the anticipated fashion, Victor fell into a light sleep and he was restful. He also spoke, and thus started De Puysegur's experiments with the peaceful hypnosis that we know today.

Davis practiced 'psychometry'

Isis – Egyptian goddess of Fertility

Jean Martin Charcot

Benjamin Franklin

Franz Anton Mesmer

Ben Franklin with Mesmer's baquet

By suggestion to Victor while in this new-found light sleep, De Puysegur was able to lift Victor's affliction from him by suggestions of peace and relaxation and by suggestion that his pain was dissipated.

Something else occurred with Victor while in his hypnotic state that heightened the Marquis's interest and activities even more. As it is said, Victor was not very bright in his normal conscious state; but when magnetized, in a trance, he became brilliant and his level of intellect was astonishing. In his hypnotized state he outlined the treatments that would cure the ills of other people that De Puysegur was attempting to help. Andrew Jackson Davis and Edgar Cayce both did similar things.

De Puysegur's discovery and use of "artificial somnambulism" demonstrated to the scientific world that a state in appearance similar to sleep could be brought to exist in a perfectly coherent and conscious person, and that while in this state a person's afflictions might well be affected.

The Marquis's work became weakened; however, as he took it upon himself to make statements that he could not prove. As the world was then, and is now, if you make claims to the extraordinary experience in life, you lay yourself open to ridicule from the blind side of the human experience. It's easier to conform to the objective than to acknowledge the subjective. De Puysegur took the chance and expounded upon phenomenon that he claimed to have encountered but could not prove. His claim to witnessing such things as clairvoyance, and also the transference of thought, weakened his work and his stature.

Modern medicine today does recognize the phenomenon of the transferring of one person's feelings and activities to another, and Dr. Carl Jung has alluded to it in his writings, having written an entire book dealing with it, and has even shared one of his own experiences in one of his writings. We will explore this when we get to the chapter addressing Dr. Jung. In the meantime, I will say that I, without question, have experienced that which Dr. Jung talks of and have found the phenomenon to be just that. It is a subjective reality in a world of objectivity, and the danger is ever present that if one says too much, "they'll call you crazy." To these thoughts, I hope you are in curiosity, because you, too, may be walking the fine line of awareness that separates the realms of the little known from that which we think we know.

Edgar Cayce considered that Andrew Jackson Davis, Victor, and himself had in common the gift of the extraordinary. I consider that many of us have in common, in large or small ways, the extraordinary gift of being willing to consider the little known and consider ourselves a part of it.

A Jesuit priest named Father Gassner was, at the same time that De Puysegur was gaining acclaim, making his own waves in the south of Germany. His methods were of a spectacular nature, and so were his cures.

This man was a player of theatrics within his Church. If you were seeking his help, you would find yourself in a darkened room adorned with black drapes and lit with nothing more than one weakly flickering candle.

To this scene would enter Father Gassner, as the drapes drew open in automatic fashion to his dramatic entry, carrying aloft in outstretched arms a crucifix adorned with studded diamonds. Peering deeply, searching depths of the patient's eyes, he would, with sudden and startling voice vibrating and echoing the room, command "Detur mihi evidens signum praestigiae praeter naturalis, praecipio hoc in nomine Jesu!" Soon the patient would fall asleep, and with this the Father would banish the "evil spirits" that were in the patient's body.

M. Scott Peck, M.D., author of nationwide best-selling books that still sell today, acknowledges for modern medicine, for modern society, for modern man, and for the doubting skeptic, that the human person can be and often is influenced and even possessed by unseen entities. The descriptions in his book of exorcisms that he personally witnessed are accepted reading to the "normal" of our society, but it takes a person of position and of recognized achievement in his profession to elevate such things to a level that public and public authority can view with credence.

Such has our world become, such is the secular dominance of materialism and objectivity, that "scientific and scientific assumption" can hide or discredit or overwhelm the reality that God revealed in the Bible and reveals to whom he chooses.

The awareness of the extraordinary was certainly extended to Edgar Cayce. One thing that he is noted as relating in regard to the sleep state that he would induce in himself had to do with his ability to return to normal consciousness.

Cayce stated that without a person being with him and interacting with him during his sleep, he might go so deeply into this other realm that he might not be able to return. He would physically die!

Father Gassner is reputed to have created a physical state in a young girl that resulted in a doctor declaring the girl dead. Her physical functions were said to have ceased at the suggestion that Father Gassner had given her that she would die for a short time but that he would bring her back.

In this experience, it was said that Father Gassner demonstrated to the physician that he could, by suggestion, cause this girl's heart rate to accelerate and decline. The girl awoke on Gassner's commands from her "death." Her muscles jerked in spasm as she came back, and she sat up smiling and declared that which might or might not be believed. She said she was reborn and that a miracle had taken place.

Regardless of the degree of credence placed upon such stories, Gassner was a clever hypnotist indeed and used it to further the ends of increasing both his and his Church's position of respect with an illiterate populace. Consider the Egyptian priests.

In 1841, an English doctor by the name of James Braid established the name hypnosis. He himself at first contact with magnetism was more than a skeptic, but after very minor experiences came to accept the phenomenon as real. He is credited with being the first to recognize that physical agents could induce the sleep state and tied fatigue of the optic nerves as connected with inducing the state within the subject.

Braid's work was rejected in England but was given credence in France, where a Professor Azam was impressed with his work and confirmed his findings. Azam added to the knowledge of hypnotic effect by stressing to the scientific community that anesthesia could be induced by suggestion in hypnotic sleep, and that the pain and shock of surgery could be reduced by such means. Ironically, Azam's work was rejected in France but accepted in England.

The physiological concepts of hypnosis were formed during this time, and they are the basis by which modern concepts find their foundation.

We might allow our minds to drift a little from this categorizing process of development and speculate a little about the Egyptians and their ability to perform surgery in what we call ancient times. We already alluded to the priests using hypnosis in the worship of Isis. Is it also possible that it was used in medical processes? The human is human, then and now; of course, now because alchemy is so advanced, I think there are those who tend to forget that human is God's creation and not the creative realm of imaginative ego.

In 1876, another physician, a Dr. Burcq, who practiced at the Salpetriere Hospital, which was the center for neurological research, recall the name Dr. Sigmund Freud, who made further discoveries in the hypnotic process and formulated the basis of use of objects, shiny objects, as applicable to the induction of the sleep state. His studies evolved from an accidental incident with a hysterical patient who fell into a hypnotized state while inadvertently staring at a polished door knob made of brass.

Another doctor of fame later developed the revolving mirror for use in inducing a somnambulistic sleep in people.

Another French doctor who was famous in neurological achievement further advanced the world's knowledge of hypnosis in 1878. Dr. Charcot and his students proved that several stages of hypnotic sleep exist and that, with each stage that manifests itself in the individual, varying symptoms occur. After four years of research, he presented his works to the French Academy of Sciences. His presentation is yet today considered the highest academic value in the field. He presented his works under the title of *On the Distinct Nosography of the Different Phases Comprised Under the Name of Hypnotism.* The conclusions of Charcot's presentation have been verified to the majority of extent.

These people are certainly not the only ones that contributed to the science, but they represent the progression of advancement quite well.

There are three stages of hypnosis, as follows:

> *Light Hypnosis* - The person will droop his head and breathe heavily and also will find distraction to be disturbing. The person will be extremely drowsy but not feel affected. Their compliance with suggestion remains only to the simple. In this state, the person is fully aware of that which is going on around him.

> *Medium Hypnosis* - This is the most often used state in hypnotic involvement and is useful for almost all purposes. In this state, the person is subject to a distinct obedience and does not resist suggestion readily. The hypnotist is able to influence all of the person's senses. The ability of the hypnotized person to relive or feel events suggested by the hypnotist is pronounced,

and post-hypnotic amnesia can be induced while in medium sleep. Light anesthesia can be involved, also, for the relief of pain and for some surgeries.

Depth Hypnosis - A person in a deep state of hypnosis wants to be left alone because the feelings experienced are so intensely pleasant. They do not want to listen to or comply with suggestions and do so only after repeated persistence overcomes their reluctance. The person's countenance shows the expected signs of sleep, and with this, his heart rate and respiration are considerably lowered. In depth hypnosis, it's stated that major surgery and painless amputation can occur.

A clinic in Germany, The Heidelburg Clinic, has indicated that thousands of women have given birth using hypnotic methods.

Recall that hypnosis requires several elements.

    A.   Heightened Suggestibility

    B.   Impulse

    C.   Voluntary Submission

A formula that is constant is the actual mechanism of hypnosis; and if followed very carefully, hypnosis must follow:

Misdirected Attention

+

Belief

+

Expectation

The Hypnotic State

(1) *Misdirected Attention*: The mind must concentrate on something that is not relevant to the actual effort of hypnosis.

(2) *Belief*: The person being hypnotized must have confidence in the ability and integrity of the hypnotist. He must believe he will surrender to him, and he must believe that hypnosis is a valid reality.

(3) *Expectation*: The person being hypnotized must expect that each successive step will work and lead to the next step, building block upon building block.

(4) *Imagination*: Belief and expectation are combined by imagination into an irresistible state that establishes an exacting course that supports the hypnotist.

The depth to which a person sinks in the sleep stages is dependent on the degree to which the person is willing and has the ability to comply with suggestions.

A sort of conditioning also occurs in an individual who has been hypnotized. There is a serenity to the hypnotic state that brings a desired state of relaxation. The relaxing experience of one's first hypnosis will negate the need for imagination, and thus belief and expectation will loom eagerly forth in pursuit to the feelings that fill a person in tranced sleep.

Suggestion may be given or presented to a person in four different fashions; and because of this, inadvertent or frivolous encounters with what is a very serious science is something to guard against and be aware of. When you combine the aspects of revelation and contact to the unknown by some individuals when in a hypnotic sleep state, then one should be easily able to ponder for himself the implications of playful or abused encounter with hypnotic suggestion.

Suggestion can be given by four methods:

First, and important to remember, is the indirect import.

Second, and imparted by complete dramatization, is the direct method of suggestion.

Third, and requiring many repetitions to be accepted by the person being hypnotized, is suggestion with dramatization.

Fourth is the reconditioning or re-education method. In this method of suggestion, the hypnotist imparts to the person who is hypnotized a new habit pattern to replace one that is less desirable.

Desirable is an interesting word and should be considered on the basis of who is determining what is undesirable. If you were a man such as Andrew Jackson Davis and the hypnotic state brought with it contact with another realm of understanding, then suggestion to enhance the contact or expand the perimeters of encounter would probably be desirable to you and to those associated with you or those seeking your help.

On the other hand, a person in our society who might make claim to contact or experience with the unknown might find it undesirable to make known the reality of his experience, lest they be called crazy. Dr. Carl Jung was such a man, a world figure of acclaim whose biography can be found in the *Encyclopedia Britannica*. Interestingly, in that commentary to his life and his achievements is a statement that his last work, *Memories, Dreams, and Reflections,* which was his autobiography, is one of his best.

What the encyclopedia does not say is that he would not allow it to be published until after his death. It does not say that it contains extraordinary accounts and revelations about his own spiritual awareness and encounters with the unexplainable. Nor does it say that childhood revelations that might be deemed a little unbalanced are relived and described.

Davis, Swedenborg, Cayce, Philippi, Rasputin, De Puysegur, Victor and others had the courage to give to those around them, and subsequently the world, the opportunity to learn, experience, and grow from their often troubled experiences. Open to the ridicule of the secular world and the religious world, their life's experiences are our guideposts to the realm that hypnosis seems to touch upon or tap into, depending on some unknown reasons to life's revelation.

It takes courage to lay open one's soul to others, and as this work comes to its ultimate conclusion, you may well ask yourself, "With who does the mantel of courage rest, and who are all the rest?" It's easy to hide beneath the doctor's mask 'til death becomes your mask, to sit and judge and expound your theories to other's experience. Society credits the theories and discounts the experience; it is the way of objectivity. I doubt that this will change—one cannot move such authority—it is too protective to its own.

Research into the actual physiological state of a person in hypnotic trance is interesting, also. Where a person might consider that the body has become asleep, the opposite is true. Heart and lung activity has been measured in extensive testing, and it has been found through electrocardiogram and respiratory studies that during hypnosis both activities are similar to being awake. Blood circulation has been monitored, also, and again, with cerebral circulation the waking state was most closely resembled. Brain waves measured by electroencephalograph are similar to those in a waking state, and the patellar reflex conformed, also, more closely to awake than asleep.

From this it can be said that hypnotic sleep is not sleep in the general term. It is, however, also not being totally awake physiologically either. The state of hypnosis does evidence a physiological depression such as might be noted from being under the influence of alcohol or drugs or possibly anesthetics. The aspect of relationship to fatigue also exists.

As the hypnotic state begins, the pulse drops, blood pressure drops, and a sudden short constriction of blood vessels occur in peripheral vessels.

It might be speculated that this constriction accounted for the jerk that Andrew Jackson Davis would experience as he was being magnetized. Being magnetized and being hypnotized bring about the same state of hypnotic sleep. Davis used a magnetizer or conductor to induce the trance state in him.

The conductor was very important to the entire effort as shall be illustrated shortly. When one is being magnetized to trance state, the three elements of misdirected attention, belief, and expectation are the necessary components, just as with the suggestion method.

To magnetize a person, the conductor makes "passes" at the individual. This means that with the use of the hands, he will, without touching a person, move his hands in a rhythmic fashion starting at the head and passing down to the stomach and not having them more than one to three inches from the person's body, make repeated moves until the person falls into the sleep state.

We have looked at descriptions of three stages of trance state that are the accepted norm to hypnotic involvement. These are that which one can expect to encounter in having involvement with a hypnotist of modern function. Andrew Jackson Davis, however, describes *four states*.

Andrew's revelation to the hypnotic process and state of being is presented to the searching person from a state of hypnotic trance and with his conductor and scribe. Word for word, it follows, and the enlightenment if believed is quite revealing. The text is taken directly from his dictation of *The Principles of Nature, Her Divine Revelations and a Voice to Mankind* by Andrew Jackson Davis, "The Poughkeepsie Seer" and "Clairvoyant." The work was printed in 1881 as the thirty-fourth edition and transcribed in July of 1847 by Mr. William Fishbough his scribe, with a medical doctor, Dr. S. S. Lyon being his conductor.

There are properly four magnetic states. In the first, no particular phenomena are witnessed, only that, the external organs being in some measure divested of their ordinary share of magnetism, a feeling of dullness pervades the system. Persons in this state lose none of their senses, but are susceptible to all external impressions. They have also the full power of muscular action; and if situated nearly midway between the first and second states, they are inclined to happy feelings. And all phenomena witnessed in this state, are only of a physical nature: But in the higher states, the phenomena consist in the development of the mental powers.

The next state, or the second, manifests itself through the mental organization. The patient still manifests his intellectual faculties, but is deprived of all muscular power. The pupil of the eye expands, and that organ refuses to act on the brain. The tympana membrane and cavity of the ear expand and refuse to perform their wonted action. The extremities are somewhat cold. In the latter part of this state all sensation and feeling is destroyed, so that any surgical operation can be performed without giving pain. The patient in this condition appears mentally associated with the operator. All the external organs being closed, there is no possible means of receiving impressions from without; but all phenomena are produced through the medium which exists between the operator and the patient. Hence there are sympathetic, incoherent, and indefinite accounts received from the mind of the patient, which are analogous to the impressions of the man previously spoken of, who seemingly recognized external realities during his moments of dreaming. Thus the phenomena are of a mental nature, and are a natural production of the mind so situated.

12 "The ear is not entirely closed to sound in the first part of the third state. The patient can hear indistinctly, possesses the power of speech, and partly of muscular action. About the middle of this state the ear is completely closed, and all impressions made upon the brain from external objects, are at an end. The patient is then placed in an unconscious condition so far as the external world is concerned. Divested of his ordinary share of magnetism, he possesses just enough to perform vital action.

In this state there is a strong sympathy existing between the operator and his subject. The chain of sympathy which connects the mind of the operator with that of his subjects, is animal electricity—the same fluid which is the agent of all muscular motion. It is through the agency of this fluid that magnetic sleep is induced. The operator sits down with the determination to put his subject to sleep. All the powers of his mind are concentrated on the subject. His will being exercised to this point, the electric fluid passes from his own brain and nerves, to the brain and system of his patient, and forms between the two, a chain of sympathy. The one, then, is completely subject to the control of the other; and in this manner you may easily account for all the phenomena witnessed in the sympathetic somnambulist.

In this state the patient is wholly unsusceptible to any tangible or physical connection, no feeling existing upon the surface. The magnetic medium is far less active than in the previous states; but the negative or muscular forces are still preserved. At this crisis the mind is extremely susceptible of external mediums which connect mind to matter. Hence the subject appears to see and hear, and to perform many wonderful and mysterious things, during this condition of the mental faculties. This is a state of still higher mental development, and of consciousness or perception of mediums. This is often supposed to be the clairvoyant state; but it is not. It stands in analogy to natural somnambulism; only one is a phenomena induced by magnetism, and the other is a similar mental state, but naturally produced by an inactivity of the magnetic medium or sensation. The magnetic subject has progressed in his mental capacity toward the state known as death: for the positive power does not remain, while the negative or muscular does remain—and the increased perception of the mind is through the medium of its own association.

Passing from the third to the fourth state, a still greater and higher mental manifestation will be observed. About midway between these two conditions, the mind loses almost all of its sympathy which attaches it to the system. At this time the chain of sympathy existing between the positive and negative, is nearly disconnected. The mind becomes free from all inclinations which the body would subject it to, and only sustains a connection by a very minute and rare medium, the same that connects one thought with another. In this condition the patient progresses into the fourth state. Then the mind becomes free from the organization, except as connected by the medium before mentioned; and then it is capable of receiving impressions of foreign or proximate objects, according to the medium with which it particularly becomes associated. The body at this time is dormant and inactive in all its parts, except the negative, or muscular and vital action, which is constantly kept up and controlled by the united forces of the operator upon the operatee.

And this stands in analogy to that natural state of physical disunion known as death. Death is produced by the loss of both forces; but the clairvoyant state is produced by the blending of the forces of the two persons, and making them physically equivalent to one. The mind, in the first case, loses all of the medium which connects it with the body: the latter is the same state mentally with the former, with the exception of the medium referred to. All the phenomena are seen, and do exist, with every being. Their healthy state is the magnetic state, and the various conditions and developments of the mind during sleep, until death, are analogous to the various phenomena induced by magnetism—only one is an ordinary manifestation, and the other is a further development of the same principles and laws which constitute and govern animal organization.

The science is thus explained; and the phenomena and appearances, which may be invariably expected, may thus be generalized. But particulars and minutia will vary exceedingly, according to the various dispositions and organizations upon which the magnetic condition is induced. To particularize would require an indefinite length of remark, consisting of individual observations and isolated inductions.

It is important to recognize that in this text regarding the statement "animal electricity," animal is referencing "human."

Andrew's bringing forth of "the principles of nature" dictations resulted in a very large volume of printed material. I find it interesting to note that people who espouse this extraordinary contact with other realms of existence quite often bring forth great amounts of so-called revelation to the unknown. Emanual Swedenborg wrote enough to comprise an encyclopedia, as did Davis and Cayce through their scribes.

Swedenborg brought forth a "New Christian Doctrine" and through others' interpretation or adherence to his precepts has quite probably influenced the course of modern medicine.

Davis has fallen to obscurity and finding his works requires a not recommended effort in the metaphysical aspects of society. Edgar Cayce identified very strongly with this man, as has been stated, and both he and Davis devoted their efforts in life to helping people. Cayce indicated, as a matter of fact, that misuse of this gift of clairvoyance and telepathy would cause it to withdraw, "it" being the contact to the spiritual realm of life.

Another man, who was also a medical doctor, brought forth a volume as large as our Bible. It, too, is claiming revelation to mankind from a source of knowledge and creation beyond this physical world. The writing of his book spanned ten years of effort on his behalf, and he claimed that it was all a result of "automatic writing." This book, too, is nestled in the metaphysical and is generally not to be found in the presentation of information openly displayed in that sector of society. This book, which I once owned, eventually brought such fear to me as to the spiritual influence associated with it, that I actually took it one night, in the middle of the night, to a distant dumpster and deposited it there in what I consider to be its proper resting place. In the span of several years that I spent researching this effort, I encountered a copy of it in an old and used book store in the college shop area that is notably part of the university involvement of Michigan State University in Lansing, Michigan. Within its pages, I had found something that I considered relevant to the function of evil, and I wanted to look it up again. It required great force for me to even touch it, though I did, and then left it to its repose.

I believe it would be naive to consider that all that springs forth from the supernatural that claims revelation and enlightenment to mankind is of good and of God. Edgar Cayce was a very religious Christian and knew full well that while he was asleep he was in contact with another aspect to life. He feared all of his life that that which he touched and which touched him might be of evil and not good. It is a question that all should ask if they choose to look beyond the objective aspects of life. Edgar Cayce's reading brought nothing but good to people and in such, he was motivated to continue the readings to the very end of his life. The Bible says to try the spirits to see if they are of good. Edgar was a man intent on good.

I haunted many bookstores and libraries in researching this book, some in both the college cities of Ann Arbor and Lansing, Michigan, and found a spattering here and there of revelation to understanding. Cities of academia seem to have a greater depth to them in areas of diversity to thought than found in cities were the diversity is focused more to survival or existence.

In a different old bookstore in Lansing, I was rummaging through the bindings that both bind and enhance our lives, and I came across a book that I gave pause to purchasing. As I thumbed and scanned the pages of a volume as large as a *Webster's Collegiate Dictionary*, I pondered whether to buy and include part of its content and concepts. I chose not, and I believe with valid reason. I don't now recall the exact name of the compiled work, but it was a dictionary written in quite proper synoptic presentation. As I thumbed page after page of mounting travail, I realized with shocking understanding the danger that modern medicine has brought to the lives of those in our society who venture to live or even attempt to understand the aspects of a spiritual or unseen guidance.

The book was one which provides names with which to label people. I dare say there is a name within its pages that forms a label for every person I have ever met. It's a very proper book, surely of great interest within the medical community that deals with the mind, for the names and labels are for the minds of people, formulated no doubt through time to represent the "science of theory." Without the "science" of alchemy, I suspect the "science" of theory would yet be well and properly confined to the legitimate practice of psychiatric medicine within the bounds of the proper hospital. Hospitals past and in many cases now staffed with the very sincere—not the boundlessness of open society, not the courtrooms of justice where we could all live our lifetimes in want of the agreement of the marching cadres of those creditable to the "science of theory." The book was one dictionary of mental disorders, and as I scanned its pages, I shook within at the thought that man has the audacity to judge and name and label their fellow men. Easily, anyone who could read and view another's actions could label the labelers.

Edgar Cayce is credited with making this comment, at the exposure to a description of Andrew Jackson Davis and Victor. If he and they were together alone with a patient, in company with a doctor respected by scientists, and Davis and Victor and Cayce himself gave readings that agreed, and the doctor in examining the patient agreed with the readings, then the scientists would declare the doctor to be a fake and a fraud and hang him, and he and Davis and Victor would be run out of town.

Before Cayce made this comment, his son, Hugh Lynn, had surmised that if the scientists were to become aware that Davis and Cayce did exactly the same thing, they would have to recognize the validity of the events.

Cayce's final reaction was to close the book that started Andrew Jackson Davis' trek through life's exposures—being *The Principles of Nature,* etc., and from which I have been quoting—handed it back to Hugh Lynn, and as he went back to his fishing, said that Andrew and Victor and he should be left to rest in peace.

We return now to the aspects of hypnosis and most specifically magnetism as experienced by Andrew Jackson Davis. We find in the introduction to his first work of dictation from a magnetized state that was to be published, a description of that which he evidenced and experienced, as presented by his scribe, Mr. William Fishbough, in July of 1847.

Keep in mind that Edgar Cayce very deeply identified with Davis.

We will now proceed to describe the process of the production of this book and the phenomenon therewith:

In the first place, the magnetizer and the magnetizee are seated in easy positions facing each other. The ordinary manipulations are then performed, from three to five minutes being required for the completion of the process. A sudden convulsion of the muscles, such as is produced by an electric shock, indicates that the subject is duly magnetized, immediately after which his eyes are bandaged to protect them from the light. He then remains speechless for some four or five minutes, and motionless, with the exception of an occasional sudden convulsion of the muscles. One of these convulsions at length brings him to a state of external consciousness, and gives him perfect command over the muscles of the system and the organs of speech. He next assumes a position inclined either to the right or to the left, and becomes cold, rigid, motionless, and insensible to all external things. The pulsations become feeble, the breathing is apparently almost suspended, and all the senses are closed entirely to the external world. This condition, according to his own explanation, corresponds almost precisely to that of *physical death*. The faint vital forces still remaining in his system, are only sustained sympathetically by the presence of the magnetizer, whose system is by an ethereal medium blended and united with his own. If while he is in this condition the magnetizer should by any means lose connection with him, the vital movements of the body would cease, and the spirit would be incapable of re-entering it. As he himself has informed us, in this report he is different from any person we have ever seen while under the magnetic influence. His mind is now entirely freed from the sphere of the body, and, consequently, from all preconceived ideas, from all theologicalisms, and from all influences of education and local circumstances, and all his impressions are received from the interior or spiritual world. His perceptions, conceptions, and reasoning powers are now immeasurably expanded. His spiritual sight, freed from its material obstructions, now extends to worlds and systems innumerable, and he feels that he has almost ceased to be a member of the human family on earth, and is a member only of that great Family of intelligent beings which inhabit universal space. He is thus elevated above all the narrow, local, and sectarian prejudices that pervade the earth. His philosophy is only that which is involved in the laws and principles which control the Universe and mankind unerringly, and his theology is only that which is written on the widespread scroll of the heavens, in which every star is a word, and every constellation a sentence. He associates familiarity with the inhabitants of the spirit-world, and the diversified knowledge cultivated by them is rendered accessible to his mind. The associated spirits and angels of the "second sphere," are, as one grand Man, in sympathetic communication with him to transmit knowledge to mankind on earth, which they perceive the latter are for the first time prepared to receive. Thus exalted, he gives forth his impressions of truth as it actually appears to him, without reference to any of the beliefs, philosophies, theories, or sectarian prejudices, that exist in the world.

Having thus access to all the knowledge of the Second Sphere combined with that of the first, such truths as are appropriate to communicate flow spontaneously into his mind, these being at the same time arranged according to a natural order of sequence. As soon as a distinct impression is thus received, the spirit returns again to its material habitation, and employs the organs of speech to communicate it to those present. A few words only are uttered at a time, which the clairvoyant requires to be repeated by Dr. Lyon, in order that he may know that he is understood. A pause then ensues until what he has said has been written, when he again proceeds; and the passage into and out of the spiritual state occurs at an average of about once every sentence.

His diction is of the most direct and simple kind, and his ideas seem usually to be clothed in those words which first present themselves.

His phraseology is not a subject of interior direction except when nice distinctions are to be drawn and great precision of expression is required. His style is much such as he would use in his normal state if a knowledge were imparted to him or the subjects on which he treats while in his elevated condition. His grammar is therefore defective; and although, when it is necessary in order to properly embody an idea, he employs technical terms, and even foreign words and phrases, with the greatest facility, he sometimes mispronounces, yet not in such a way as to obscure his meaning. Correctness might have been attained in all these particulars, yet labor on his part would in that case have been immensely increased, by making all those minutiae matters of interior investigation. His great object was simply to present the idea, leaving the niceties of the verbal clothing to be adjusted by myself, with the restriction that the corrections should be such as not to destroy the peculiarities of the general style and mode of expression.

His enunciation was characterized by a peculiar breathing solemnity as though every word gushed from the depths of the soul; and his simple, pure, and unaffected manner, was impressive in the extreme. If we wrote to say it seemed that the very atmosphere of heaven surrounded him, and that angels were continually breathing their thoughts through his organs of speech, the expression would appear to be prompted by a heated enthusiasm; yet a phrase less expressive would fail to convey an adequate idea. This remark applies also to all his philosophical and spiritual conversations while in the abnormal state.

The time occupied in the delivery of a lecture varied from forty minutes to about four hours, and the quantity of matter delivered at a sitting varied from three to fifteen pages of foolscap closely written. There were one hundred and fifty-seven lectures in all, the first delivered November 28, 1845, and the last (*viz.*, "Address to the World," which comes first in the book) was delivered on the 25th of January, 1847."

When Andrew had finished his presentation, he gave instruction as to the corrections and preparations for printing, which were meticulously followed by Mr. Fishbough.

To the surprise of everyone connected with the bringing forth of Andrew's effort, Mr. Fishbough makes this comment:

Immediately after giving general directions as to the correction and publication of the work, he voluntarily, in the presence of a witness, and contrary to the expectation of everyone, renounced all claim, direct and indirect, to any portion of the copyright, and the proceeds of the sale of the work, simply claiming a reasonable compensation for the time he had been employed in its delivery.

To me, the sources of all such dictations that claim a spiritual origin fall within the category that the Bible alludes to in instruction to the individual to "try the spirits." If we recognize that God is spirit and believe such, then spirits exist of both good and bad. The individual has to make for himself the decision of what to pursue in life's learning experience.

The volumes that exist from Davis and Cayce and Swedenborg and Nostradamus alone and each to themselves could consume a lifetime of study. To me, the reasonable and appropriate source of knowledge and understanding to become a part of is the Holy Bible. Each page brings with it a feeding of the spirit within and a growing advancement toward union with God.

As I encounter each person—Davis, Cayce, etc.—the awareness builds within me that truth and help and knowledge can proceed to mankind through such people, but I also recognize the open avenue to deceit that could be represented by that which comes from a realm of the unseen, and continually strive to keep my guard up and my eyes up as well. It is good practice and advice. As you read on, I would hope that you keep the thoughts in mind, also.

If we back up now to where we left off in the self-stated description of the four stages of hypnosis and carry forth with Davis's sleep state explanation of that which he experienced in giving his presentations from a clairvoyant or physically examining entrancement, we find further depth of understanding to ponder:

> To particularize would require an indefinite length of remark, consisting of individual observations and isolated inductions.

> A great question now presents itself for investigation: Is there such a thing existing as independence clairvoyance? I answer, there is. You ask for proof. Such you shall receive by the following investigations.

> It is well, however, to understand the meaning which is applied to the word independence. If you mean self-existent, abstract, indefinite, and without any connection—then the expression means nothing: For in this sense there is no such thing as independence. But if the word is intended to mean free from direct instigation, then it has meaning; and to it this signification should be attached. I am compelled at this time to explain and reveal the mental phenomenon as I experience it; and the reason to familiarize it to the mind will be given hereafter.

> It was admitted that the body is in negative subjection to its operator—and also that muscular and vital action are still sustained, yet in a less degree of

activity than during the self-possession of the forces of motion. The body so situated is dependent for its activity upon one source, while the mind or the intellectual quality is dependent upon another. While I am examining (that is, examining the diseased, with a view to the application of remedies), I am directly dependent upon the close connection of the physical, and the steady and intense cognizance of the mental. But when the independent condition or crisis is produced, the body assumes an inclined position. It becomes cold, rigid, and unsusceptible; and hearing and all the physical organs are torpid and inactive. But when the body resumes its natural position, hearing returns, muscular motion is commenced and active, and the organ of speech is also in full exercise. Each of these powers must be in operation in order to communicate externally what the natural organs are seemingly cognizant of. This dependence is not what is termed sympathetic, but it is in reality a situation which that word will express. The medium existing between thought and thought, between mind and mind, and between time and eternity, is only active pervading medium which I am dependent on for the conception of thought, and for that perception of all things of a refined, ethereal, or spiritual constitution. This is while the activity of the body and mind appears to be sympathetic or dependent. I am not impulsed or impressed by the thoughts or feelings of a foreign person, though I am cognizant of them through the medium above termed ethereal. The independent condition is when the body manifests the external appearance of rigidity, etc., above described; and in this situation only is the term "independence" applicable.

From the induced state of "independent clairvoyance," Davis interestingly brought forth comment about Emanual Swedenborg, Aristotle, and others. Again quoting from *The Principles of Nature, etc.,* we find what I consider to be interesting revelation, if it is to be taken as such, and that is for the pondering of the mind.

As Davis in hypnotic trance continues, keep in mind that at this point in his life he had all of five months of formal education.

It is impossible for anyone to enter voluntarily that state in which he can view with clearness things belonging to a sphere of existence higher than the natural world. Were such a thing to take place, that moment death would necessarily and inevitably ensue. For this state can not be entered without a loss of one of the controlling forces of the system; and if this force is not supplied by the system of another, the natural functions of the organization would cease, and the spirit could not re-enter it after it had once departed. Independent clairvoyance, therefore, must be induced by the action of another system, by which the positive power is extracted from that subject. To sustain life, this is supplied sympathetically by the system

Aristotle

of the operator; and so long as this is the case, there is a rare and subtle medium of sympathy existing between the mind and the body, by which the former finds its way back to the latter after a temporary absence. If this medium were destroyed, the mind could not return; and it is impossible to go voluntarily into the independent state of clairvoyance without destroying it.

This is an important paragraph to make note of. As we approach Dr. Jung and Dr. Richie, the experiences that they personally relate may be considered to relate in some ways to the aspects of the separation of life.

Continuing:

> To some, however, it is possible to go voluntarily into a state in which the mind is greatly developed, and made cognizant of principles and truths pertaining to this mundane sphere. This sometimes happened with a well-known Grecian philosopher (Aristotle) during his hours of slumber, he often received impressions which led him to extensive generalizations; and such was the source of those excellencies in his works which have so long been the admiration of the world. He was in the habit of wearing particular kinds of stones about his person, imaging that these had the virtue of inducing this condition of mind.
>
> A celebrated orator (Demosthenes) of the same country frequently went into the same state of mind. Some of his best impressions were received during his hours of slumber. These he would subsequently systematize and carry out to their legitimate results: and the ability for which he was distinguished may in a great measure be referred to this source.
>
> A distinguished ancient physician (Galen) also received impressions in the same way, which led him to analyzations of the properties of plants and to the discovery of their medicinal applications, which before had been locked in secrecy, and which must long have remained unknown, independent of this source of discovery.
>
> A similar mental phenomenon often happened in a still more perfect degree with a noted Swedish philosopher and psychologist (Swedenborg) who flourishes within the last century. His impressions were more extensive and distinct than those of either of the others to whom I have referred; and by these means he was led to extensive generalizations on the animal kingdom,

which are true." [Keep in mind that animal means human.] "He also had visions of the future state; but not being in independent clairvoyance, these were not in all respects perfect. Yet to some extent they were true—and were valuable as being the best that could be received under the circumstances.

Besides these, several Chinese and several Germans, and other writers who have had the most influence upon the world, received the leading ideas which characterize their works, in the same way.

Such impressions were of the same species with those which I receive, though theirs were received through a different medium, and were measurably clouded by the organization.

ell, well, well, one person claiming and claimed to be clairvoyant, commenting supposedly about several prominent figures in human history and adding to the mystery of man's existence through the ages.

Searching the mysteries of mankind's stuttering advancement often brings unexpected contact with potential explanation to man's attainment of knowledge. Think back to the comments regarding Thomas Edison and think ahead to our coming discussion of Dr. George Richie's experience that gives claim to the realm of the dead.

When we venture to talk of Cayce, we're going to look at his ability to instantly "read" a person's character or state of being. In discussing Davis, we find a similar but definite pronouncement of Andrew's insight into other people. Mr. Fishbough in his introduction to Andrew's first book describes him in the following quoted excerpts and alludes also to Andrew's nature.

The nature of a person, being selfless, is indicated as a necessary state of being for a person to attain contact with the realm that both Davis and Cayce claimed attachment to. The following quotes are important, also, then in regard to the very basis of understanding that characterizes the clairvoyant attachment to the spheres of spirit.

Mr. Fishbough states:

The expression of his countenance is mild placid, and indicative of a peculiar degree of frankness and benevolence; and from his eyes beams forth a peculiar radiance which we have never witnessed in any other person. This is especially the case in his moments of interior meditation and mental expansion. His inferior passions are only moderately developed, and are completely under the control of reason and the moral sentiments. During daily intercourse with him for eighteen months, we have never known him to manifest the least degree of anger or impatience, though we have known him to be severely tried.

We are having here painted a picture of a very controlled, very placid man, a characterization of an individual that you could easily term as being your "neighbor." If all were of this disposition, it would be a peaceful world indeed.

Quoting further now to Andrew's insights, Mr. Fishbough says:

> He is very fond of congenial society, though he is peculiarly sensitive to what are in his book called the "spheres" of certain individuals, or the influence or atmosphere emanating from them. Thus he is instinctively either attracted to or repelled from a man on first coming into his presence, and from the same cause he generally forms a judgment of human character at first sight, which, as to accuracy, we have seldom if ever known to fail. This sensitiveness to spheres forms a striking trait in his character.

To this commentary about the seeing or knowing of "spheres" by Davis, it is appropriate to point to the modern science of Kirlian Photography, which is (Aura)" the actual photographing of what appears to be an energy emanating from a living thing, a plant, a person. It is the seeing through the image of the photographic plate, the aura of life, or maybe life itself.

The imaging on the plate can see also in this fashion that which is not physically to be seen as part of our objective world. A torn leaf with part missing yet emanates the glowing form of the whole, or a person missing a part of the body shows the form of the image of the whole.

If a photographic plate can tell us of the existence of such, can it be possible that the eye of a gifted person can also see it. I believe most women feel it. I believe if a woman opens herself to her inner self, she is in awareness of that which Davis saw, but she in feeling. Discernment is her choice. I see it in the eyes of women I encounter all the time. It is part of the reason that women value contact with the eyes so highly. Some cherish it; all crave it. The avenue is to their soul and their heart, and it is said that some women can almost experience the climatic ecstasies of orgasm by sharing the contact with the right man's eyes. When a woman has opened herself and found that which she seeks in another's eyes, in another's person, her eyes belie the guise and point to surprise. It is the spirit that is life, Davis claims the seeing, women know the feeling, and it keeps us all reeling within the feeling; I like it, and you probably do, too, if you will admit it.

The descriptions of Davis are pragmatic, the writing is somewhat dogmatic, but the feeling can be automatic and break through the static of objective existence and open the realm of personal growth to aura's unknown. How long have you known?

To continue now with Mr. Fishbough's description of Andrew:

> His imaginative faculties are well developed, though not so as to form a prominent trait in his character. A supreme love of truth is the central point around which all his moral faculties revolve. Hence he holds himself entirely open to conviction from all sources of information, and is ever

ready to abandon preconceived opinions, however ardently cherished, the moment he finds they are erroneous. It is from this cause that he manifests the utmost unconcern when his pretensions are attacked.

So we find that Andrew was open-minded and unpretentious. With five months of formal education under his belt, we can, of course, assume that these traits were certainly not the result of exposure to the evolving world of academia.

Farther on in the description we find:

That all his leading mental operations and outward actions appear to be governed by a species of interior prompting. Upon the whole, therefore, he may be considered as a most amiable, simple-hearted, truth-loving, and unsophisticated young man, being disconnected from all sects, parties, creeds, and denominations, and governed solely by his own intuitions.

Such is a description of his character while in his normal state, as it has appeared to us during daily intercourse with him for the last eighteen months.

Davis is further described as being a person who exhibited a great indifference to things that are of no particular importance.

From these descriptions, it's not hard to form a mental picture of the character and person that Andrew was. What I find to be intriguing to parts of this is that Dr. Jung identifies aspects of the human makeup that definitely apply to Andrew's evidenced nature.

I don't consider the presence with and in Andrew to be extraordinarily different from you and me. What I do consider to be notable is that Andrew apparently listened to those inner urgings. Those aspects of person and personality that Jung might call the number 2 personality, or Dr. Dyer might call inner directedness, or a lady might call intuition, or I might call the awareness of a spiritual directedness from within *and* without, when recognized, link the subjective world of spirit to the objective world of flesh. The more you open and allow yourself to perceive, the more you will.

Cayce alludes to being focused to objective or subjective. Each has its own sphere of feeling and influence to a functioning person. Each sphere is interactive to the other, but is of itself. The Bible tells us we are blinded to the realm of spirit. I think we've become blind period!

The activities that were most important to Cayce, and of considerable importance to Davis, centered about their ability to interject themselves into the medical-physical aspects of helping ailing people. We find a description of Davis's activities in this regard also in Mr. Fishbough's introduction to Andrew's first book. It proceeds as follows:

We also at the same time heard him examine a number of patients while in the clairvoyant state. While in the latter state he appeared as if metamorphosed into a totally different being. The human system seemed entirely transparent to him, and to our utter astonishment he employed the technical terms of anatomy, physiology, and materia medica, as familiarly as household words! Our surprise was equally excited by the exceeding clearness with which he described and reasoned upon the nature, origin, and progress of a disease, and concerning the appropriate means to employ for its removal. From infallible indications presented, we saw that there could be no collusion or deception, and no such thing as receiving his impressions sympathetically from the mind of the magnetizer.

This description of Andrew's medical involvement is almost identical with that associated with Edgar Cayce in its relationship to the aspect of presentation to the conductor of medical information. Neither man was a doctor, though Davis became one late in life; neither was educated to even a lower level; and neither came from a medical background.

Continued further now:

In February, 1845, Mr. Davis being (with his magnetizer) in Bridgeport, Connecticut, attending to such patients as required his services, formed an acquaintance with Dr. S. S. Lyon (Dr. Silas Smith Lyon), the magnetizer connected with him during the delivery of his book, and who was at that time a successful medical practitioner in Bridgeport. Dr. Lyon had previously been an unbeliever in clairvoyance, but the evidence of its truth, as presented in the case of young Davis, proved too powerful for him to resist; and under a deep conviction of its importance, he did not hesitate to render it his open encouragement, and to avail himself of the clairvoyant's advice in the treatment of some difficult cases of disease then under his charge.

As we've searched through the surface of the volumes attributable to Davis, I think it's evident that something extraordinary existed with him, and I think further that if a person were to delve deeper into his dictations while he was in hypnotic trance, that the biblical commandment of trying the spirits to see if they are of God might again be stated as well in order.

Claiming a contact with an inner aspect of one's being, or contact with that of another sphere of existence on a spiritual plane, requires deep personal scrutiny by the person contemplating the study of the mystery of the unseen and little known.

I myself do not doubt that Davis, when in trance actually touched the world beyond this consciousness, but I do question the total validity of what was presented by and through him. Part of my skepticism finds itself rooted in two places.

The first involves Dr. George Richie's experience, later to be discussed; and the second has to do with information that was obtained in the book that so frightened me that I threw it away in the middle of the night.

Recalling from it that it distinctly stated that nearing and at the end of an age, the world of spirit that is most immediately present, following the movement away from the physical body by a person who has died, becomes out of synchronization with the proper order of things, so to speak. Individual spirits do not progress to levels beyond this worldly sphere, but rather remain in contact with this physical world and attempt to influence it through yet living people, either by entering into them or by influencing through them from the sphere of the spirit.

We are at the end of an age, by biblical prophecy and by astronomical movement. Christ is about to return, and it is about to be the Age of Aquarius. A total change to mankind's direction is about to occur, and it is as much spiritual as it is physical.

By the doctor's "automatic writing," it was stated that that which affects a righting of the spiritual process is the changing of the rulers of the spiritual sphere. According to the Bible, and in my belief, the changing is to occur by the predetermined plan of God Almighty as he saves both the planet and mankind at this time from total destruction at the hands of our unruly selves. Keep in mind that Christ has power in heaven and hell and total rights to the inheritance of the earth. These are not small things. The small things are found in the meager contact and revelation within the clairvoyant's writings.

If the clairvoyant could write with infallibility, which I don't believe they do, then considering that the revelations they present are of such depth and volume to the subjects addressed, they would lend themselves to intense depths of both secular and religious study. Change of awareness would occur on large scales, and the truth would become known by the scrutiny of the masses.

Only that which is revealed of God is of total truth, and the test of a prophet is in that totality. To me, a person has to fall back on his inner self, to the inborn knowing of good and evil, to discern that which is of good and that which is of evil.

Where Edgar Cayce was concerned, he made statements that if that to which he would become connected with spiritually was put upon to be part of something that was not of good, but of evil or evil purpose, that the spirit would withdraw itself from contact to both, end the abuse, and protect itself, thus thinking we to be part spirit. The warning within ourselves should be heeded as well, not ignored or rationalized to continuance of pursuit. It is a dangerous thing to walk in His knowledge, to walk in His grace, and tempt His patience. The entire creation is God's, us inclusive and finding that out the hard way will not be very pleasant.

It's generally considered that an age lasts for some two thousand years, and we commonly hear that it is now almost two thousand years since Christ established His new covenant with His chosen people, being those who have and will accept Him as having recognized the calling of the Father and have been found by Him.

To the second advent of Christ, those who have been called and have accepted are looking with intense anticipation, and rightly so, for the changes that are to occur in mankind's existence are both physical and spiritual in nature, and Christ will be here shortly to bring it all to be.

Melchisedec preceded Christ in influencing mankind as well. In the Bible, we find little written of him, but that which exists is deeply revealing to both him and Christ.

As with Christ, both are alive today and forever more. Melchisedec's presence here in identifiable person, if he is a person in the sense that we perceive people to be, finds identity some four thousand years ago, two ages ago, if one counts by such thoughts.

His name is mentioned in the Bible in Genesis Chapter 14:18, Psalms Chapter 110:4, and in Hebrews Chapter 5:10, and Chapter 7. He is described as being "without father, without mother, without descent, having neither beginning of days, nor end of life, but made like unto the Son of God; abideth a priest continually."

Christ has a Father, as do all of us. Some of us have the same Father as Christ, others have Satan as their father, but Melchisedec has no father.

Christ is described in likeness to Melchisedec by this verse: "After the similitude of Melchisedec there ariseth another priest. Who is made not after the law of carnal commandment, but after the power of endless life." Further the Bible says of Christ, "The Lord swear and will not repent. Thou art a priest forever after the order of Melchisedec."

At the time of Abram, later to be called Abraham, Melchisedec was the "King of Righteousness, King of Salem, which is King of Peace;" Salem is considered to be Jerusalem and I believe that no coincidence could be the reason for such association and descriptions of being.

Abram paid tithes to Melchisedec and by biblical explanation thus did Levi also, because Levi is described as yet being in the loins of Abram at the time (unborn).

The subjugation to this man by God's chosen person is more than evident. The Bible does not tell us what happened to Melchisedec, and I certainly wonder.

The Bible tells us that this prophesied sequence that we are now living is to be the final one. Once this progression of events has been fulfilled, the earth and heaven as they exist today are to pass away, and God is going to provide a new heaven and a new earth to be inhabited by a peaceful creation.

Because it says this is to be the "last time," I ponder how many previous times actually existed. Considering that this time or this age is concluding with Christ's return, and considering also that living as inhabitants of the earth under the travail that Satan and his host are inflicting upon us ends, and that Satan will again be loose for a short final time to deceive the nations before this earth passes away, is it not possible that the present losing of evil is the, or part of the final losing from a prior age? The age that Melchisedec ruled, just as Christ is to rule the coming age. If you follow the line of thought, it is food for thought and offers possible explanation to man's previous existence on the planet that is both evidenced and debated.

If the Bible did not mention and describe Melchisedec and did not directly associate Christ with him, and did not identify Salem which is probably Jerusalem, God's chosen city on earth, then I would be the first to admit that I am all wet, but it does and thus possibly lends credence to the doctor's writings or at least part of them. They claim a recording of a twenty-five thousand year history of man upon this earth, with the rule reportedly changing by ages of about two thousand years. To my knowledge, he does not, however, mention Satan as the source of the evil that plagues man in the midst of his own evil nature that he doesn't recognize.

Trying the spirits as the Bible instructs is always paramount to life's ventures within ourselves and in exposure to others. This world is made up of the good, the bad, and the ugly; and it's going to get uglier before it gets better.

I've ventured away from Andrew Jackson Davis a little but with deliberate intent. We live in a world that is spiritually and physically connected, and all that is being addressed either is here, was here, or is going to be here. So each aspect is of its own importance and bears looking at; and the first thing to look at are God's warnings within the Bible to not learn their ways, and to not partake of the company of those who do. They are those whose knowledge and heart and source of strength and power is of the devil. God gave us the ability within ourselves to recognize the meanings of these instructions and to make the choice of heeding or rejecting.

Andrew had other traits that I consider significant. He had this certain nature to him that was indifferent to "things of no practical importance." He was sort of a pragmatic individual and was not even concerned with where he had been born. His earliest recollections were of Hyde Park, Duchess County, New York; but his father indicated "that he was born in Blooming Grove, Orange County, New York, and that on the 11th of August 1847, he will be 21 years of age. From Hyde Park, he removed, with his father, to Poughkeepsie, on the first of September, 1838."

He was also a person who allowed himself to be guided by his own intuitions, what Dr. Wayne Dyer today calls inner-directedness, what a lady might call intuition, and what I call a recognition of the presence of spirit within.

Continuing with thoughts to Andrew, some repeating, some new, he can be seen as a man who sought and loved truth, and he evidenced a very mature depth of judgment. Association for him was not so much with his peers, but as it was by his choice, with older people of experience, and he preferred the company of but few people. It's said that his mind was very inquisitive, and it led him to read controversial religious works; he also found himself to be confident in discussions with a minister.

Painting this picture of Davis evidences a very controlled person who was unpretentious when attacked and whose sense of levity also found itself subject to this restrained characteristic. To all of this is added his definite concentration of thought; he was given to abstraction.

The man is given to you to ponder.

To conclude this chapter of revelation to some of Andrew's mysteries, I'm going to quote yet another segment of his first book. This I find to be profound to life's struggle and in part a breathless amazement to aspects I have too much lived and now fear because of it.

> Man, who has now approached to some degree of knowledge, feels sustained
> by surrounding beings who wonder at his indulgence. He becomes lofty,

dignified, and vain. He assumes a spirit of arrogance, and with an air of pomposity takes the stand of a foolish critic. He will complain of the great laws which compose and govern the universe, and dare to suggest alterations and improvements in their operations. He will laugh at the appearances which the world manifests, and assume the ground which nothing but ignorance can prompt him to maintain—daring to sneer at the great laws which govern this and other worlds, when in reality he has not the capacity to comprehend the component parts of one atom that goes to compose the universe!

There are, however, some lofty and noble characters in the world. They do not hesitate to sacrifice their individual interest for the interest they feel in Truth. Possessing a high sense of conscientiousness, and a deep solemn veneration, the very elements of moral philanthropy compose their nature and desires: and these, with intense and patient deliberation, search deeply into the causes of the social effects which are visibly manifested. Their interest is involved in exploring, investigating, and revealing, the cause that products the disunion and disorganization which spread persecution throughout the world, and which genders vice and misery, and consequent personal and national wretchedness. Such a one, with the best feelings and actuated by the best of motives, dares to lift his voice against the causes of the prevailing evils in society. He does this with firmness, and yet with a feeling of philanthropy and benevolence. He addresses himself to the world in the mildest language. He states the truth with simplicity yet fearlessly; and his thoughts are not contracted to one particular society or state, but he speaks forth his irresistible convictions to the world. The world opposes him with its varied interests, individual, sectarian, denominational, and political. These weapons are hurled against him with anger, and the fire of indignation and wrath is set against his efforts; and he is finally obligated to leave the field as a reformer, and retires in despondency and heartfelt wretchedness! He no longer feels life a blessing, but longs for the dissolving elements that compose his being to terminate their work. Discouraged with the experience of this life, he seeks for a future. He arrives, through analogy, at the conclusion which he sought, stops breathless and amazed, and sinks to be known no more! And is this free thought and unrestricted inquiry?

The man who presumes upon knowledge which is merely superficial, is praised and approbated. He maintains the sentiments of the institutions which cover the land. He freely enters and breathes their atmosphere, when he has an internal consciousness and irresistible conviction that it is deleterious to the world. He not only assumes all this, but he is sustained in his assumptions by the strongly fortified denominational institutions to which he personally adheres.

And there is the meek and lonely reformer, who feels the moral convictions of his nature, and claims an atmosphere of light and liberty to express them—and his voice is hushed; his influence is arrested by private and public denunciation! And is this free thought? If truth exists, why is it closed to all examinations of a free mind? If truth one possesses, why should he be afraid of investigation?"

The reason he should be afraid, as I believe it to be, can be grasped in the phrase, "Be careful, they'll call you crazy!"

Village of Poughkeepsie, 1835.

IN 1835 THE VILLAGE OF POUGHKEEPSIE, NEW YORK WAS WELL
ESTABLISHED ON THE BANKS OF THE HUDSON RIVER.
THESE PERIOD PHOTOGRAPHS THAT SPAN THE YEARS FROM
1850 TO 1902 ARE A FINE DEPICTION OF 19TH CENTURY SMALL
TOWN AMERICA, AND ARE PROVIDED COURTESY OF THE
DUTCHESS COUNTY HISTORICAL SOCIETY IN
POUGHKEEPSIE, NEW YORK.

THE NORTHERN HOTEL, LOCATED ON THE NORTHEAST CORNER
OF MILL STREET AND WASHINGTON, BRINGS A RUSH OF EXCITEMENT
AS ONE DRIFTS TO 1862 AND A BEAUTIFUL PLACE.

THE COBBLED STREET AT THE CORNER OF MAIN AND GARDEN,
IS STEEPED IN TRADITION IN 1863.

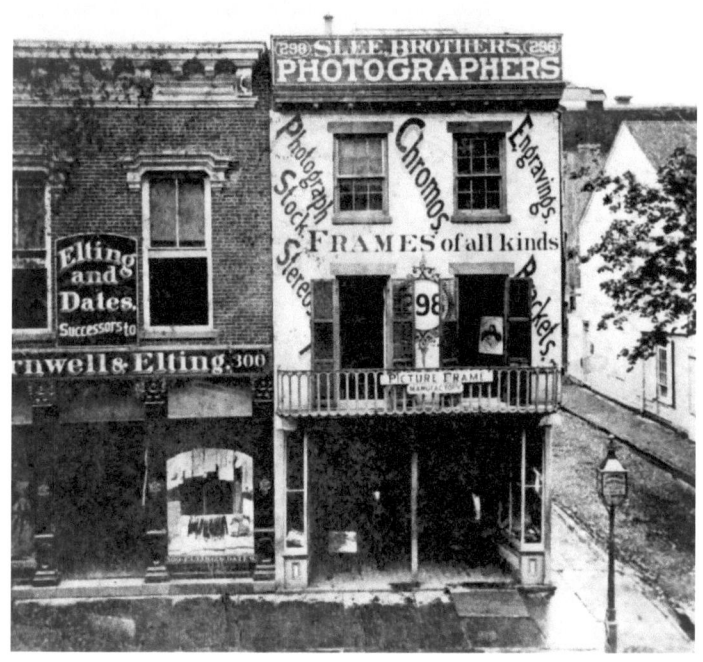

AT THE CORNER OF MAIN AND LIBERTY, ENTERPRISING AMERICA
IS SHOWN IN FINE FOUNDATION IN THE YEAR OF 1860.

THE THIRD DUTCHESS COUNTY COURT HOUSE
Erected in place of the Court House destroyed by fire in 1806.   Demolished 1902

**THIS DUTCHESS COUNTY COURT HOUSE SERVED THE COMMUNITY
FROM APPROXIMATELY 1806 UNTIL 1902**

**BUILT IN 1856 AND SHOWN AS IT WAS IN 1906, THE ALSON WARD
HOUSE AT 254 CHURCH STREET IS A FINE EXAMPLE OF THE
RESIDENTIAL CONSTRUCTION OF THE PERIOD.**

CHRIST CHURCH WAS BUILT IN 1774 AT THE CORNER OF MARKET AND CHURCH STREETS, AND REMAINED UNTIL 1889.

MAIN STREET LOOKING EAST FROM LIBERTY, 1853

A PICTURE OF ANDREW JACKSON DAVIS REPRODUCED FROM
A ENGRAVING AND AS IT APPEARS IN THE 1946 YEAR BOOK
OF THE DUTCHESS COUNTY HISTORICAL SOCIETY.

CHAPTER 6

EDGAR CAYCE

<u>Born March 18, 1977 - Died January 3, 1945</u>

"Modern Mystery"

The Most Accessible and Well Documented

Psychic in History

O'SHANNADOA, OVER THE VALLEY FOR SEVERAL HOURS FLEW THESE
THREE CLOUDS, PARALLEL TO THE SKYLINE DRIVE, ON MY DRIVE
TO VIRGINIA BEACH AND THE EDGAR CAYCE FOUNDATION,
DUE SOUTH IN WHAT WAS AT FIRST A CLOUDLESS SKY.

THE CLOUDS HAD HELD THEIR FORMATION, AND ALMOST IN TOTAL
THEIR FORM, AS HOURS PAST AND MILES WERE TRAVELED.

AFTER COMPANY IN TRAVEL ON THE WINDING SKYLINE DRIVE,
I LEFT IT TO MOVE EAST AND TOOK THESE PHOTOGRAPHS
LOOKING WEST TOWARD THE MOUNTAINS.

AS I FINISHED TAKING THESE PICTURES, THE CLOUDS BEGAN TO
CHANGE. AFTER SO MANY HOURS OF MOVEMENT IN WHAT WAS FOR
THE SAME HOURS A CLOUDLESS SKY, IT WAS AT THE VERY LEAST ODD.

Edgar Cayce

CHAPTER 6

EDGAR CAYCE

<u>Born March 18, 1977 - Died January 3, 1945</u>

"Modern Mystery"

The Most Accessible and Well Documented

Psychic in History

Approaching Mr. Edgar Cayce requires delicate steps and quiet tones, for found in this man is the life of the common man. A deeply devoted Christian, his faith in God and pursuit of the hope that Christ offered brought him to read the Bible through once for each year of his life. At the age of fourteen he had already read it through several times but with little understanding. He considered, though, that the person within him was finding its craving's needs in the pages of God's word and felt its promises to be true.

He was a devoted family man who raised children and found friends of faith in those who surrounded and touched his life. Today such people can still be found walking and working in his lingering shadow at the Edgar Cayce Foundation in Virginia Beach, Virginia.

Edgar Cayce walked a path throughout his life that is oh so familiar to most of us. His was a life of financial trepidation. Born on March 18, 1877, on a farm in western Kentucky to parents of America's strength and America's struggle, his education formally ended at the age of fifteen and he was never considered to be the brightest of students. Without depth of education to any specific profession and without family influence to aid in his pursuits, Edgar walked his own mile in life. With this, Rasputin, Victor, Davis, Phillipe, and Cayce shared a common thread to life's realities in their beginnings, and as we will see, to considerable extent in their lives.

As a young boy Cayce had asked his dad to obtain a Bible for him. So it can be said that Edgar's pursuit of knowledge and God was of an inner desire and not something that was forced upon him. The aspect of self desire and eventual willingness to put self and ego aside to a desire to help others opened the door to a life of giving and healing for this man, through channels of spiritual encounter, that are more soundly documented than for any person in history.

I made deliberate effort to travel to and view for myself the buildings and encounter the people that today are the Edgar Cayce Foundation. This foundation along with the Association for Research and Enlightenment and the now accredited Atlantic University are a soundly established part of Virginia Beach, Virginia.

While I was there, though I did not attend, Mr. Dannion Brinkley, author of the best-selling book, *Embraced by the Light*, made a presentation; and the following week, Dr. Raymond Moody was scheduled to do the same. Dr. George Richie also is no stranger to the staff of the foundation and their triplicity of presence to this extraordinary place added to my experience and encounter. Though I met none of them, I respect all of them for their courage to tread the paths of life's questions in a world that can be overwhelmingly vicious to the realm of the spirit and the mind.

Cayce, like Rasputin, like Dr. Carl Jung, like Andrew Jackson Davis, and as Emanual Swedenborg had an encounter with the spiritual world that set the stage for the importance in their lives, that made their lives important to those who would seek to grow and understand, in some small ways, life's mysteries.

Edgar's encounter came at the early age of thirteen in 1890. He had built himself a lean-to in the woods on his family's farm, and it was there that he would sequester himself and read the Bible. It was a special place to him and reading the Bible was very important to him.

While reading the story of Manoah, he felt a presence with him and looked up to see a woman standing before him. Before she spoke, he thought it to be his mother who had come to remind him of his chores. When she spoke, the brightness of the sun and his having been concentrating so intensely on the book were overcome by awareness that it was someone else.

The woman's voice was a melody in its softness and clarity. She told him that his prayers had been heard and asked him of what he desired most of all and indicated that it might be given to him.

With the focusing of his vision to the woman, he noted something on her back, and that shadows cast outlined the shape of wings. Understandably he was frightened, but she just stood there smiling and waiting. Fearing but speaking, he said to her that he would like to be helpful to others and that he would like to help sick children. These were his greatest desires. It was the desire to be as a disciple of Christ. Without answer she was gone, and Edgar hurried home to relate the experience to his mother.

He was afraid that he was reading the Bible too much and questioned whether he was going crazy from it, as he thought some might do. His mother took the Bible from him and read a passage from St. John in reassurance that it is God who is to be trusted. The passage she chose says,

> Verily, verily, I say unto you, whatsoever ye shall ask the Father in my name, He will give it you.
>
> Hither to have ye asked nothing in my name: ask, and ye shall receive, that your joy may be full.

Edgar spent a nearly sleepless night that night, and in school the next day he was dull beyond his normal dull and listless as well. This combination along with his natural inability to spell words with any proficiency brought the ire of the teacher upon poor Edgar when he couldn't spell cabin. The teacher, who was also Edgar's Uncle Lucian, made him stay after school and write cabin on the blackboard five hundred times. As I sit writing this, I am without too much effort recalling my stints at the blackboard as well. It's not something one forgets through time, and I doubt that Edgar forgot, but I wonder if he forgave?

Later that day Lucian had spoken with Squire Leslie Cayce, Edgar's father, and when Squire came in that night he was furious and considered the family disgraced because he had been told that Edgar was stupid.

Determined to rectify this deficiency in spelling ability, he took Edgar into the parlor after supper along with his spelling book. Determination can mean very little in the face of reality, and the Squire's efforts with Edgar were failing miserably. At ten o'clock Squire Cayce's frustration vented itself as he slapped Edgar out of his chair and to the floor. Picking him up and trying for another half hour resulted in Edgar being knocked from the chair again. Slowly getting to his feet from the floor, he was tired and sleepy.

Sitting again in the chair Edgar thought he heard something through the ringing in his ears. Within himself he heard words, and the words were in the voice of the lady he had encountered the day before. He listened and she was saying to him that if he could sleep a little, she could help him. There is a saying, "Any port in a storm," and poor Edgar was not fairing well in this one. He begged his dad to allow a rest for a few minutes, and he consented and retired to the kitchen. When he left, Edgar curled up in a chair and placed the spelling book under his head and promptly fell asleep.

When his dad returned he found him asleep and grabbed the book, waking Edgar. This brought the statement from Edgar that he should be asked now, that he knew the answers now.

Edgar was astounding in the suddenly-found ability. Not only could he spell the words his father asked him to spell, but he could actually picture each page of the book in his mind and relate the content and spell all the words.

One might speculate to the reaction of Edgar's father. It could have been one of amazement or one of exasperation, and that Edgar ended up on the floor again is testimony to two things. First, and most important to me, is that his dad really didn't know him very well or he would have found the wonder in the event that I find in it and possibly you. Second, I find wonder that such social pressure existed amongst the ordinary people of a farming environment. It is no crime now or then to not be bright or not know how to spell, and yet Edgar, though deeply reading the Bible, found wrath for his faltering efforts at education.

The learning session ended and Edgar was sent to bed, where under the covers he prayed thanksgiving to the lady of the vision and held his spelling book close to him.

The next morning, Edgar told his mother of how he had placed the book under his head and that he knew all that was in it. At Edgar's insistence, she quizzed him on his lesson and found his knowledge faultless. She told him the lady was keeping her promise to him.

Edgar took his book and his knowledge to school with him and was not lacking in his ability to spell every word asked of him. His knowledge to other areas of study was yet lacking, so he decided to try the same thing with his other textbooks.

A sleeping miracle

Sleeping on them under his pillow brought the same miraculous results. Edgar could see every page in the eye of his mind and would recite verbatim the content of each page when asked a question by the teacher.

Impossible not to recognize the remarkable change in Edgar, Uncle Lucian promoted him to the next grade and made Leslie, his dad, aware of the change in Edgar.

Edgar was no dummy to presenting the image of hard study to his classmates and continued to carry his textbooks home with him to promote the image. He slept on them frequently to be sure of sustaining the knowledge; though he thought once was enough, he wasn't taking any chances.

The Squire questioned him as to what was going on and specifically asked of the sleeping business that Edgar had professed to him. Edgar assured him that all he had to do was sleep on the books and that when he woke up he would know the entire content. Leslie, pondering the circumstance, commented to Edgar that he hoped he was not crazy.

This was Edgar's beginning to knowledge that life exists beyond this life's *normal* awareness, and his selfless nature opened the door to a life of giving to others and a life that gave little to him in material ways.

His gift and giving would ultimately open the door to scrutiny by the law and courts. His picture in company with his wife, Gertrude, and his secretary, Gladys Davis, would be published in the New York Times as they sat in court, in what was obvious desperate concern to the judgment of official-DUMB upon them. Though acquitted, the trauma was evident in these simple people.

Edgar did not follow the farming life, and by 1900, he had worked in a dry good store and a bookstore. In that year, he and his father formed a partnership and became salesman for "Woodsman of the World Insurance." It was a fraternal insurance that was readily purchased by members of a certain fraternal order, and it was easy to sell to the new members of the fraternity because it was so reasonably priced. Edgar would travel from town to town during the week and be home on weekends. Edgar was also representing his former full-time employer in Louisville as a salesman for their specialty books, checkbooks, ledgers and such. J. P. Morton and Company was the large bookstore where Cayce was a salesman, and thus he was both an insurance agent and a traveling salesman in western Kentucky while residing in Hopkinsville.

It was during this time that he felt ill. He had been suffering from severe headaches and had obtained a sedative powder from a doctor. Taking the medicine in a hotel room some forty miles distant from his home, Edgar became unconscious to his actions and did not regain awareness to them until he had been taken home by a friend, Mr. Ross Rodgers.

Rodgers had found him dazed and wandering about in the railroad station and helped Edgar to travel with him.

Two doctors were attending to him and had concluded that the sedative had shocked the nervous system and that the cold of the day and his open coat and loss of hat caused a sore throat that brought hoarseness with it. It was April 18, 1900, and Edgar could barely be heard above a faint whisper.

Gertrude Cayce

Gladys Davis

The next day, he was recovered to an ability to work, but his voice was still hoarse. A Dr. Manning Brown, who was the specialist in throat disorders in the area, became involved as Edgar's condition continued. He mentioned something about aphasia. He had no solution and was given permission to call other specialists. All efforts failed, and weeks turned into months with no improvement. Edgar one day drew the conclusion that there was to be no remedy for his plight.

Unable to speak, he could not return to being a salesman, and he did not desire to return to farming. His dilemma to employment was solved by an offer made to him to become an apprentice to a local photographer by the name of W. R. Bowles. This he readily accepted and found solitude in the quiet of the darkroom in the studio.

It was a time in his life when he was able to contemplate his life and relationship to God. He had considered becoming a preacher, something not difficult to do in what even today is called the Bible Belt of America. Edgar's mother always wanted him to become a doctor.

It is very appropriate to call this man a man, as the courage to live the conviction of the knowing of one's self in any society is the courage of a man in the eyes of those willing to open theirs, and Edgar lived his conviction. He had taught a Sunday school class in church, and a mission group was attributed to him as well. Edgar tried to live as a true Christian and was not a person of pretense. His mother had said to him that preachers expect other people to be virtuous, but Edgar expected it of himself. Edgar Cayce was the kind of a man that fit the mold of a description to life that my grandmother lived and had brought with her when she came to this country.

Of the many things I am grateful to her for, watching her live, and thus by example given to me, is the saying well known within me that: "You should keep your own door yard clean before you worry about someone else's, and if you try to do so, you'll find little time to spend on someone else's."

Edgar was about to embark on a life of minding his own dooryard while giving to others that which was given to him, and relevant to this type of life. Dr. Carl Jung told of an encounter in his room with a departed spirit. He wrote in one of his books of his departed friend, seen by him sitting in front of radio that was playing, listening to the broadcast. His friend turned to him, and in part, said to him that to live a life of helping or service to your fellow men was the best life that could be lived.

What Edgar encountered next is such as has occurred with far too great a frequency and with unknown effect to people's lives. I've written frequently in this effort of the realities of hypnotic trance and suggestion. I've alluded to the aspects of its development and use to help people, and of its abuse by the use of it to entertain people at the expense of others and possibly to bring harm to unknown victims of its powers of indirect suggestion.

In Edgar's time and town, being 1901 and Hopkinsville, Kentucky, a man in a traveling troupe would entertain at "Holland's Opera House." He was "Hart the Laugh King," and the people of Hopkinsville would flock to the opera house to see and be part of his show.

Hart would bring entertainment to his audience with both a professional troupe and by including the local gathering in his act. He would also do something that might be considered an extension of Dr. Carl Jung's "transference." Skeptics of Hart's considered the possibility of fakery, but with such a man one never knows. To put credence to his

A spirit visits Dr. Jung

demonstrated ability to find an object hidden in town by a selected local volunteer, he would put on quite a show with his blindfolded eyes, sitting in a carriage with two horses, on either side of him a man holding his wrists, and by his instruction, they would follow the exact route taken by the volunteer and, never failing, would locate the object.

To such a man, either in legitimate ability or experience, or pure hoax, fell the ability to hypnotize people, and thus the main part of his act can be related.

In his professional troupe he had a man that under hypnotic trance could remain rigid enough to allow a rock to be broken upon his chest by the blows of a blacksmith's hammer.

His audience participation involved gathering a group of townspeople from those in attendance, and with them on the stage, he would make passes at them while speaking to them. Passes, you recall, are associated with magnetism and Mesmer, words are associated with Puysegur and hypnotism.

Hart did not have an elaborate set or props or robes. Neither did he use lights or dazzling objects to tire the optic nerve, at least not in his act.

Those who succumbed to his efforts remained on the stage. Those who were not affected returned to their seats. Edgar had gone up on the stage with a group, but he was one of those who returned to the audience to watch as Hart would instruct the hapless victims in antics that brought uproarious laughter to the opera house.

If the Laugh King's efforts with the groups failed, then he would attempt to put the audience under by droning "sleep, sleep, sleep" from the stage while sitting in a chair and swaying back and forth. This would be followed by his entering the audience to seek those who had fallen into a trance sleep. He would then awaken them by making passes in front of their face while speaking quickly.

Hart's abilities as a hypnotist were quite evident, and how deep his knowledge went is a matter of speculation. He did not claim to be a therapist; but hearing of Edgar's travail, he offered to cure him for two hundred dollars, saying that if he did not affect a cure, he would accept no money.

With the offer, we can assume that he had knowledge of earlier efforts to cure the ills of the sick by hypnotic suggestion.

Dr. Manning Brown thought there would be no harm in trying, and he was aware that earlier in his life Edgar had prescribed a poultice for himself that cured him of the effects of an injury. What was to be expected now left an open-ended question.

Edgar was about to make more history for the medical community. He had already become a continuing curiosity to visitation by doctors from a great diversity. A doctor from Europe had even looked at him. Now he was about to evidence the same results that were demonstrated in the clinics in France where Dr. Sigmund Freud had made his observations and participations to the process of hypnotic therapy.

Awareness had sprung from the earlier efforts in Europe that some patients who were debilitated in a normal conscious state, when induced to a hypnotic state of at least the second level or stage, would evidence the absence of the debilitating afflictions. The condition of distress would return when the patient was brought out of the trance state. Recall here that the second stage of hypnotic trance is that most often used in hypno-therapy and that the third stage creates a state of depth in which the hypnotized person is very difficult to reach and becomes very much "inner directed" in the euphoria of experience.

In Dr. Brown's office, Edgar and Hart embarked on an effort of hope. Hart, making passes, using suggestion, and employing optic fatigue helped Edgar into hypnotic trance. While Edgar was hypnotized he was able to speak in his normal voice, but when Hart brought him out his hoarseness was still present.

Again and again the effort was made, and each time the result was the same. All of Hopkinsville knew of the experiments, and the local newspaper began reporting on the event. News of Hart's efforts reached South Kentucky College and a professor of psychology, William Girao, who asked permission to attend and was invited.

Taking his notes of account and clippings from the paper, Professor Girao sent them to a Dr. Quackenbos in New York City.

Dr. John P. Quackenbos was a strong advocate of hypnotism as a medical tool and believed and espoused it to be the future of medicine. He considered that the subconscious could be directed to cure and heal the person of illness.

Hart's theatrical bookings necessitated his leaving, but he would occasionally return to the same results. He believed that Edgar would not go beyond the second stage.

In the autumn of 1900, Dr. Quackenbos made his way to Hopkinsville and to Edgar. At first the doctor could not move Edgar beyond the second stage. Dr. Quackenbos then, in intense effort, set out to induce a deep sleep. Using intense deep suggestion, Edgar responded and went into a very deep sleep.

A person when induced to hypnotic trance and left there will eventually awaken as though waking from a deep sleep.

Dr. Quackenbos had no intention of leaving Edgar in a deep sleep, but Edgar had other ideas, and the good doctor's effort to draw Edgar back to this objective reality failed miserably. This resulted in a gathering of two physicians and much fright.

Edgar didn't care about all this fuss; he merely slept on and on and on. Edgar slept in disregard to all efforts to wake him for twenty-four hours (not a bad snooze if I do say so). It's not known if Edgar yawned when he awoke naturally, but his voice was still as it had been, even though he felt fine.

A certain new difficulty now arose in that Edgar now could not sleep at all, save for a catnap here and there. Dr. Quackenbos was in distress again until Edgar, in a few days, began to sleep properly.

Having returned to New York in a quandary and contemplating the events, he wrote Professor Girao, being convinced that a solution existed to Edgar's circumstance.

Edgar was nervous, tensed, and given to being fretful since he first became the focus of experimentation. He was also losing weight and his parents feared further efforts, considering that both medicine and hypnosis had failed to affect a cure.

Dr. Quackenbos in a letter—no doubt he knew of the four-thousand-patient Salpetriere Hospital and the neurologists Charcot's efforts there as well as the experiments of Janet. He may well have known of the Nancy School and the work of Liebault and Bernheim there.

He stated also in the letter that patients in France had shown powers of clairvoyance while in a state of hypnosis, and thus we might conclude that the names de Puysegurs and Victor Race were no strangers to him.

From this base of knowledge, though not openly espoused lest he be called crazy, Dr. Quackenbos that if the hypnotist suggested that the patient talks about himself at the point that he was taking over, possibilities existed to revelation. His statements could easily be related to de Puysegurs experiments with Victor.

Everything now was in a state of chance; Edgar's condition was worse than when efforts to help him started; and one can imagine the concern to further experiments after Edgar had slept for twenty-four hours. It is one thing to sit and write of such things, or to sit and read of the events of another's trauma. It is a far distant realm the person and people experiencing them live, and I feel within me now a little of the apprehension that must have been known to those walking the precipice of the unknown. I doubt laughter echoing the hall of the opera house echoed within them.

Hopkinsville had its own hypnotist, a man whose wife ran the millinery store, who was a frail and thin person who studied by correspondence such things as osteopathy and therapeutics by suggestion. Edgar's sister, Annie, worked for his wife, and from her Mr. Al C. Layne learned that the professor and Edgar were looking for a hypnotist.

Layne requested an opportunity to try and help, but Edgar's parents were afraid for his health and concerned that they would drive him mad.

Al Layne was not an imposing figure and did not cut the metal of someone that confidence might be easily bestowed upon. His ill health made judging his age between thirty-five and forty hard to do, and he hardly weighed one hundred and twenty pounds soaking wet. His graying hair also added to his image of age.

Consent was finally given to try, and a date of March 31, 1901, was set. Edgar was twenty-four years old. On that Sunday afternoon at 2:30, Al Layne arrived at the Cayce home, and with himself, Edgar's dad and mother, and Edgar, effort and part of modern history was to be made.

From this day forward to the end of his life, Edgar Cayce's life would be a mixture of contact with the realm of the spirit and the realities of the flesh. He would live his life in contact with that, which being of the spirit, remains obscure to our objective understanding, but to evidenced events exists. Edgar, a devout Christian, was about to have his faith tried by the specters of life and ultimately found solace within the knowledge that what he did helped other people. Helping others was that which he had asked of the lady whose wings not only cast a shadow but overshadowed Edgar.

Mrs. Cayce was nervous as Edgar suggested to Layne that, rather than have him attempt hypnosis on him, that he instead put himself to sleep in the same fashion that he did when sleeping upon a book. Edgar suggested that once asleep Al Layne could attempt to speak to him. Layne agreed, saying that such would be a form of what he termed auto-hypnosis.

Edgar indicated to Layne that he had observed within himself that in previous efforts to hypnotize him, it was not the effect of the hypnotist that put him to sleep, but rather it was his thoughts that did so.

Edgar had observed within himself that which is a now known and accepted concept of the hypnotic process.

Edgar lay down on the family couch and proceeded to put himself to sleep. Layne watched his breathing deepen, and then he seemed to sigh deeply. Layne then began to speak to Edgar. One could imagine the apprehension in Edgar's parents as Layne suggested to him that he see his body and look at the affliction that was causing his loss of voice. Edgar was asked to speak in his normal voice.

I would think that one could have cut the air with a knife in that room while waiting for minutes brought first silence, then mumbling, then a clearing of the throat, and next Edgar's normal voice.

In what was to become an oft-repeated introduction to a physical reading for someone, Edgar indicated that the body, his body in this case, could be seen. Those present were not prepared for Edgar's response. There was not even a pencil in the room to use when Layne said to the squire to write down Edgar's statements.

Edgar began a diagnostic dissertation about the condition of his body. He stated that his ailment was the result of nerve strain that was causing a partial paralysis of the muscles of the vocal cords. He said that the condition was psychological but that it was producing a physical effect. Edgar continued and stated that while still in his sleep state the condition would be alleviated by suggestion that the circulation increase in the affected parts.

Layne firmly stated that his circulation was to increase and that the condition would be removed. There was silence now as they watched his throat, not knowing what to expect. Leslie loosened Edgar's shirt; and gradually, his upper chest and then his throat began to change color, first pink then gradually to a deep intense red. Two minutes passed into twenty before Edgar spoke.

Clearing his throat, Edgar broke the silence, declaring it to be all right now and that the condition was removed. He instructed Layne to suggest that the circulation should become normal and that he should awake. Layne followed his instructions, and they all watched as Edgar's color changed and he awoke. Sitting up, he coughed, spat blood, and then in tentative voice spoke. Grinning and allowing himself further brought tears to his mother and a seizing handshake from Leslie.

If this were a movie, it might bring tears to some in the audience. If it were fiction, it would make a good story line, but this is neither fiction nor a movie. It is not medicine as we know it either. It is mystery, it is man groping at his existence, it is one man touching, what is for objective man, the frontiers of a reality he finds difficult to accept and in ways frightening to anticipate.

The Bible tells us that our eyes do not see all that is to be seen of His creation; and from study and belief and experience, I have grown to know it to be true.

A condition exists to that which Edgar and those clairvoyants before him shared in helping to others. The condition is that a person has to be able to set aside his total ego, his total dwelling upon self and concern to self. Somehow this helps to open a door to revelation.

To this moment that changed Edgar's life, there was added a new mystery. Four events that Edgar experienced could be attributed to what medicine today might call the paranormal. In medical terms, *para* means abnormal and for me if someone can tell me what normal is, I want to shake his hand, buy him a drink, and then tell him I don't believe him because he doesn't know any more than I do, and I can't figure it out. Edgar's first was the vision of the lady; second, the voice of the lady and his sleeping on his books; next came his describing the composition and application of a poultice to cure a delirium that had overcome him at having been struck at the base of the spine by a ball (the description came from him in his conscious state of delirium); and now fourth in a self-imposed hypnotic trance, he interacts with a conductor as though in the third stage of hypnosis; or perhaps beyond to Davis's fourth stage, he experiences a curative phenomena to his medical travail.

Next, we find this fourth phenomenon extended to Mr. Al C. Layne to remedy his well-diagnosed ills of many years.

Layne was obviously anxious and intent as he accepted Edgar's gratitude, and then suggested that Edgar try to help him with his ills. After much discussion between them, they agreed to attempt a reading on him through Edgar the next day. Edgar's mother was apprehensive, but he put it in the context of doing good, of helping others, and within the sphere of moral right, she was able to accept the suggestion.

The next day, Edgar put himself to sleep again and while in trance, diagnosed Layne's illness, told medications to be used, what diet to follow, and indicated what exercises to do. When he awoke and read what he had said, a deepening of the mystery came upon Edgar.

He had never studied anatomy or biology. He had no knowledge of physiology or chemistry and had never worked with drugs or in a drugstore. He didn't even know if the drugs he had said to take were patented medicines. One could imagine the concern that must have been felt regarding his possibly affecting another person's health and well being.

If Layne had become more ill or even died as a result of such activity, the thought occurs that more than social ramifications might well have occurred.

Nonetheless, Layne immediately tried the remedies and was so much improved within a week that he was urging Edgar to try his new-found ability on other people.

If we refer back at this point to Edgar's delirium when he was hit with a ball at the base of the spine, and relate the Sanskrit words of Chakras, Pranic Forces, and Kundalini as words associated with yoga, and most speculatively Edgar's plight, it opens avenues of curiosity.

The aspect of losing within one's self, forces of energy by mental activity to the Sanskrit words mentioned, and alluding to Cayce's delirium, the base of the spine is specifically mentioned as associated with Kundalini, a power of electrical force that is said to lie at the base of the spine and that is in constant readiness to spring forth into the body.

The energy is said to be awakened within the body by exercise, concentration on nerve centers, and breathing. This can be described as a dangerous practice; and in some readings where possession was indicated, the possibility exists that the people possessed had been experimenting with this spiritual unknown and got into trouble.

Supposedly, this energy once released from the base of the spine is said to travel up through what are called "Chakras" to eventually radiate from the top of the head.

Chakras are said to be seven vortices and are associated with the passage of psychic energy. They are stated to be along the spine and in the head as well. In the practice of yoga, these "Chakras" are reception points for "vital energies," also called "Pranic Forces." Such forces are said to initiate action in a person. These energies or forces are said to be psychic in nature rather than physical and in referring to yoga as the basis of information. The reference to the practice of yoga is regarding the mental contemplative aspects, not the physical exercises.

Chakra's, Kundalini, and the word Moksha are also found in the eastern manual of love, *The Kama Sutra*; and some western writers have alluded to Tantric and Taoist practices in the arts and pleasures of nature's spiritual and physical union between a loving woman and man.

Both Indian and Chinese tradition holds that the physical body is a complexity of nerve centers that are called "Chakras." It's believed that in the melding of spirits, the release of "Kundalini" comes from the passions of lovemaking and that this crimson energy is coiled at the base of the spine.

The ancients claimed knowledge that, through a practiced sequence of training of the mind and body and the unrestrained sharing of one's total person with the person of one's love, an ecstasy of union in spirit and body could become the shared joy of love's desires and fulfillment.

The Taoist festival of love that leads to such release requires several days of devoted and directed opening of the spirit and enjoyment of the flesh to achieve, and the path to final release of love's embrace is one of touching and stroking, bathing, and caring that shimmers in the glow that two people should share if both can smile in each other's eyes and yearn to surprise.

The ancients believed that the rising release of this energy in the body fortified one's spiritual, mental, physical and emotional health. In accomplishment to this, the energy had to be made to flow from Chakra to Chakra. As it flows, it vitalizes and energizes.

Religious belief also has its say in the melding of spirit and flesh and Kundalini, for some schools presented thought that through this bliss of two in being one, the raising and control of Kundalini could be a path to ultimate salvation. This release from the cycle of life and death was given the name Moksha, and Moksha is also the word used to describe the ecstasies of loves releasing fires as a woman climaxes to the passions of her lover's embrace.

The deliriums of love's intended release and pleasured moments in orgasms pantry of delight is not imagination to our speculation, and as we are traveling these pages and moments of contemplation and revelation to the being of our being. The frailty of Edgar's person in distress from injury could give us the thought that life's mixture of experience is leading somewhere, and enjoying the traveling is something that could be more deeply done, and more cautiously viewed within the midst of spiritual and physical forces that we little understand or control.

In some Cayce readings dealing with "possession" of a person, he alludes to an involvement of certain yoga mental exercises as opening the person to disincarnate influence or actual intrusion to a person. Keep in mind that Jesus Christ confronted throughout his ministry the forces of Satan possessing or influencing ordinary people. Recall again that they even spoke to him in awareness that their time of torment was coming and that it would be but a short while before their freedom was removed and torment was to come upon them.

To this awareness of disincarnate beings and the dangers of opening one's self to their influence, Cayce alluded to automatic writing and self-hypnosis experimented with by individuals as being a very dangerous activity as well.

Interesting, also, to this description of inner energy being present and available for action, the Rosicrucians Order addresses mental exercises that are intended to give rise within a person to such energies.

I know a man with whom I had worked for many years who involved himself in the Rosicrucian Order. He, on two occasions at work, demonstrated that both the presence of such energy in an individual, himself, and also the ability to direct it toward both a living person, me, and also a magnetic object, my dad's old U.S. Army compass, was a reality and not a fantasy. I had been considering joining the Rosicrucians and, as a result of these two encounters, chose to pass that activity in life.

In the involvement with the compass, I had been showing it to a couple of fellows at work, as it is rather novel. The arrow points south instead of north, as in a mistake in manufacture— the polarity was established opposite to the correct application. It is a conversation piece, and that's what we were doing when this fellow walked up and said, "Here, let me see that," and took it in his hand.

I didn't know what he was doing, but he did. He went through a breathing exercise and then began moving his finger around the crystal of the compass. He started with the needle pointing away from him, and when he stopped, he had, *in successive passes* with the needle fluttering around toward him a little more with each stroking of the crystal, brought the magnetized needle to very nearly move 180° and point toward himself.

For me, this was an absolute first-hand demonstration of the ability of a person to effectively transfer an internal energy into a physical effect. I still have the compass today, and I have never been able to move the needle.

This man was not only a Rosicrucian, but he had also studied hypnosis and is in holding of a certificate that indicates his qualification to practice hypnosis. He had studied under a very accomplished hypnotist in obtaining this certificate.

Thus with me there is a personal understanding of the term "magnetism" and the existence of forces within the body that we don't normally acknowledge in presence or that we ignore.

On another occasion, this man demonstrated to me, without warning, the ability to transfer something from his person to mine. We had on previous and numerous occasions discussed the aspects of one person transmitting to another a strengthening force. Such was also part of his knowledge awareness from the teachings of the Rosicrucians. The man walked up to me and went through the same breathing exercise that he had done when he moved the magnetic needle in the compass. This time, however, instead of initiating any such activity with an object, he formed the tips of his fingers into a specific configuration, as I recall, omitting one or two from the formation. Suddenly he moved his hand to touch me in back of my ear and to the lower portion. At his doing this, and taken totally by surprise, *something* flowed from him and *into* me. Whatever it was did not move along the surface of my skin, it penetrated to what felt like an inch or two inside of me.

Needless to say I was startled and somewhat unnerved for a moment. He offered no explanation as to what happened but was not surprised by my saying that something had happened.

Another man I worked with in the same place was also a member of the same order; and he, though knowing of the other man, was not in any open running friendship with him. This man had actually traveled with a group to Egypt and the Great Pyramid at Giza. By special permission the group had obtained from the Egyptian government, he and others in the group were initiated into the Rosicrucian Order in one of the chambers inside the Great Pyramid in a private ceremony.

These events were enough for me. The biblical events, both past and prophesied, that involved Egypt in relation to God's chosen people, the evidencing of an unexplainable presence of energy and its application to both a material object and a living person, were enough to cause me to run, not walk, in a continued pursuit of biblical truth.

Because of those and other experiences in life, I can relate to Edgar's concern to his circumstance. He, being a man of deep Christian belief, was facing in Mr. Layne a difficult choice.

Mr. Layne pushed Edgar to apply his newly-evidenced ability to others, and for money. Edgar consented to the endeavor but refused to take any money for his involvement.

Layne had set up an office, and Edgar would give readings for people to aid them in dealing with physical difficulties. Applying the same technique of putting himself to sleep that he employed with placing books beneath his head, Edgar was able to respond to questions from Layne, who could now be called a conductor, to effectively locate the person for whom the reading was to be given and be able to respond to interactive communication. From this beginning, through to the end of Cayce's life, when he gave a physical reading for someone, he would have to know the location of that person in order to locate the body on a spiritual plane.

A spiritual consciousness associated with Edgar could proceed to a described point, even if it was on another continent, and address that person's body, while communicating about that body to the conductor who was in the presence of Edgar's physical body.

Edgar was to later make statements to the effect that, without this conductor acting in unison with him; he might not be able to return to his physical body. In effect, his physical body would die. If you think back to the commentary in the chapter dealing with Andrew Jackson Davis about hypnosis and the conditions described there, one can note a similarity of circumstance in Edgar's case.

From this halting beginning, Edgar's life would proceed from one struggle to another. In the world of finance, he would never be a prosperous man, let alone a wealthy one. In the world of family, he would live at times in trauma and hope. To his abilities in the supernatural world, he would remain true to his Christian faith to the end. He would, however, in this area come to believe in the aspects of reincarnation as a reality. Edgar was to become associated with people that today we would describe as having a knowledge and belief in metaphysics, though he himself knew nothing of this.

Eventually Edgar began to give two types of readings. One was the physical, which dealt with the condition of the body and a person's health. The other was a "life reading," and this dealt with the makeup or involvement of the person's spiritual being or the psyche.

The accuracy of Edgar's physical readings, though not infallible, would eventually result in the actual building of a hospital in Virginia Beach, Virginia. The building exists yet today and is part of a three-building complex that sits on the main street that most closely parallels the Atlantic Ocean. At the time of the hospital's construction, one would have considered it to be on the shore of the Atlantic Ocean.

The three-building complex houses the legacy of Edgar's contribution to our knowledge of the existence of spirit and spiritual realms.

The hospital was dedicated on November 11, 1928, and the dedication speech was given by Dr. William M. Brown of Lexington, Kentucky. His address was the principle one, and his presence is a strong indicator that Edgar Cayce was no stranger to the medical profession. Dr. Brown was Professor of Education and Psychology at Washington and Lee University. Considering that this hospital was built for the purpose of treating people based on the physical readings that Edgar would give for them while in hypnotic trance, Dr. William M. Brown's presence was of no small significance then and now.

Then the reality was alive and part of everyday life, part of suffering people and hope, at times where there was none. Now we have mechanized medicine and doctors of psychiatry who will be more than happy to give you a label, if you are willing to step to the wrong side of their conceptions of objective reality.

If you were to travel today to Virginia Beach and visit the facility there, you could read for yourself numerous newspaper articles that appeared in front page presentation of Edgar's person and of those close to him.

One such article dates from October 1, 1910, and appeared in a paper in New York, New York. The *New York Times* presented two pages of pictures and commentary about Edgar and his gifts. The article originated in Hopkinsville, Kentucky, and reports on a paper that was read in Boston the previous week before the American Association for Clinical Research in Boston.

The presentation was one of Dr. W. H. Ketchum of Hopkinsville, Kentucky. The front page headline on the paper describes a Kentucky man, who doctors claim can describe diseases while in a hypnotic state. They describe his ability as an inexplicable psychic power that they consider to be marvelous, and that's just the gist of the headline.

The article says that the young photographer, while in a self-imposed hypnotic spell, is the focus of widespread discussion in the medical community *throughout the country*. Notice that the article says country, not county.

He is described as having a wonderful psychic power. *The term wonderful is used.* I know in my life the meaning of the word *sickness* as well as the meaning of the word *wonderful*. Edgar was at this point in his life "labeled" wonderful in his ability.

Edgar's name was not specifically mentioned in the context of the paper that the doctor had read before the association, but little time was required for people to identify the man as Edgar.

Dr. Ketchum and Edgar were not described as strangers; as for two year's time and nearly one hundred cases past and diagnosed by Cayce for Dr. Ketchum, the diagnosis had not once failed.

There was no showmanship to what Edgar did, no lilac robe as Mesmer wore, no self-withdrawing curtains as Father Gassner used, no amphitheater such as at the hospital at Salpetriere where the learned medical profession would gather to watch the experiments in hypnotic demonstration, and no elm tree such as De Puysegur used as a setting. I'm going to speak of Victor and the elm tree shortly.

Cayce was in no way a showman. He was given a gift; he knew that's what it was, and he gave of it to others.

The hospital contained thirty private rooms and was financed primarily by an enthusiastic follower of Edgar's reading, Mr. Morton Harry Blumenthal, who was a New York stockbroker.

Construction of the hospital began after the "Association of National Investigators" was formed in 1927. The Association was headed by Morton Harry Blumenthal and to it Harry was to turn the $200,000 hospital over. The hospital was dedicated November 11, 1928.

Interestingly, it was an effort to expose Edgar as a fraud that brought Dr. Brown to see Edgar. Hugh Lynn Cayce, Edgar's son, was attending the college where Dr. Brown was involved. The doctor had made the statement that he could expose any charlatan, and Hugh Lynn, knowing his father not to be, had suggested he look into his father's circumstance. Obviously, since Dr. Brown gave the dedication speech for the hospital, he found more to Edgar than a person of deceit.

As the construction progressed, Dr. House of Hopkinsville prepared himself to take charge of the hospital. Dr. Thomas Burr House was a medical doctor and an osteopath (that's two doctors in one). The hospital was actually more extensive in its facilities than was the ordinary hospital.

The building had been designed to be a home for the patients if the circumstance was appropriate. There was a porch that was glassed in during the winter and screened during the summer that covered the front and the sides of the building and provided a very beautiful place to rest. The huge lawn stretched to Atlantic Avenue, with the ocean beyond. A graciously furnished living room that was very large was a comfortable repose and, with the library and lecture hall, diversion and study could be part of a convalescence. The building also contained a vault to house Edgar's readings and offices for research workers who were involved with the Association's other activities. Temporarily, the hospital was to be host to the psychic research aspects of Edgar's mystery. To the rear of the building was built a twelve-car garage with servant's quarters, and they also built a tennis court.

The day following the address, the first patient was admitted, and the hospital operated until February 28, 1931. It closed as a result of the nation's financial distress.

Dr. Ketchum

The Depression might not have closed the hospital if Edgar's warnings had been heeded for a longer time. It seems that Edgar forewarned the men who were the financial minds behind the hospital's existence that financial travail was pending. The men actually followed the advice in the warning for a number of months, but then decided there was nothing to be cautious about. Shortly after, they again ventured forth, the stock market crashed, and so did the hospital. The stock market is one place where a continuously positive attitude is not the thing to have. In Edgar's lifetime, the hospital would not be regained.

I find it to be a very interesting and perplexing thing that Edgar was never put into a hospital setting again. One would have thought that the proven advantage of his ability would have been explored and utilized by the medical profession. Edgar continued to give readings of accuracy until his death on January 3, 1945.

From the point that the *New York Times* published the articles about him as a result of Dr. Ketchum's presentation, through the time the hospital functioned and beyond, people from all over the country contacted him for readings. Often in the readings, Cayce would direct people to doctors he did not know, with advice to treatment.

As Cayce had given readings through the years, certain patterns to treatment for varying illnesses evidenced themselves, and this knowledge was part of what was put into practice by Dr. House, the nurses, and dietary staff at the hospital.

Things that Edgar prescribed then were not different in category than that which is today's approach to medicine. He gave instruction for growing hair and for lotions to treat skin conditions. There were concoctions to act as antiseptics in the intestines and diets to aid health. Also prescribed quite often in the readings were medical mechanical devices that existed at the time. His readings also directed the creation of such devices.

Cayce's readings helped drug chemists with formulas for ailments whose composition never existed; or in some cases, the formulas once concocted would be used to treat something the chemist had not intended. Where have I heard that before?

Edgar had an involvement with a chemist who had been working on a formula to administer iodine internally. Interestingly, this man was psychic from birth and had the habit of "sleeping on his problems." He came to Edgar for help, and by some means the formula was perfected, either by the readings, or his dreams, or his efforts. The product was marketed as "Atomidine." This chemist was described as being a learned Hindu, Dr. Sunker A. Bisey. In distinguished fashion, he had earned his doctorate in chemistry from Oxford University in England. Oxford University is not a shoe factory.

After the product was formulated, the readings indicated that it should be used as a preventive measure in times of disease to combat infantile paralysis. This was never the intended use that Dr. Bisey foresaw.

In our chemical world that was called for centuries alchemy, advances that made major change to the world we live in today sometimes found their origins with one person. A man of Bohemian descent who was born on September 7, 1829, was such a person.

He was descended from a Bohemian noble family that lived in a town near Prague named Stradonic. His education was first directed toward architecture in studies at Giessen. A man named Justus Von Liebig came to influence him, however, and he changed his course of study to chemistry. The year of 1851 saw him leave Giessen for Paris, and one year later he was in possession of his doctorate.

He worked in Switzerland for a short time and then in London with a John Stenhouse. In this association, he met many of the leading chemists of the day.

Later, he had his own small laboratory in Germany and lectured at the university in Heidelberg. In 1858, he became a professor at Ghent. In 1895, he was raised by William II of Prussia to nobility and, at that time, took the name Kekule Von Stradonitz. He lived until the thirteenth of July in 1896.

Credited to this man, a circumstance of resounding note can be found in another documented relationship between the objective realities of our modern society and the evidenced subjective relationship that can help direct the course of man's history through such as Kukule.

To a great extent, the poisoning of ourselves and our world has its center at the discovered formula that bred organic solvents into our modern world and our lives.

The man who discovered this formula, Friedrich August Von Stranonitz Kukule, had been seeking for a long time the key to his efforts but to no avail. His eventual discovery has brought into our lives such products as paint, lacquers, and varnish. Printing inks, plastics, and synthetic fibers are directly associated with his discovery. Gasoline, degreasers, and dry cleaning fluids are also noted to his advancement of knowledge.

One can readily see the implications wrought upon us by this man's efforts. The discovery can readily be seen as one of revolutionary change to our world of material products.

His discovery has found itself related to me as occurring through two given stories of exposure. Both are similar to the subjective, but as to which is exactly correct I remain unsure.

One story has it, through Dr. Carl Jung, that Friedrich Kukule, in his deep struggle to achieve the breakthrough, eventually had a dream that saw a couple dancing in a certain fashion, joining and separating. The dancing couple of the dream, when recalled in waking consciousness, bore direct relationship to the chemical configuration that represented the basis formula for Benzene.

The second story has it to be that a linked configuration of rings appeared to this man in a manner similar to that which Thomas Edison experienced. Recall now, Edison became aware that in the twilight of sleep a revealing awareness would come to him from within.

The linked configuration of rings that separated and joined in specific fashion resembled the chemical depiction of structure that was basic to the discovery of the formula to create Benzene. This discovery led to the chemical family of organic solvents.

It seems to be a given to history that one of these stories is correct, and maybe both, as in each case of description the circumstance was presented without reservation as fact.

I've often wondered at such moments in history and contemplated individual achievement. In school, I recall pondering the discovery of pasteurization and the struggle that had ensued and marveled also at the directed intensities of Charles Lindberg.

August Kekule

Often I thought that something of higher directedness might be involved; and now, after so very much deep study, I believe that what Dr. George Richie saw in the second portion of his experience of death is incredibly valid.

Richie encountered in his directed tour of death's avenue by a person he considered to be Christ, a room or area that was peopled by individuals in spirit who had yet a desire to achieve to this world. They were quiet, dignified, scholarly, and intensely directed to their efforts of constructive attention.

It was taken to be by Richie that before these people would go beyond this stage in spiritual existence; they needed and were being provided the time and opportunity to personal fulfillment in attachment to earthly objective, material things.

Richie noted a specific apparatus that was being constructed and after his return to earthly physical life and after the passage of many years. He had occasion to find himself in awareness that the apparatus, seen while in spirit form, had now come to recent discovery by humans. A new machine in a new field of science, the use of radiation for peaceful purposes had been seen by Richie in two separate but interrelated worlds—separated by the dimensional difference that divides flesh from spirit, separated by the span of years to what was evident development in one world, to be brought to another, and possibly separated by the biblical statement that you cannot serve both God and Mammon. Mammon was a Syrian God of riches and wealth, earthly pursuits.

Food for thought and possibly a reflection on Cayce's readings indicates a succession of appearances in fleshly life by a soul before it completes its journey on earth. Development to the knowledge of life seems to be coupled to a release from material ties and attainment of a higher state of being.

The Bible says that man perishes for lack of knowledge, and Pilot asked of Christ, "What is truth?" In the midst of growing knowledge and sought-after truth, we should keep in mind that this world, the things of this world, and the knowledge of this world are to all pass away and that the promise of God is to a new world for those that accept Christ; and Christ's message is that you put nothing or no one before Him in your mind, your heart, and your spirit, your total person.

I think that through the lives of such as Cayce, we are being given a glimpse of the lower aspects of God's creation, and that through the study of the Bible first, as Cayce did, these little windows of para-normal revelation second, and ourselves thirdly, we can focus to a higher knowledge and spiritually profitable direction of life's traveling.

Each time something such as Kukule's experience manifests itself in our world, it brings to light the reality of God's influence and directedness to the course of man's wild ride with destiny.

Such cornerstones of discovery are actually cornering mankind to the fulfillment of prophetic finalities.

It is certainly not without regard for the good that has come from these revelations to mankind that comments are being made; and as we return to Cayce's revelations, it can be said that right now in our time a practicing physician is applying the knowledge brought forth in Edgar's readings to treat psoriasis, and the help that is being brought to people in affliction to this God-awful disease is exceptional to modern medicine's ability to treat people.

If you were to travel to Virginia Beach and visit the Edgar Cayce Foundation,... you would find that on the second floor of the building, in the lobby area outside of the library, there are several showcases that are devoted to this reality. Photos of actual patients are on display, and one can easily see that Dr. John O. A. Pagano of Englewood Cliffs, New Jersey, is in fact helping people through Edgar's readings. I would readily say that both the doctor and the patients are in gratitude to Edgar's courage and confidence that what he was doing was the right thing to do.

Being face to face with and in the presence of reality is without question a dimensional experience that transcends our electronic world. Many things transcend this materialistic world that envelops us.

I traveled to Virginia Beach specifically to further research this book and to take photographs. To this, I was added the bonus of meeting a number of very nice people who, as I encountered them, are living and working in the midst of an experience as well as a place. Each is in his own way continuing Edgar's legacy by supporting the efforts of the organizations there, and each is in his own way enhancing his life by the contact with the people that come there. I found it to be a very pleasant encounter because the people are pleasant.

Approximately one hundred people are employed there and many others volunteer their time. The combination results in affording one the feeling that a person is not just visiting the business of Edgar's legacy, but that the business of his legacy is alive.

I had known about the foundation for more years than memory allows recall and had contemplated going there several times.

Being as I am, in terms of subjective awareness at times, I often wondered and was concerned that my going there might open aspects of life to me that I might not be prepared to accept or possibly handle; and as I have encountered, I am glad that I went at this time.

I did not go there seeking the subjective in experience and, as a matter of fact, the agenda that I had planned had me totally focused to the mental pursuit of gaining quick and accurate information.

Because I was so totally focused, what happened to me there has added another deepening event to my person, and my scope has again expanded. Little do we know and even less do we see.

When I arrived at the Foundation, it was a very beautiful day. The sun was bright in a blue sky that was scattered with clouds. The lighting for photographs was perfect, bright but not glaring, with just a few shadows. With this, I decided that rather than making straight the encounter with people, I would envelop myself in film and lenses.

I allowed myself to become lost in what I was doing. There are many different angles to consider in addressing three buildings and a garden, and my concentration had become totally focused to picturing the pictures. Having taken quite a number, I found myself in a slight pause, standing in front of the original hospital building that has been re-obtained following the loss in the Depression and now contains administrative offices and a school of massage.

I was about forty feet in front of and just to the right of center, if one were facing it, to be more accurate. I was standing at an angle to it, looking to the main building which lies farther towards the right and towards the ocean from it.

To this setting and without anticipation to anything save taking the next picture, I suddenly found myself not alone. I was yet alone in person, as no one else was in front of the hospital, the nearest people being down the small hill and by the entrance to the main building, some good distance away.

This experience I will remember as long as I exist, for I have never felt a warmth like it before at the source. Not to the source, but at the source. For without question, the source was living, present, in multiples, and at least three, but I think more.

Such warmth, such a loving, embracing, encompassing warmth I cannot describe, but first, before it a presence felt, singular I think and close, two feet away and just to my back and right side. It was a quick feeling, not a seeing of anything with the eyes, not the touch of flesh to flesh, but rather the embrace that love is, that peace is. To this knowing of presence, as though summoned, yet there already, others were with me and upon me, not in me. There was no effort in any way felt that intended intrusion to my body. The that which was, was with me.

If there was a direction to be thought to these added present, it was to my left front side and toward the front of the hospital. Their movement was not like movement but like presence to presence. It was as though they were there but yet came to me, also. It was like nothing I've ever known before in total. Although once before, a very similar feeling I might recall, but the circumstance was totally different, yet I wonder.

The warmth of the total persons with me now became just that, total; and I knew it was people I was feeling. I had been and was being doused without interruption with caring-loving-goodness, total goodness. It was the essence of peaceful, helpful joy, and it was joy to be in and with. There was total absence of trouble, and I wish I could be in it and covered by it and part of it now and forever. I fit right in, and I was welcome, and I was glad that I was welcome.

The feeling behind me was, or seemed, slightly different than the feelings in front. A little bit of authority behind for just the slightest of instance and then the same. You might almost equate it to a coach being doused in Gatorade by the team. First, a quarterback or other coach behind and then the players from the front. Different but all one, first but together, a slight distance, yet there all along.

There is a sadness within me as I write this, as though I had something very precious and lost it. How I had it, I don't know; and how I lost it, I don't know either. I just know. Christ said that he went to prepare a place for us and that we could not go where he was going. If that which he has prepared is that which I felt, or if that is what we are to feel, then it is true that we know not the magnitude of his gift to us.

I wanted to speak out loud, to say "Hi" or "How are you?" or "*Who are you?*" But even I have some limits to what I will do. Usually, I hesitate little to think out loud when I am alone; and on occasion, such activities if not monitored closely can overlap the presence of others. This brings at times an odd look and, for me, a chuckle within. A shallow perception is had by too many, I have found. Society is programmed to conformity.

I thought the questions within but did not ask them within either. I was too busy controlling the urge to open outwardly, while being taken to the moment. We are an odd creature that can think and feel at the same time; and as I felt, I thought that I did not want to do anything that would impinge on the contact to come with the people and place. If overheard or seen in gesture, odd it could easily have been. Sometimes it's tough to know and not let it show and yet to grow.

The feeling lasted for its time in time, and then left me to me. Less than a moment but more than none. If a minute passed, I would be surprised, but, oh, how it is prized! And how I have grown in size.

As suddenly as it came, it ended; and I stood in wonder and wondering—who, how, what and why? It was an exceptionally beautiful sky.

I encountered people of many persuasions in this place, staff, volunteers, and people visiting as I. Some whom I encountered brought sadness to me. This had been a place of healing, and I encountered those who were in obvious pursuit of that yet, and this made it for me a place of sadness as well as wonder.

Occasionally, a pale colorless face, and on some so young, brought reality home to me, for I did both feel and see the real reality! A joyous place with many a smiling face, a somber place if one watches the struggled pace. My, my, we live 'til we die and wonder why.

Available in their bookstore and their library are readings and information about that which Edgar revealed regarding many ailments. Some information can be purchased in organized form, and all of his readings are available for research and study.

In researching further this effort, I encountered something that raised my eyebrows a bit, and now I wonder to possible validity. I found a claim made in regard to Edgar's readings. It stated that, while in trance, Edgar quite often suggested that in trying to understand the subconscious mind one should read *The Law of Psychic Phenomena* by Thompson Jay Hudson. The book was written in 1892. I personally have never seen it or attempted to obtain it, and I'm not suggesting it be sought as I don't know its claimed origins.

The book that I read paraphrased certain statements from Hudson's book that I think can be paraphrased again to give an extremely accurate commentary to an aspect of subconscious function.

Dividing the two realities of the subjective and the objective, each is influenced usually by separate sources, the objective by the five senses, the subjective by the subconscious. Our conscious mind looks to reason and logic and external awareness. The subconscious differs as it looks to internal appearance.

Reality for the subconscious is that which from a subjective viewpoint seems true. It's said that objective reality rules the conscious mind, while the subconscious is in a state of servitude to subjective reality.

Both operate on principles; one reasons logically, and the other functions by suggestion. Recall that hypnosis functions by suggestion and misdirected attention. Bear also in mind that psychiatric treatment can function with suggestion given as indirect in nature.

The book quoting Hudson states that if we talk to ourselves, that which we say is accepted by the subconscious as truth. It says that if allowed freedom, this suggestive power can function against us. The statement is such that negative thoughts directed toward ourselves are registered and accepted as reality by our subconscious. The opposite of this is said to be true as well. The subconscious also accepts the positive and can contribute to bringing them to be.

One can see here the manifestation of the power of suggestion through what is actually an interactive involvement of the total person all the time, though we don't always consciously recognize the inter-activity.

This is obviously not an explanation of what the subconscious is; it is, however, a certain commentary to its existence.

What raised my eyebrows to this particular commentary was associated with the fact that since childhood, I have considered it "normal" to talk thoughts to me, either within or without, not to just think thoughts. I do both, and I have thought for many years that I have a closer than average contact with the subconscious. This is significant in that more than one source—Cayce, Jung and others—have alluded to a universal unconscious mind that we are all tied to, and to which some are possibly accessing, knowingly or unknowingly.

In contemplating these things, I stumbled on an interesting correlation between conscious and subconscious, but connected to both presented realities, objective and subjective. In self-awareness training sessions, a memory retention exercise is presented. The people participating are asked to associate a series of things to remember with an image imagined in the mind. Each item to be remembered is to be mentally imagined to rest on a certain part or place on the imagined object or in the setting. By association between the two, recollection is helped to retention.

The approach is objective in that the conscious is striving to retain memory in logical fashion, while it is subjective in that imagination is being told within one's self to create an imaginative inner image. Thus, by the presentation of Mr. Hudson, we can speculate to the addressing of both aspects of being; we can see the interaction between conscious and subconscious.

As for me, the exercise never really worked well. It did for others, but memory for me is something with which I've always struggled. I don't think my subconscious is so easily manipulated by my conscious. It seems with me that I know things that I don't really know and yet they are objectively correct. It's as though the knowledge is there, but I never really learned it or in many cases never studied it. I would imagine psychiatry has a whopper of a label for this if only I cared.

I do care about the label that Edgar Cayce puts on it, and that label is reincarnation.

The word *quandary* is appropriate here. Believing in the promise of Jesus Christ, one finds, or at least I have found, troubling moments in considering Edgar's experience, my experience, and the descriptions of Dr. George Richie's book, *Return From Tomorrow.*

Edgar had given "physical readings" for people for about 20 years, when on August 10, 1923, he was asked to do something different. That different was to answer questions about the person in a reading, rather than the body of the person.

Edgar was a devout man of forty-six years, with forty-six readings of the Bible to his credit, who found himself shocked by the statements that were read to him when he awoke from the reading. The words brought question to the source of his information and fear to him that things had gone wrong.

The Bible says that it is appointed unto man to live once and then to die, and then to be raised to judgment and either everlasting life or the destiny of the Lake of Fire with Satan and his host. It's simple and straightforward.

In over two thousand "life readings" that followed the one on August 10, Edgar had presented through him descriptions of successions of lives lived in the physical plane by the people he was giving readings for. He found circumstances that in his hypnotic state he described as "possession," people being "possessed." He talked about the development of the soul through successive opportunities to develop toward a higher spiritual existence, and he stated that a new source of information was brought to bear in giving the readings.

He claimed that his consciousness traveled to a distant place that contained books that held the records of each soul, every word spoken, every deed done in each life lived; and he claimed that the books were open to him and to anyone else who could or would seek the records. They are not private but rather universal in nature.

This description strongly sounds like the biblical "Book of Life" from which each person is to be judged in the final "judgment" when the book and the books shall be opened and each person's life is to be revealed. For me to say that they are one in the same I surely cannot, but I wonder.

In one of Edgar's readings he described his journey to the place of records. He said that first a narrow bright line of light was followed; and on either side of the line, a fog or smoke shrouded a large number of figures. They seemed to be calling for help and beckoning him to come to them. As he continued the traveling, it began to clear, but the beckoning continued. He felt they were trying to avert his purpose. Cayce's continuing on eventually saw the figures become more like shadows, and they were urging him on now instead of attempting to slow or stop him. Eventually, the figures became clearer, but now they were self-involved.

As the light had appeared, Edgar stated that he had felt that he was leaving his body. Now as he had traversed the light and the figures, he was approaching a hill. Situated on the hill was a mount upon which a temple sat.

When Edgar entered the temple he found himself in a large room that housed the books which contained each individual's records. They were open to him, and it was merely his task to select one and read about the particular soul he was seeking information about. Keep in mind that Edgar gave over two thousand recorded life readings.

Edgar considered that this experience of travel was possibly a description of what it is like to die, and he equated the Apostle Paul's statement of "Whether in the Spirit or the flesh, I cannot tell."

Edgar revealed this in a talk that he gave at the hospital in 1931. Edgar's experiences are not distant history as one can see.

Edgar's reading brought forth from these books the basis of one soul's repeating appearance in this physical plane.

Dr. George Richie's book, *Return From Tomorrow,* was inspirational to Dr. Raymond Moody's efforts in investigating near-death experiences, which led to *Life After Life* and other works by him.

Dr. Richie's own presented experience of dying and returning to this life offer some added insights to what possibly can happen when a person dies.

Dr. Richie had died of natural causes while in a U.S. Army hospital. The moment came before he had become a doctor, and to me his subsequent continuance to becoming a medical doctor and a psychiatrist, coupled with his freely relating of his encounter, carry great weight.

Richie experienced immediate consciousness when he died, and it was to such an extent that he did not recognize that he had, in fact, died.

He traveled first in a circumstance associated with his thoughts and activities of importance in a physical involvement, but eventually discovered that he was a spiritual being rather than a physical person. He could see and hear *both* physical and spiritual beings relating to this physical existence. The spiritual beings at this depth of encounter were interacting, or attempting to interact with physically alive people.

The physically alive people were not cognizant of the presence of spiritual beings, yet Richie saw them to be all around them. They were attempting to interact with the physical people, attempting to communicate with them, *and attempting to possibly enter into them.* This last item is of great importance because it involves "auras" and consciousness. Edgar and Andrew Jackson Davis and Kirlian Photography (Aura)" saw auras or show auras, and George Richie saw auras around the physically living people that he encountered while he himself was dead. Those spirit beings that he saw did not have an aura surrounding them. I'll discuss auras further as we continue this revealing and interesting peek into the unknown.

Edgar gained information while in trance from three stated sources. Physical reading generally came from a direct contact between his spiritual person and the body of the person for whom the reading was being performed. Edgar would have to know the location of the individual to make contact, but that contact could be anywhere on Earth, and traveling to that location in spiritual form would take but seconds. Edgar could also make contact with departed people for information, but this was not usually done unless the person obtaining the reading requested it. There were times, however, when assertion from the departed spirits brought forth comment or communication that was not the primary objective of Edgar's efforts.

In this regard and relating to George Richie's experience, Richie saw many departed spirits in his earthly contact. They were around the living, seemingly attempting to yet experience more of fleshy life. Edgar, on one occasion, commented to someone, while in a fully conscious state, that they were literally in the presence of thousands of such beings; beings having been once living physical people. Have you ever felt a presence of that which you did not see and denied the feeling or wondered at it?

I have, when my dad died. On the day that he died, their house seemed to be filled with a raging anger that could be felt but not seen. It was frightening. We left the house unoccupied for a short while following his death, partly because of it. He fought desperately to live through a massive heart attack and did not make it. I don't think he was very happy about it, and I suspected then and now even more so, that it was he who was felt.

Thirdly, Cayce identified the records of individual recording in a universal openness as a source to the revelation of the development of each soul and to such he was given access, and from such he came to believe in what is called reincarnation—that progression by which a person, being a soul, grows to a higher level of development. Keep in mind here that in a tranced reading, Cayce said that for a Christian there is only one way. For me, it goes without saying, that way is Christ, and that development is that He and His sacrifice be accepted. In light of what is revealed by the experience of death and paranormal occurrence, the statement in the Bible that you cannot serve God and Mammon is given definite definition.

Interesting to me, about me, is that now for approximately two decades I have sought knowledge of what death really is. That search began with my dad's passing and has not stopped throughout these years. At his passing, I was starkly confronted with how little time I had devoted to understanding the questions of life. Oddly, though I set out to study death, I began to learn about life. I started to study the Bible in earnest. I read the Lost Books of the Bible and the Hidden Books of Eden. I attempted Elizabeth Kubler Ross and looked closely at the Tibetan Book of the Dead. Delving on, I studied the revelations of biblical relationship in the Great Pyramid of Giza's construction and looked at the denied prophecies of St. Malachi. With Erich Von Daniken and Hal Lindsey, I trouped with the masses in life's quest. Two decades now spanned and with the last three years of this writing, depth of pursuit and intensity, I've proven to myself that it's been revealed to me that that which you are reading is no fairy tale.

Cayce himself came to believe that he himself had been reincarnated several times, and I feel for him in the struggle such would have brought him. I feel also for myself in the struggle that such thought brings me, because with struggle, one wonders at the term *instinct*.

One can function from "instinct" without thought, but what is it? One can function also from impulse, but what is it?

George Richie, in the first phase of his experience with the realm of the dead, had vision, being dead himself, of a barroom scene. He was watching the physically living, with their auras, and the spiritually living without an aura. The spirit beings were trying to enjoy the normal rancor of the place along with the fleshy. They were having a problem though, because they had no solid body to interact with solid people or solid material. They could not lift a drink, though try they would.

In this scene of transparent and solid, Richie observed something of, in my opinion, great significance. Significant in that Christ cast things out to people, significant in that Cayce did at times identify a state of "possession" in a person he was giving a reading for; significant in that modern psychiatry identifies at times multiple personalities in people. The last is very important to Richie's observation in the barroom scene.

George Richie observed the aura of living people as it opened up at the head and shoulders of an individual when that person would fall unconscious. This opening seemed to allow one of the nearby "dead people" to pounce on the head or face of the unconscious person and quicker than the eye could see, disappear as though it had entered the person. Allow your imagination to wander a little and maybe you'll consider that the term "living dead" is possibly more than a joking phrase.

Richie speculated that maybe the halo or aura is some kind of a protective shield that somehow changes with lack of conscious being.

Auras (Kirlian Photography)" for me first became a matter of consideration not from the spiritual aspect of life but rather from a scientific. Kirlian Photography (Aura)" gained its name from two Russians who advanced it in 1939 and it has been studied since that time.

Two Soviets, Semyon and Valentina Kirlian discovered that by a simple process of using an electrical charge that is passed through regular photographic film, a person's aura will be recorded on the film if the person or part of the person is placed in contact with the film.

It has been revealed through continuing research that the aura will vary in color, intensity, and configuration as the physical and mental person varies in condition.

Two examples of this would be that if a person is physically healthy and relaxed in mind; the aura will be recorded as being a deep blue. The same person, if photographed in a state of excitement, will show a marked difference. There will be thin spindles flaring from the person's aura that is now red and white in color.

In 1970, a Dr. Thelma Moss traveled to the Soviet Union and observed aspects of the Soviet research with the Kirlian process. When she returned to the United States, she and her associate, a Mr. Kendall Johnson, constructed apparatus to perform their own experiments.

Using twelve volts of electricity and a high frequency of 3,000 Hertz, they too were able to photograph an aura of people on ordinary Kodak film.

Another phenomenon associated with the effort that they made revealed that, not only could the aura be photographed, but also that two people photographed at the same time on the same photographic plate (fingertips were used) would show evidence of repulsion or attraction between varying individuals. Join a dating service, and you might well read in their literature of "chemistry" between people. Chemistry may well be physics instead. at least, physics as seen in the photo and felt in person.

Magnets have a polarity within them that attract to opposite and repel to like fields of energy. Mesmer used magnets and magnetism in his experiments, and Andrew Jackson Davis was, in his early years of adventure to the realm of the spiritual unknown, magnetized.

Davis also was reputed to be able to tell the nature and character of a person by feeling or sensing the "atmosphere" of the individual, and as you recall, in later life, had merely to touch a person's hand to gain knowledge of that person's state of being.

Professor Moss is to be given much credit for opening the door to western research a little wider for all of us.

A Dr. Tiller is also to be given credit for returning from a trip to Russia with the knowledge that when a person dies, the finger tips will glow for several days before losing life's living shroud.

The "Shroud of Turin" that many believe to be the burial cloth of Jesus has an image imparted to it that has defied the explanation of the world's best scientists as to its origin.

The shroud, or corona, or aura is also without explanation to the living, about the living, but representative of the physically alive. Two mysteries, possibly interrelated, possibly not, but both are revealed to the human eye in best image by an unusual process of photography. The Shroud of Turin, by causing a negative to show a positive, the aura by involvement of an electrical field related to life, Christ is without beginning and without end, never dead, but given to a physical body to die in the flesh. Edgar claimed to be able to see, with his naked eye, the auras of people. It is a claim that some people make, though not many. I don't know if Edgar ever saw the Shroud of Turin, but I would surely be curious at what he might have seen had he. I've rambled a little here, but it doesn't hurt to do so occasionally; a little thoughtful mystery doesn't hurt occasionally.

In the matter of auras, science is actually trailing Edgar; and what I've related to was lifelong, everyday awareness to Edgar.

Edgar actually developed a code, if you will, that he related to each individual. The code encompassed aspects of color, mixture, intensity, and configuration. The appearance of absence of aura, Cayce came to equate with pending death.

To the last I will comment first and relate to an instance that Edgar shared with us that involved a personal moment.

It seems that Edgar was shopping in a store that had several floors to it and an elevator to reach one's destination. He was on the sixth floor and ready to leave. The elevator was nearly filled with people to the point that when Edgar's turn allowed a crowded place. He stepped back and declined entry at the seeming darkness within the car and defrayed to studying some nearby displayed apparel. The cable that suspended the elevator compartment snapped, and all who were riding, less Edgar, plummeted to their death.

In later thought to the tragedy, Edgar realized that he had noted something unusual besides the darkness at the moment he gazed at the people in the cubicle. Recalling, he realized that all the people had no aura about them. When I read this, I had an involuntary moment of recollection to the bouncing step of a school teacher from New England on her way before the T.V. world to destiny, a destiny shared by six others. I wonder if at such moments we all see too little, and if the challenge of life is really a challenge to all.

The phenomena with Cayce's ability to see auras is extensive and compelling. The aura is definitely associated with Dr. Richie's presented experience in the spirit, in the barroom, and to him identifiable spirit persons were seen to possibly enter physical persons at the opening of the aura. Cayce stated that in talking with a person, that should the individual make comment to a prejudice attained in a former incarnation, an image of an individual would appear within the aura of the person, and that image would be like in appearance of one from the era being represented as consistent with the personality the person supposedly was then. Each time, the time frame of comment might change, the image might change, and six or eight changes of the figure in the aura might occur during an encounter of several hours of company and conversation. Are you in contemplation? I am! Whose life? When? *How? Have you ever felt a compulsion?!*

Edgar had given a life reading for a friend of his; and in that reading, it was revealed that the friend had supposedly in another lifetime been an English monk. Edgar's friend in spoken assertion to a group of people alluded to an aspect of English history; and at

Cayce's near miss with death

the time that he did, Edgar saw an image of a young monk in his aura. The reading and the incident were at separate times, and for Edgar, the incident helped him to accept the information of the readings.

To me, within all of this, questions abound. They abound not only because of personal experience within myself, but also because of experiences with others that have no *real* (objective) answers. Yet, subjective explanations might abound to that which a being is in being. We have:

First, the appointment of God that man is given once to live and then to die, and to die to the final judgment.

Second, to awareness that Christ cast out demons from people who were in possession of those people.

Third, that Christ, and the Apostles, and the Prophets recalled through God's grace and power, people from the dead.

Fourth, Cayce in giving readings at times found that "possession" of the individual existed.

Fifth, the Catholic Church recognizing the possession of people and actually performing, to my understanding, exorcisms to cast out "demons" from possessed people.

Sixth, the Catholic Church recognizing what are called "inner locutions,." these being the awareness within a person that a knowledge or information is being presented or passed to a person from a spiritual source.

Seventh, Dr. M. Scott Peck, psychiatrist and best-selling author recognizing and believing that people can be possessed and influenced by that possession, and that people whose faith in God is strong enough can influence God to cast such things from people, and that once cast out, extended psychiatric effort helps to maintain the re-established person.

Eighth, Dr. Carl Jung, who extensively worked to identify the make-up of the human person and who came to identify for us the anima and animus, and the number one and number two personalities of a person as aspects of being human that he believed in, and that I am not in dispute to, but rather am finding myself more and more tuned to as life's experience continues. Also, we know that Jung in his autobiography *Memories, Dreams and Reflections and Reflections"* identifies personal aspects of existence that point to the influence of previous life experience.

This could be continued later, but for the moment, suffice it to say that existence as a physical person is in concert and conflict with a spiritual aspect of being that possibly is of more than one form of being. The aura would seem to be an identifiable and close to tangible representation of some aspect of the term "life."

Cayce's lifelong association with viewing consciously the auras of people led him to be a very discerning person. He came to believe that the basic deep colors that he might see in a person could change as the person changed in development, and that also outside influence could change the evident colors.

An example given by Cayce is that one man that he had contact with had a beam of light projecting downward to his left shoulder. The light was multi-colored, being made up of red, white, blue, and green. Cayce considered that in a circumstance such as this, some information was being given to the person through inspiration. Cayce queried him and found that he had previously been a writer but was now teaching and lecturing. Recall now Ernest Hemingway and what he discussed as "The Juice." "The Juice" was when he had the flowing inspiration to write fluidly, quickly, unhindered by the surrounding life and for extended periods. Not having "The Juice" meant calculated plodding to bring product to effort.

Have you ever had the juice? Have you written or talked with inspiration, possibly without prior depth of knowledge or feeling? If you have, what do you suppose Cayce might have seen in "your aura?" Think about it; what I'm talking about regarding the existence of aura can be seen in pictures of photographic creation. It's not a fantasy or deniable subjective suggestion. Kiss someone you love and sparks literally fly on film!

In our present time, psychological studies have been done regarding the influence of color on people. The military has done studies as well as the private sector in pursuit of understanding a little deeper the mysteries of life.

Edgar believed that the color of aura a person was projecting could be reflected by the color clothes they predominately wore and by the color of items that they would surround themselves with. Thus, if true, then Edgar Cayce gave insight to all who chose to contemplate the possibilities. He also seemed to give consideration to a woman's added sensing, a sensing that can get a man in so much trouble, believing that a woman can feel if a color is right for another person, especially another woman. The expression of a color looking so good on someone may well be a reflection of a matching of one's aura to one's attire. Thinking back through life now, I recall occasion when in early marriage my wife would literally bring the chattering, bustling, feminine activities in a ladies' dress shop to an admiring halt by considerable multitudes. It used to amuse and delight me because I knew all the in's and out's of the figure that was cutting the figure in the colors that all thought ravishing. I, for one, believe Edgar was right; I can still see the heads turn and hear the voices quiver to the blessing of one color and not another. Dress shops can be a lot of fun and high adventure with the right woman, figuratively speaking. I think Edgar had an eye to such moments, given that excitement and vitality intensify the glow that ladies show.

If we use Edgar's gained knowledge as a base, then we'll see that a lady dressed in blazing red will drive you both 'til you're dead. More towards the pink and with less maturity, she'll think, but look good in the pink. If deep red is there, deep suffering you'll share, so beware. If red is the choice, it may well be time for a quiet voice.

If green is to be seen, then know full well it's the color of those who might help you be well. Cayce claimed that doctors and nurses wear it well. It's friendly, it's strong and if tending to blue, trusting, too. Care should be taken to the lemony side; she may harbor deceit inside. So said Edgar, not me, from flying purses I flee.

Mind you now, if yellow she likes, she's mentally right; a deep well of good care if to the dress she'll compare. Helpful and happy and so quick to learn, you'll soon discern that worry's not her plight and this woman's a beautiful sight. If a little ruddy, the yellow it be, a little bashful you might see. To the red side of yellow, Edgar saw indecision that might allow others to lead.

Edgar's seeing of auras, if reflection of person, seldom showed totality, unless there was deep reality. Gray is the color of illness, and to this one I can speak to my own personal experience, for I have lived the transition from blue to gray and now returning it would seem, it's more than a dream. To become ill can cause one to fall still and wonder to the strength of will. From dominance in my lifetime of blue, gray took over. An odd change, I thought, and then my health was wrought. Reading now that deep blue is health, too. A strong spirit and unusual, too; deep blue is moody blue. Deep blue has a spiritual mind that might sing or write a cause to fight, has been my plight. Steadfast with a mission, but with gray transition and a new mission of admission to vulnerability unknown, a lesson I've learned, and it's deeply burned. For Edgar was right, with blue there's less plight.

To the pale blue, depth is not great; but the struggle is right and talent's a fight with maturity in sight. A blue in the middle is a person who will not speak.

If a seeker you seek, the colors are indigo and violet they've chosen, turning to deep blue once they've stopped supposin'.

Purple can be bearing, at least to Edgar's baring.

If orange is the color, then consideration you'll know; it'll show along with the glow. A thoughtful person this is, and it's not show-biz. To the golden is self-control but toward brown won't care, even on a dare.

White, white, white, it's out of sight, the color of the chosen, perfect if seen. Edgar believed that if a perfectly balanced soul were seen, the person would have an aura of pure white. He believed that Christ had such an aura and thought that to be the strength to its cause, considering all auras an effect, that would have brought death to anyone who would have touched Him following His resurrection at the tomb. Cayce thought it to be the reason for Christ having warned that he should not be touched before He ascended to the Father. He believed that the vibrations from within him that were evidenced by the pure white color would have killed as if one were electrocuted.

Whether Edgar is right or wrong, I don't know; but I believe the "Shroud of Turin" bears the image of Christ; and Edgar's awareness of the reality of auras and their representative relationship to the internal person gives pause to me to consider a possible relationship.

Edgar's seeing of auras had a very practical bent to it that is striking and revealing. This practicality focused to the speaking of truth. Cayce came to recognize a visual phenomenon within a person's aura as revealing the telling of a lie or a deception by the individual.

Edgar would see within the person's aura above their head, a shooting streak of lemony green flash horizontally. He never knew it to fail in its revealing nature and thus it gave him an uncanny advantage in dealing with everyone in the normal course of life.

I find it of extreme interest that people who espoused phenomenon of mind such as Rasputin and Jackson and Cayce, each possessed within that extraordinary ability very practical senses. Rasputin, as you recall, could see a person holding a stolen object; Jackson could read a person's character; and now Cayce could discern a lie. It's said that Cayce could also know the cards held in another person's hand and that few would play cards with him.

Edgar noted that a person's aura was most heavily concentrated about the head and shoulders. This is significant when placed in the light of Dr. Richie's observation of auras about those in the barroom who fell unconscious, and whose aura then opened in a rolling or peeling fashion starting at the head, thus apparently allowing the entry of, or possibly allowing the entry of what he perceived as, the fellow dead that he himself was with.

If it becomes practically possible to readily perceive a person's aura in the present or future, then application to the development of children may take a giant step forward. Edgar came to equate the shape of a child's aura with certain circumstances regarding the child. The position had bearing as well.

A child whose aura was shaped like that of a chain rolling in the areas of both the shoulders would denote a personality with a will all its own.

An aura that rolled about the head in a manner of a crown would reveal one who would accept instruction through perception and be very reasonable in person.

Cayce gave further example by saying that if instruction would come to a child only through a great deal of exposure to example, then the aura will be a definite figure with various colors and sharp points evidenced.

The advantage of such a knowledge to an individual would surely be a boon to parenthood, and an educational system that could separate and direct children to their most rapid area of achievement would certainly create a more balanced approach to learning and contributing to socially enhancing behavior. A child that is not quick to respond to verbal instruction would not find the pressures to learn through such means as pressing. What Cayce was really seeing were natural abilities, and all such abilities contribute in one way or another to man's advancement.

Recall the comments in the chapter addressing Andrew Jackson Davis that allude to the ability of a person to build upon and enhance another's initial ideas or inventions, while yet another would be able to initiate activities from mere inspiration or idea. Cayce's observations may well be a harbinger of predetermination to the two types identified by Davis.

Cayce noted further in regard to color and configuration that, in seeing the green glow of a person devoted to healing, that sympathy could be expected from one whose green quivered as it rose. Also, he noted that should a person be a leader or director of some sort, their auras would be sprinkled with light in the form of hooks.

Edgar's observations indicated that a person's aura showed constant change as the mental and physical state of a person changed. He gave accounts where change of significance occurred in a matter of days and within those days smaller variation as well.

A child's nature revealed to Cayce

Hidden Shadows

Edgar's shared ability to see the glow about a person in a color revealing fashion ties together the continuous relationship of spirit and flesh, subjective and objective, within each of us, and adds yet another morsel to life's twinkling mysteries.

Many have taken an objective approach to understanding the presence of the aura. One such approach involves the aspect of what has most commonly been called "Kirlian Photography, (Aura)" " named after two Russians, Semyon and Valentina Kirlian, who are considered pioneers in the systematizing of the process and experimentation with what also has been subsequently named electromagnetic discharge imaging (EDI), electro-photography, electro-graphy, and radiation field photography. Their experimentation began in 1939.

Semyon was working as an electrician in the city of Krasnadar. While working in a local research facility, that has also been referred to as a hospital, he noted that a high frequency massager for patient treatment emitted a small electrical discharge between the patient's hand and a glass electrode. Semyon was curious as to whether he might be able to photograph the unusual happening.

He constructed a device that he thought would allow him to do so. The electrical discharge burned his hand severely, but he also captured an image on a photographic plate.

Thus began the Kirlian's encounter with the pursuit of a photo phenomenon that saw its origin with a man named Nicola Tesla in 1880. Tesla was able to produce and photograph what was termed corona discharge by employing the use of a "Tesla Coil."

Research in the use of this process of photography has been pursued both here and abroad, and development in diagnosis of medical condition has evidenced itself in numerous studies. Also, the sector of industry testing for physical properties, in conformity to structure, evidences researched effort.

One very interesting revelation that has notable content is that those places on the body that are identified as acupuncture points actually can be located through this photo process. The intensities of light that are given off by the points are definably evident, so much so that denial of a patterned energy flow through the body is a difficult thing.

The presence of aura, and the evidencing of energies flowing within the body, are given an expansion of understanding within the realm of the ancient art of exotic massage. Within this long established practice that is based in the sectors of Tantric and Taoist teachings. We find awareness that the sensual art involves the three aspects of mind, body, and soul.

The knowledge came to the West from India and China around 2,000 BC and has part of its basis in the cult of the god Dionysus. It's found in these teachings that touch between a man and a woman not only satisfies the sensual desires, but also is believed to be food for the soul.

Famous people of influence in the western civilization of the time praised the art of sensual massage as having a power of its own. Both Greeks and Romans mingle together and include Plato, Homer, Socrates, Hippocrates, Herodotus, Pliny, and Julius Caesar.

The physical and mental benefits of massage eventually began to fall into disrepute, and by the time of the Middle Ages the pleasure had turned to the belief that it was an unhealthy practice. The Middle Ages can be called dark for many reasons.

Nikola Tesla

Hippocrates

In Tantric and Taoist beliefs we find that the body and mind are closely connected, and thus one can affect the other to major degrees. The mind, if ill, can make the body ill. The body, if ill, can make the mind ill. "Mind-Body" is often associated with Chinese visualization of a person's being, and thus physical massage affects both mind and body by calming the mind, while visualization in the mind relaxes the body. It's believed that the conscious mind is linked to the imagination by such visualizations as well.

The harmony of relationship is a basis to relationship within this mind and body, and between a woman and a man sharing each other. The body was honored by the ancients as being the temple of the soul. Thus, by Tantric tradition, when lovers touch, it is with respect and reverence to each other.

Tantra is associated with gods and goddesses while Taoism is associated with the energies of yin and yang.

"Tantra" origins are from about 5,000 BC and are from India, and it means "weaving," bringing things together. Also in India, "yoga" is spiritual practice and the Sanskrit word means "union." With this, Tantra can be described as a "sexual union."

This "union" according to the ancient Eastern traditions, when associated with erotic massage, involves both "energy" and "aura."

In beginning a massage, two fundamental things are addressed. First is harmonizing, and second is removing negative energy.

Harmonizing is the first step to forming a mystical intimacy in which two feel to be one. Without describing the total stepped actions, it can be said that in Taoism and Tantra it is believed that a very subtle "energy body or aura" surrounds the physical body.

Rubbing the hands together briskly is believed to focus this energy in the hands and invigorate it. This promotes a greater stimulation in the massage. Placing the palm of the right hand *on the base of the spine* and the palm of the left hand at the top of the spine at the neck and closing your eyes, the mind is then tuned into one's partner. Awareness of the partner's feelings is focused too, and loving thoughts are sent through the hands.

It's believed that the "subtle energies" in the body are stimulated and controlled by the mind. Next, it's to be imagined that a flow of energy passed down the left arm, through the palm of the left hand, flowing down the spine to the palm of the right hand, completes a circle that unites both people. The partner is asked to help by visualizing the energy flow as well.

Removing negative energies is next, and in the next step in the pleasured union of a man and a woman the aura is addressed.

It's considered that the aura, just like the physical body, gets dirty and requires cleansing. It's believed that "negative energies" are picked up by the aura each day from exposure to the world around us, and that also our own negative thoughts and feelings contribute as well.

Cleansing the aura is done by monitoring one's feelings to the time it "feels right" and then moving both hands from the spine and placing both hands on the back of the partner's head very softly. From this beginning, with ever so light a touch, the hands are swept down the entire body and off at the feet. This sweep is done several times, gradually involving the entire body. At the end of each sweep the hands are gently removed to one side, and as though flicking tiny droplets of water from them, they are shook into empty space. This is believed to remove any negative energy that has been picked up by them from their partner's aura.

This opening to each other begins the exotic massage and is in definite recognition to the existence of the aura and energies within the body. Keep in mind that 5,000 BC is the date associated with this awakening.

The closing to an encounter of lovemaking that erotic massage can lead to and encompasses also lends itself to this inter-involvement of aura's and energies and is fascinating for sure.

In the glow of the moments following the melting of love's passions, a final massage can be shared before slipping into the embrace of sleep in the embrace of love.

This is described as "massaging the aura." It is done as the most delicate massage of all and ends the love-play.

It involves massaging your lover's aura, and the process does not encompass touching. The hands are held, palms open and toward your partner. Keeping them two to four inches from contact with the skin, a circling sweeping motion starts at the head, and gently and slowly is moved down the body.

It's possible that the sensation of heat may be felt in the palms of the hands as they are moved so delicately over the aura of one's partner. The sensitized state is very delicate in the person being massaged, and that person may feel the aura being massaged, though the skin is not touched.

When the massaging pass has been completed, the hands are once again flicked into empty space to remove unwanted energies that may have been transferred from the aura of the sharing partner.

Taoism further addresses the aspect of energies by relating to yin and yang, and in the chapter devoted to Dr. Carl Jung, speaking to his belief will further enhance our understanding.

Today, a scientific explanation exists regarding the creation of photographs produced by the Kirlian process, but none yet exists that explains the ability of Edgar to see auras of people who were not deliberately or inadvertently exposed to an electrical field.

To briefly state what happens in the artificially created Kirlian environment, one finds that the object of attention is ionized (electrically charged) by exposure to an electromagnetic field, and thus is created an acceleration in gas molecules surrounding an object. The electromagnetic field also frees electrons from the surface and accelerates them along with positive ions. The particles that are accelerated and charged collide with molecules and atoms that are neutral. This creates additional ions and electrons. After positive ions build up in sufficient volume, they re-combine with the electrons. When this occurs, red, violet, and ultraviolet light is emitted; and on a photograph, the discharges can be seen as light.

Experimentation with Kirlian photography has shown that it can be used to monitor ions as they change in living tissue, and members of the scientific community believe that physical and psychological changes in organisms can be followed by observation.

Known factors that can affect the image on the Kirlian photo include moisture content within a subject or object and temperature, as well as surrounding gasses. Other physical factors exist along with the intensity of electrical charge, the type of film, and type of subject in contribution to the variables. Progressive photographs of a leaf as its physical condition changes, or other organisms as they change, will change the aura in color and intensity. So there is evidence that life's changing conditions are effecting to the scientific explanation of process that brings creation of the aura and its visible representation on film. The film merely shows the effect of the cause, and Edgar considered the aura which he saw to be an effect generated by a cause within the person. Edgar had a distinct advantage to this revelation because he could continually watch the evolution of change to a person and their aura, and thus could relate one to the other with personal intimacy. Being intimate with Edgar in life's proceedings must have been quite an experience.

He espoused an ability to know, from trance-induced statement, one's physical condition and how to effect curative efforts, one's past history as a soul, at least in part, and to be able to relate that past history in his conscious state through revealings seen in the aura of a person he was in company with, making immediate statement in conversation or activity. The physical state that might be revealed in trance could also be reflected by aura presentation. A person's initiatives in life could also be reflected in the aura that he saw, and that same aura could reveal to Edgar if a person he was talking with was presenting a deception. The tranced information could reveal pending trouble, such as the financial travail of the stock market crash that caused the loss of the hospital; and on top of all this, in his early life, he could sleep on a book and know its contents. This is quite a list of extraordinary things to be associated with a man of such deep Christian beliefs.

As we've been looking at magnetism, hypnosis, and auras, both natural and artificially induced by the existence or creation of electromagnetic fields, at this point, looking at the human person in relation to life's electrodynamics is most appropriate.

Cayce's ability to recognize a person's physical state by natural observation of a person's natural aura might be in some ways duplicated by artificial means. In the sector of medical diagnosis, three areas have drawn my attention.

The first area of medical attention relates to the efforts of one Dr. Ion Dumitrescu, who is a Rumanian medical doctor. The doctor indicates that he had done a medical screening of six thousand chemical workers and used Kirlian photos of their thumbs as the diagnostic tool. He was looking for malignant tumors in these people and, as was confirmed by conventional testing, the evidence of forty-one of forty-seven revealed by photographs showed undeniable probability of relationship. The doctor also believed that those remaining six patients would soon show conventional evidence as the tumors he believed present grew in size.

The corona displayed by those afflicted was one of a bright image emitted by the unhealthy tissue. Contrasting to this, those with healthy tissue emitted a dark image.

Cystic fibrosis has also evidenced itself in Kirlian diagnostic efforts. Two blind studies done at the New York University Medical Center by a researcher there named Leonard

Hidden Shadows

W. Konikiewicz, who was also the director of medical photography at Polyclinic Medical Center in Harrisburg, Pennsylvania, and Dr. Benjamin Shafiroff, M.D., associate researcher at the University, effected a diagnostic success of eighty-eight percent and eighty percent respectively in C. F. Homozygotes and C. F. Hetrozygotes. Though not absolute, the evidence is not ignorable.

The researchers found that electrolytes in the sweat of C. F. patients is eight times that of a normal person; and if you recall, moisture is one of the variables associated with variation in corona image. The electrolytes cause the difference in corona appearance, which shows to be an uneven light emission about the finger that can be broken and crumpled, also. Twelve of thirteen clinically known cases were evidenced by photography and thirteen of fourteen known carriers showed repeatability of the process.

The third area involves the diagnosis of schizophrenia, and again, evidence indicates that the artificial introduction of an electromagnetic field in photo application reveals a corona discharge that varies from a significant blue in healthy people to a patchy or nonexistent no corona condition in a person who is ill. Under the fingertips of the ill person, a red coloration that lacks any structure is shown. The results of the study were presented in 1982 by Dr. Vitto Ria Marangoni at the International Congress of Medical Physics in Hamburg, Germany.

The coloration that appears in the photos is considered to be a result of ultraviolet light that is created by the electrical discharge, and that also the silver crystals in the various layers of photographic film react to the ultraviolet light of the emission and thus create color as well. If one wants to eliminate the corona effect, it can be done almost completely by filtering the ultraviolet light.

Color can also be created by varying the type of film and altering its contact with the surface to which the electrical charge is induced.

Predominant influence can be affected to a Kirlian photo by regulating conductivity, pressure, and moisture.

With a wide variety of variables, it can be readily seen that continuity requires skills, knowledge, and precise regulation of equipment and process.

As I've studied this developing field of research photography, I've concluded that, in fact, a person's physical condition is reflected through the revealing corona. I've also concluded that though calculated scientific approach explains a great deal about artificially produced corona effect, there is no scientific explanation regarding the ability of one such as Cayce being able to see a natural corona.

That does seem to be the bottom line regarding coronas.

In looking at Kirlian Photography (Aura)" , I stumbled on something that might relate to Mesmer's magnetism. Thinking back to the commentary regarding his efforts and his equipment, we can recall that he actually used what he claimed to be magnetized water in a baquet and the effects of people coming in contact with both him and his procedure would bring about disruptive behavior.

In 1983, a R. Baker made a discovery regarding both the pineal and pituitary glands. The revelation that emerged was that close to these two glands there lie magnetic deposits.

The pituitary gland exerts a key influence on the thyroid gland, which in turn regulates the metabolism in the body. The metabolism is in turn a key factor in the total function of the body.

Symptoms of mental distress as well as physical problems can come very readily from a malfunctioning thyroid gland.

In 1961, two men associated with this nation's veterans' hospitals had opportunity to study psychiatric admissions to eight state psychiatric hospitals. Dr. Robert Becker had worked with electricity and bio-magnetic fields with bone healing, acupuncture points, and salamanders, and espoused curiosity as to whether the bio-magnetics in humans were influenced by external fields.

Dr. Becker, along with Dr. Howard Friedman, who was Chief of Psychology at the V. A. Hospitals, studied twenty-eight thousand patients over a period of four years. In those four years, sixty-seven magnetic storms occurred on the sun. The doctors found that following each storm the number of admissions for psychiatric care increased significantly.

It was reported by Dr. Becker that a possible relationship exists between the magnetic deposits lying close to the pineal gland, the magnetic storms, and the admissions.

It is common knowledge in our society that sleeping in a north-south configuration within the northern hemisphere, one's head to the north, or in the southern hemisphere, with one's head to the south, brings a better night's sleep.

Looking back through medical history, one finds that the treatment of ailments by applying directly to the body various ferrous and non-ferrous metals was a commonly accepted practice. Ferrous metals definitely interact with magnetic fields and could easily bring influence to a biological system sensitive enough to be affected by a magnetic disturbance on the sun.

We seem to be living in a very delicate body that is being treated by our electrical society in a very indelicate manner. The world is running to mood and mind-changing prescription drugs to balance life; and I wonder at the prophesy in the Bible that states that in the final days before Christ returns, the world will be filled with madness. Are we creating our own madness and not knowing it?

In Edgar Cayce's biography, *There is a River,* one finds an interesting statement regarding the pineal and pituitary gland.

Edgar identified, while in trance state, a configuration that at the time I read it I found puzzling and still do. Edgar said that the human being is imparted with three minds, the conscious mind, the imaginative mind, and the mind that is of the soul, which rests with the spirit. Each mind interacts with the other in progression or system. When I read of the progression, I pondered the aspect of my person that at times will be confronted with a statement or question that requires immediate response. Oft times I will answer and then some time later find myself saying, "Why didn't I think of this deeper, more appropriate, or possibly funny thought then." Edgar offers a possible explanation by saying that thought travels from the conscious mind through the imaginative, which is also termed introspective mind, to the mind of the soul. There it is compared to all previous knowledge attained in rightness of being by that which has been and is the person at the moment. Next, the thought is related to the universal knowledge that rests with the spirit for a rightness of response.

If all goes smoothly, the thought is then returned with answer to the conscious mind. The conscious mind is the record of the present life. As the thought travels back through the system, the imaginative mind can delay and influence the return answer and thought. Imagination is not truth.

Expanding farther to these statements, in the initial traveling of thought from the conscious mind, the thought travels to the imaginative or introspective mind where it is compared with the person's previous thoughts for relationship and conditioning. Once this takes place, the conditioned thought is then transferred to the soul, which is also called the subconscious. Both the subconscious and the spirit are said to rest or be seated just above the heart in a person.

If a thought is considered constructive, as all thoughts are recorded, then it will lower the barrier that separates the soul from life's essence and will quicken the spirit. Should the thought be destructive, then it helps build the barrier up. Such destructive thoughts are rejected; and if repeated, they detract from life's essence.

The returning answers from the soul, when compared with the truth of all knowledge, move from the imaginative mind to the conscious level by means of a hunch or intuition, or possibly a yearning or reflection will bring it to a conscious level. I referred time and again to inner-directed awareness. Dr. Wayne Dyer calls it inner directedness and touts its following very heavily. Woman's intuition is to a man perplexing, and Cayce's knowledge from trance may well hold part of the answer to the mystery of the process and origin of that which can put a glint in the eye of a young lady and cause her to look and to move as though some person other than she is in mischievous motion. I personally take a great delight in watching and feeling a lady who's reading and acting to her inner self. They are delightful to me as all can be; and if they sense that you are sensing their secret. Oft times, a little grin will add to their spin, and they have trouble hiding the delight that both try to hide from sight, but to delight. That which we're describing is really the essence of life, and women are closer to it than men, without doubt.

The stated seat of each mind is what I now find intriguing in light of the aspect of medical discovery regarding magnetism and the influence of the identified glands on the psyche of a person.

The tranced information stated that the pineal gland is the seat of the imaginative or introspective mind, and the pituitary gland is the seat of the conscious mind. Each gland is recognized to have its own physical function as well. Each gland, as you recall, has been now shown to be in close company with magnetic tissue, and life within the body is an interactive, interdependent intricacy.

- The conscious mind is the recorder of this life's experiences and responses to other conscious minds. It's said to be seated in the pituitary gland.

- The imaginative or introspective mind compares thoughts from the conscious mind with past known conscious thoughts. It conditions the thoughts and passes them to the soul mind or subconscious. It's said to be seated in the pineal gland.

- The soul mind or subconscious records all thoughts and relates them to the spirit or superconscious if they are good, or bad thoughts divide the soul from the spirit.

Good thoughts are returned through the minds to a conscious level through introspective awareness at the conscious level.

Superconscious is a new term, and it relates to the spirit level and is now leading us to a commentary about Edgar's struggled belief in reincarnation.

The tranced information indicated that the subconscious mind, when it received thought or when a new experience occurred, would compare it with all thought and experience from all past lives lived by the present conscious person.

Once the thought was passed to the spirit or superconscious, it is compared at that level with ultimate or absolute truth, with the actual law itself. Pilot asked, "What is truth?"

Once all this interaction has occurred and the thought is returned to the conscious person, the person is changed from that which existed prior to the thought.

The time associated with this process of thought change is that which I was referencing about having wished I would have thought of that at the time.

One can say that in process of time, judgment for several days can be centered with the conscious mind. Time passes in "Reflection" to the initial thought and then a new opinion of extended person is adopted. As more time passes, a wise, universal and detached "Understanding" prevails. This now deeply seated opinion can, however, be influenced by future experience or thought which again traverses the same avenues to "Understanding," and thus a person grows.

The term superconscious state can be applied to both Cayce and Jackson. It represents the fourth stage of hypnosis, which can be described as the state of death. It is to this stage of hypnosis to which both Cayce and Jackson alluded to as requiring a conductor to be in sympathy with them to sustain the life function of the physical body, and to allow the return from the spiritual venture to the physical plane to relate information to this conscious plane.

Jackson moved back and forth between planes in less than an instant with each transfer of statement. Cayce seemed to be able to relate more readily from the spiritual realm but both described and experienced the same circumstance of superconscious awareness. Both knew that it was possible to die by staying in the superconscious or fourth stage of hypnosis.

Edgar's description of the progression of change in consciousness at death relates to a progressive involvement, also. He stated that when one dies and the spirit passes to the other plane of existence, that the conscious mind remains as physical and passes with the body. The subconscious that was such in the physical life then becomes the conscious mind to awareness of thought and activity. The superconscious mind of the physical experience becomes the subconscious mind, and life in cycle and growth continues.

Such came to be Edgar's belief that life was a growing spiritual experience that involved reincarnation.

Edgar also made a professing statement about what could be identified as a representation of the phenomenon known medically as the transference. It is one of my favorite subjects to contemplation and in many ways is associated with what could be called intuition.

In Edgar's biography, *There is a River,* there exists a commentary to possbily understanding the transference that I have never seen duplicated and to which I have personally lived. When you have lived something in repeating times, it is very difficult to deny the existence of it. Finding an acceptable explanation of such personal events is both gratifying and in a way relieving to a person's jogging pursuit of understanding life's mysteries.

Interestingly, a very noted European psychiatrist, Dr. Viktor E. Frankl, espouses a theory to life's motivations that centers itself about "will to meaning." I agree with him greatly in that I have spent my life, both childhood and adulthood, primarily in pursuit of understanding, and doing so as a matter of will. Most everything else in life has seemed to be sort of getting in the way of that quest. Interestingly also, I developed my own awareness of this long before I read of Dr. Frankl. You might note that a man such as Frankl might have insight to life's struggle with depth, considering he survived the mangled insanity of Hitler's concentration camps. To such a man, I would think that Dr. Freud's concepts of sexual motivation fall flaccid, to say the least. Contrasting opinions of motivation within the medical community are to me at times a reflection of who has the strongest will to presentation, which is another motivation.

Edgar's revealings regarding what Jung and Freud call the transference came as a result of information from readings that he did for Dr. Lucian H. Warner of Duke University. The requested readings centered about aspects of telepathy and evidenced that telepathy is in some ways associated with the development of the soul.

Keep in mind that a soul is not an inanimate thing, but a creation of God that is not immortal as of now, and is capacitated to life by His grace and lives the possibility of dying. To this awareness add the revealing from Edgar in trance, that communication or telepathy occurs between the minds of two people when time and space are lower than the state of consciousness that both share. The perception of both conscious minds are connected or mingled through and in the subconscious of both and become the same within the subconscious of both.

It is an interaction of one or both conscious minds acting with the subconscious which is now one linked mind in both, that creates the link between each individual's conscious mental perception. The subconscious is primary and the key to receiving the thoughts, feelings, or awareness of activity that the transference is labeled to be. The individual subconscious can either receive or send or do both. Edgar said that some are good senders and some are good receivers, and that some are both.

There are individuals in a state of development who might be more developed to sending and those who are better tuned to receiving the subconscious transmissions of the others, according to Edgar. The aspects of this linking of minds can become so intense that the transfer of physical feeling of presence, one with the other, can occur. Thought is easily transferred. Any emotion helps set up the transference and is also felt by the receiving person. The physical activities of the sending person can be seen within, and felt by the receiving person in somnambolic flash or burst that lasts but seconds or parts of seconds. They are instantaneously recognized and understood by the receiving person.

The activity can be involuntary to both, and Cayce indicated that when two people are in love and in a state of mutual understanding, transmission can occur between minds *without* a conscious awareness of it. Cayce's statements were very specific in identifying love as a major contributing factor in the linking of minds.

My personal experience with this intuitiveness is such that I believe it fully true that such occurs. The aspect of love is also associated with openness of person to person. A conscious lowering of resistance to a premonition to event opens the door to depth of knowing of the other's thoughts. Edgar made statements to the effect that if two people set up a specific time and made conscious effort to communicate, that over a span of some twenty-plus days, a channel could be established between those sincerely seeking the other, and that the involvement of love and understanding help as well. It's actually quite swell!

The trance generated information went on to further state that a pathological continuity also exists, and the parameters of "Eugenics" establish the necessary physical conditions to facilitate the telepathic state.

Whatever the reasons, the reasoning to a person who can look to their life's experiences in this extraordinary area of consciousness and relate actual objective events to experienced subjective thought, or awareness of thought, has a distinct advantage to advancing their inner perceptions of the "real world" that is really a combination of the steadied propensities of the seen and the immensities of the unseen. In a way, I feel sorry for those who deny the latter and place themselves in pursuit of the clatter.

Edgar Cayce identified himself strongly with two men, Andrew Jackson Davis and Victor Race. I've talked about Andrew Jackson Davis already to considerable extent and written of Victor Race a little as well. I think it interesting to continue the comments to Victor, as little seems to be known or written of him.

In traveling to Virginia Beach and to the Edgar Cayce Foundation to research this effort, I gathered some additional knowledge of Victor in the library at the Foundation.

If you recall, Victor was a Frenchman and came to be known by the discoveries of a follower of Anton Mesmer, the Marquis de Puysegur. Prior to the trip to Virginia Beach, all that I had encountered regarding Victor and the Marquis merely referred to Victor by his first name, not including his last name, Race, and the indications were that only one man was associated with the name de Puysegur.

I found that the de Puysegur's of discovery actually referred to two men. The de Puysegur brothers were French Army officers, both of whom had been stationed in Paris at the time Mesmer was a person of notoriety. Both had become interested in Mesmer's work and both had joined enthusiastically "The Paris Society of Harmony" that existed in support of Mesmer's works.

Retiring from their service in the Army, they returned to their estates near Soissons and to a life that afforded considerable leisure. The leisure afforded them also the opportunity of concern for the well-being of the villagers. Their involvement in the "Society of Harmony" and exposure to Anton Mesmer's endeavors in treating people by the practice of magnetism soon found them experimenting with their own approaches.

These men, being pragmatic in nature, as having been instilled by military careers, carried this stellar approach into their involvement with magnetism as well. In the social pomp of Paris, the trappings of solemnity with pink robes and curtains of quality in quantity, along with music to penetrate the soul, were fine refinements to the fastidious of society.

In this rural setting, such would have been possibly unnerving and even upsetting to the common people that were the subjects and participants in the efforts of healing by application of magnetism. The de Puysegur's selected a more natural and comfortable setting for their efforts.

In the village, a place of long-standing traditions existed, and to it both young and old found fun and consort in concert with nature. The village green found congregation of the older men as they gathered under a huge elm tree to discuss harvests and the anticipation of crops at sale. This much respected tree saw also the gathering of younger people who, in the evening, danced the laughter of youth beneath its embracing warmth.

Such a place of comfort and ease was ideal for soothing the ills and discomforts of people in distress, and the de Puysegur's added the magnetism of healing to the limbs that saw romance, and dance, and the business of France.

About the tree, arranged in a circle, benches made easy repose beneath the limbs from which ropes were attached that furled toward the ground, where the ends might be found by those in repose who were about to dose. In such setting, who knows to what depth of belief one might succumb. The benches were made of stone and made in circular form. Several such benches were about the tree. The rope or cord, as you will, was wrapped about the trunk of the tree and the branches, also.

The people who came to the tree for help were sick. This was not a Paris social amusement, and the village was not a place where boredom's relief was rife.

To this setting, the patients would come; and sitting in circles about the tree, they would tie the dangling cords to touch the area of their body that was in distress.

Tied to the tree in hope and belief, the session would begin. With the patients sitting in a circle, they would touch the thumbs of those next to them with their own, thus allowing the magnetic field to flow freely.

Maxime Puysegur believed, as did Mesmer, that a "universal fluid" existed, but differed from Mesmer's theory of magnetism, himself thinking it to be electric and that it could be linked with living things such as trees.

The tree, the ropes, and the benches were the full extent of the Puysegur's material objects; and the patients were never touched.

The setting and the approach were more tranquil than the Paris predecessors; and with this, those who experienced cures did so with less violence, as they were released within, to whatever it was that created such crises in people.

It was the year of 1784 when Mesmer was suffering the antagonism that spelled his future, that in Somes, the Puysegur's were to first delve to the study of "La somnambulisme par l'acte magngtique."

A peasant of twenty-three, who was the gardener of the de Puysegur's, became ill with an inflammation of the chest, and he came to the tree for treatment. When he was included in the group and had done as the others, he, however, fell into a trance that would be termed today as being hypnotized. The normal reaction to the curative efforts was that of convulsions. Victor Race demonstrated none of such. In this peaceful state, Victor, who heard no one save the Marquis, was directed to touch the magnetized rope to the area of distress. Suggestion and several episodes of this brought a cure to his ills.

Puysegur pursued the experimentation into somnambulism with those others that continued to seek help and found that by suggestion, in the curious state, cures could be affected. He discovered, also, that if he were to touch a person or the bench that they were sitting on, convulsions and suffering would result and that the soothing of his voice was all that would calm them.

Victor's somnambulistic state also brought forth, to Puysegur's initial amazement, the learned voice of medical diagnosis to the ills of others. When this which was considered by Puysegur to be a supernatural event occurred, Victor's dissertation would evidence exact medical terminology that was precise to the point that the title of physician was applied to the efforts, and Victor's abilities expanded to the point that in his third or fourth entrancement, when ailing people were given over to this diagnosis, he would immediately touch the person's body in the area that the distress lay.

Probably the best description of Victor Race comes from the lips of Maxime de Puysegur himself, in the form of a letter that he wrote to his brother.

> It is from this simple man, this tall and stout, rustic, twenty-three years of age, enfeebled by disease or rather by sorrow, and therefore the more predisposed to be affected by any great natural agent, it is from this man, I repeat, that I derive instruction and knowledge. When in the magnetic state he is no longer a peasant, who can hardly utter a single sentence; he is a being to describe whom I cannot find a name. I need not speak, I have only to think before him, when he understands and answers me . . .

Maxime believed that he had, in this mysterious way that is yet mysterious today, tapped the inner person of Victor. I've seen it stated that that which was revealed in Victor was his subconscious person or his secondary personality. Dr. Carl Jung identified very strongly with what he described as a secondary personality in a person, it being very pragmatic and pronounced. I have experienced throughout life a relationship with my own secondary personality that finds my understandings of Puysegur and Jung an expansion of knowledge and yet a wonder to existence, within the existence.

Cayce's evidencing brought forth the aspect of subconscious and what he called superconscious being. He believed, through understanding from the readings, that he traveled to the realm of the superconscious to obtain the knowledge that came forth from his also simple person. He believed that his subconscious talked with and mingled with the subconscious of others, and that all are part of a spiritual realm of universal openness to one another. Dr. Carl Jung called it the "universal unconscious," and I think the evidence of life and life's understandings bears truth to their revelations.

From this basis of discovery, the Marquis and a Dr. Ostertag established two experimentalist "Societies of Harmony" in the City of Strassburg. Mesmer opposed this action and even condemned it as being possibly harmful to the science of magnetism.

Nonetheless, Dr. Ostertag continued his experiments in somnambulism and thus moved the science of hypnosis another rung up the ladder to today's understandings. He experimented with the use of a glass ball that he would suggest that patients stare at until they would give themselves over to a "strange immobility." This was obviously a formative step toward the methods of Dr. Braid that were to occur in Manchester, England. His efforts took place in 1841 and, as you recall, though some call him the Father of the Evaluation of Hypnotism scientifically, his efforts were rejected in England but accepted in France.

Victor also evidenced, while in somnambulistic sleep, certain things that brought the Marquis to make public claims to the experiencing of thought transference and clairvoyance. This weakened the acceptance of the phenomenon that surrounded Victor. It does, however, today find itself in mirror to Cayce and Jackson in similarities of expression and experience.

The phenomenon of the transfer of thought to Victor from the Marquis while Victor was in trance is something that I have not seen as being evidenced between the conductors of either Jackson or Cayce. Actual verbal communication seemed to be necessary to convey information to both of them.

Of the three men of simple nature to life, Victor stands as the least of stature in social order and afflicted by sorrow for some reason. It was obvious that Cayce's explanation that being able to set aside self-concern opened the avenue to knowing of others and the spiritual side of life's experience.

It takes a great deal to bring a feeling of accomplishment in me, but I seem to be sitting and feeling that, by being touched by the lives of these three men, I have accomplished a great deal of personal development. I've used the term repeatedly, "Be careful, they'll call you crazy," and they surely may; but with the knowledge of these three men clattering about within, it is a very shallow concern that might be brought by very shallow people.

A man well known to our society attempted to start "Societies of Harmony" here in the United States. Does "Lafayette" ring a bell that will bring liberty to your thoughts?

At this point, it might be appropriate to step back and gather perspective to that which we have been exploring.

I've mentioned that had Sigmund Freud been a better hypnotist, the world might have followed a different course to today's being.

If we look at the basic beliefs that came to exist at the two places of prominence in France that he studied, the Salpetriere Hospital, with its four thousand beds, and the Nancy School, and consider the recorded realities of Victor and Cayce and Jackson, then it would seem to me that one man contributed more to losing a form of reality for society than did any other. There is little wonder that Freud and Jung parted to their separate ways. Jung seeming to respond to his own inner subjective nature, and Freud responding to what must

'Neath the tree, cures were known

Marquise de La Fayetté

have been inner sexual torment for him, to have forced upon the world a closure to the realm of somnambulistic revelation. Jung also helped this closure to occur by deliberately choosing to ignore its potentials because he did not understand and could not explain the phenomenon.

In the Nancy School, being a place of intense advocacy of hypnosis, it was believed that hypnosis was a subjective manifestation of the patient and that in this state of subjective presentation of self, the patient objectively became extremely receptive to suggestion. Recall the previous statements regarding the receptiveness of one's subconscious to verbal and thought suggestion given forth by the person himself and accepted to reality by the person's subconscious.

The Salpetriere school of thought brought forth that hypnosis was merely a form of hysteria and that the hysteria brought on degrees of trance that could extend from a catalepsy to a light coma.

In these years of experimentation, the aspects of somnambulism's presented realities in the area of medical diagnosis was an accepted, though not understood, phenomenon to occurrence.

Two forms of somnambulistic encounter can be had by the individual. Both have shown themselves to be effective to objective individual realities, and the failure of Freud and Jung to aid and advance the study has left few in awareness that a person can be an intuitive somnambulist as Edgar Cayce was, or that one can be a sensitive somnambulist as Frau Hauffe was. It can also be that a combining of the two subjective gifts or abilities can manifest itself in the individual. This eventually seemed to happen to Andrew Jackson Davis.

An intuitive somnambulist is one who experiences the phenomenon of subjective encounter, with those already described sources of spiritual encounter, while in a hypnotic sleep state.

With Andrew Jackson Davis, he would initially be magnetized by a conductor to help produce within him the hypnotic state. Eventually in life, as I've described, he could merely be in a person's presence and touch the individual to establish the subjective links to encounter. Edgar described this as psychometry.

Edgar's ability to self-induce the hypnotic state also produced the intuitive somnambulistic state. Both Davis and Cayce required a conductor to convey the subjective information to the objective plane. Neither, while in somnambulistic sleep, was consciously aware of the information flowing through them. Victor also fell into this category of intuitive somnambulist.

The intuitive somnambulist does not consciously know of that which is addressed subconsciously, nor does he assimilate any of the conditions or feelings of the person being addressed.

The sensitive somnambulist, on the other hand, has merely to be aware of the person's presence to assimilate the knowledge of that person's physical and emotional condition. This circumstance of assimilation can then be conveyed to another person as it is felt, thought, or exists. This occurs *all* on a conscious plane that is in cohesive accord with the subjective being.

A sensitive somnambulist is a walking manifestation of the real reality that Dr. Carl Jung describes in different ways within his autobiography, *Memories, Dreams and Reflections and Reflections"* . This book is listed in the *Encyclopedia Britannica* as being one of his best works, and it should be noted that he would not allow its publication until after his death.

Dr. Carl Jung is not the doctor next door. He is world-renowned and can be found in the *Encyclopedia Britannica*. It states that he is the Father of Modern Analytic Psychology.

One should note that the word *psychology* is associated with the *study* of the phenomenon of the mind. This contrasts with psychiatry, which is the study of the *illness* of the mind.

The first, to me, represents a healthy and appropriate approach to living and searching life's mystery as we travel the path to eternity's destination. The second, to me, represents the turmoiled struggle to deal with the negative polarities of life. Phenomenon is positive; illness is negative. The combining of the two creates a struggled mixture of one power pushing and pulling at the other within the normal human desire to be considered right to one's perceptions. Drs. Jung and Freud and Frankl could never really mix because reality for one is not necessarily reality for the other. All three were really just human beings experiencing life.

Cayce, Davis, Rasputin, Race, Phillipi, Hauffe, and you and I have and are experiencing life in the same world of human development. The phenomena of life is to each his or her own, and those who would label should be cautious that they do not obtain a label themselves.

Frau Hauffe, who lived from 1801 to 1829, had attributed to her many phenomenal things. One such encounter that is notable to relate involves a woman for whom she gave effort to help by diagnosing her physical ills. This she did to remarkable accuracy by just being in her presence, but something additional happened to this meeting.

Frau Hauffe not only diagnosed the physical and felt the physical; she also assimilated and identified a disorder that had not been the order of the woman's complained concerns.

The Frau questioned a condition in the woman's right eye and indicated an obscurity to vision and discomfort. The woman was surprised and confirmed the condition. She had for several months been experiencing the difficulty described.

The Frau's contact brought assimilation of the symptoms of the disorder to the woman's sight; and for months following the encounter with the woman, her eye was in a state of discomfort and diminished ability to see. It was as though a condition of cataract existed in her eye. It took repeated contact with people whose eyes were perfect, and the staring into those eyes for extended periods of time over several months, to restore her vision.

Such is described as sensitive somnambulism. Edgar's intuitive somnambulism was part of his everyday life from March 31, 1901, to his death on January 3, 1945.

Edgar gave of his gift to others who sought his help and his revelation to their life understands, in sincerity of person and personal fortitude in over thirty thousand physical readings and over two thousand life readings—all of which can be read in the library at Virginia Beach.

To Edgar's legacy of revelation to the unseen world of spirit, Atlantic University, which cohabits the Foundation grounds along with the publishing house of the Association for

Research and Enlightenment, now finds credibility from the objective realities we all live, in the accreditation of Atlantic University in the State of Virginia. The study of trans-personal skills and global citizenship find themselves as part of curriculum offerings there.

I've discussed magnetism as a reality to our existence, and we are all familiar with the polarity of the earth. Edgar's readings evidenced, in his physical person, an effect that somehow mysteriously mates the earth's polarity with Edgar's divisive readings, being physical or life.

Edgar could give a reading for both physical and life readings while lying in the same position, but he would experience a physical difficulty when he woke up. He would also have more difficulty with life readings if given from his familiar position for physical readings. Magnetic polarity seems to be a plausible explanation, but no absolute understanding exists.

In giving a physical reading, Edgar would lie with his body in a position with a north-south axis. Edgar would awake with a headache if he did not rotate himself 180 degrees to give a life reading. The solution to the headache problem manifested itself in a reading that gave instruction to turn around.

Edgar died on January 3, 1945; and his wife, Gertrude, followed him just a few short months later. She died on April 1, 1945, at dawn on Easter Sunday.

One has to give pause to the meaning of the word *death*. Swedenborg predicted the day of his. Cayce, it would seem, ventured there twice a day, give or take, for over forty-three years. Davis was no stranger to the same traveling in strangeness to our objective world.

I encountered belief in one lady at the Foundation in Virginia Beach that there is no death, merely a cycle to growth of the spirit in experience built upon another.

Edgar's readings shed light on certain aspects of our human being in relationship between physical and spiritual life. One such revealing is encountered in a reading given on November 13, 1937. Edgar was asked if feeling, physical feeling ends immediately at physical death. Edgar's answer was that a dependency upon the manner in which unconsciousness comes to be, as well as how the consciousness has been trained, influences the release of spirit from the physical dwelling.

Further indication is that a continued consciousness is prevalent, and it is evidenced by the fact that physically living people who are sensitive to spiritual contact know the impressions that are projected to their consciousness by the entities that are projecting, who are departed from the flesh. In addition to this sensitive knowing of the spiritual realm of the departed, they are also in like manner sensitive to the subconscious of those living in the flesh, though this reading addressed the aspect of death.

Further to the readings' comments, we find a statement that could be directly associated with the experience of Dr. George Richie. In the initial moments of Richie's death, he was not aware that he was dead. His consciousness just continued as though the flesh and spirit were still one with the other. Such was not the case, however. Richie only realized that something was amiss after a considerable number of instances of encounter with the physical realm brought no physical contact. His consciousness was not aware that he was in a state that is called death by the reading of Cayce.

The reading specifically states that individuals who have died have at times been dead for what we term "years" without becoming aware that they were dead. The relationship between Richie's shared experiences is unmistakable.

In Dr. Carl Jung's *Memories, Dreams, and Reflections*, he posthumously shared with us his near-death experience; and in that commentary to unusual experience, he relates that the doctor in attendance to him actually followed him spiritually to the realm of death to bring him back. I think Cayce would have seen a massive amount of green in the aura of a doctor who was so devoted and developed to such spiritual depth to somehow be able to do such a thing.

Keep in mind that Dr. Carl Jung is not described as being "Bat Man" in the *Encyclopedia Britannica*, as you contemplate his sharing.

A further description of the state of death in Cayce's reading continues with a comment to the appetites of physical life. The indication is that they are changed, or they become not an awareness at all to the departed spirit being.

Again, we find Richie's experience relevant in that in the barroom scene, the appetites of the flesh are the driving passions that were being evidenced by the spirit beings who had no auras, as Richie had no aura, and gave reason to conclude that possibly entry to this living unconscious was to further the fulfillment of those desired physical appetites. The fulfilling of the fleshly desires in the flesh apparently carries over to a release from such feeling in the spirit.

Richie has further encounter to such appetites as his experience continued and deepened to an involvement with a person he considered to be Christ, and a place he thought possibly to be a state of hell.

Hell was a place where those appetites of the flesh were manifested in continuous repetition to unfulfillment without effect on the recipients of the appetite's assertions. The assertions were physical in violence, all manner of sexual endeavor, and verbal abuse to others in the same state, but all with no effect to the intended victim. There was no communication between them, just being; and in Edgar's reading, in the same paragraph that I've been alluding to; the aspect of communication in the state of death is a disturbing thing to the experiencing individual. In the place that Richie considered to be Hell, communication did exist in the form of whispers or talking projected from angelic beings hovering over the people in conflict.

I wish I could say that I am amazed at the relationships that spring forth when one studies life's mysteries, but in honesty to self I am not. Too much exists from too many valid sources, and also from self, to deny the propensities of life's challenge to understanding to Dr. Viktor Frankl's quest of "will to meaning."

Cayce's reading continues with comment to the psychic forces of an entity-individual, and states that such forces are *constantly active* and that the soul-entity might not be in awareness to all of the activity. With this circumstance of constant psychic activity, the psychic force of an individual can become an individual in its own right. In a way, it would seem that what is being said is that the psyche can be of a mind all its own to the personality of activity; and with this, I wonder to the relationship of this stated circumstance in a Cayce reading for a requesting person and Dr. Carl Jung's identifying of one's secondary personality.

Jung most surely places a great deal of emphasis on one's secondary personality. He alludes to its strength of assertion, its pragmatism, its knowledge to propriety of circumstance, its difference from the normal conscious person's person, its involuntary presence in an individual, and its definite influence to those to whom it projects.

Cayce stated in trance that a person's subconscious mind in the physical becomes the conscious mind in death, as you may recall. Jung may well tap the identification of both the conscious and subconscious mind in physical life with his assertion of number one and number two personalities.

My, my, Jung, Frankl, Richie, and Cayce in step and Freud off chasing the phallus of the mind. No wonder he couldn't understand women, with women being so highly directed by the intuition of nature's depths and the psyche's warmth's. A woman is a subjective knowing in a physical glowing, and her entire being is the meaning of her being; and if the love of her knowing is given in glowing that she can't help sharing, then foolish is the man who ignores a lady's giving of that which God has given, but many there are who fail to see the shimmering star.

Cayce identified in the reading three bodies—physical, mental and spiritual—and indicated that the consciousness is not of the physical and that when that consciousness is not in the physical body that it is with the Lord, the ideal, or is present in the universal consciousness.

I asked, while at the Edgar Cayce Foundation attending a lecture dealing with reincarnation, if it was considered that the universal unconscious of Jung's description was considered to be the same as that of Cayce's description. The answer was emphatically *yes*, and the name of Rudolph Steiner was voluntarily included to the list of persons identifying the same realm of existence that is considered all parts one.

A question also within the reading deals with one oft thought or considered, and concerns cremation and the aspect of feeling it's happening to one's physical body. The answer to this finds itself tied to the appetites of physical desire that a person might cling to. The physical consciousness is tied to the appetites, and thus the duration of attachment determines the time to remaining conscious to physical feeling and event. If you feel a little queasy about now, then you're feeling as I feel.

There is the biblical statement that you cannot serve God and Mammon. Apparently, the truth to that statement can be given consideration in the aspect of focus at the point of death as we see it. A focus to Mammon brings attachment to the body and sustaining feeling. A focus to God brings detachment and flight to the promise of a place prepared for the spirit or soul to find peace with God.

Richie seemed to be approaching such a place when it was deemed appropriate to return to the attachment of physical being. From the place, two people were speeding towards him and the person with him that he thought to be Christ. Richie thought that contact with the two approaching people would have spelled the end of his ability to return to the physical body.

Keeping in mind that Cayce indicated in readings that there is only *one way* for a Christian to attain the sought after relief from the physical bonds, we can recall the commandment from the Bible that says you must love the Lord, your God, with all your heart, all your mind, and all your spirit, and from this, one's person becomes bound to God through the acceptance of Jesus Christ. I believe that Edgar was certainly a man who did this.

Edgar's readings touched many areas, and another that I found to be of hope concerned the people that were born into this world during the years spanning 1943 to 1946.

These people, who include me, were stated to be special within their own right. It's said that they would be very purposeful as individuals, and a great deal will depend on the course of their activities twenty years into their lives. The roles they are to play will be interesting in service to their fellow men, and the approaches used by them will be very unusual. I'll leave it to you to speculate the meaning of these statements from another world.

In a reading given on November 2, 1937, it was asked of Cayce how the person for whom the reading was given might complete life's earth experience in the present lifetime. Cayce's response instructed the person to show the Lord's death through study until He comes again.

Are you questioning with me the question and the answer? Did Cayce in trance tell this person that he or she would live to see Christ's return in a lifetime that started sometime before November 2, 1937? The question was direct and so was the answer.

The other night, I was watching Jack Van Impe on T.V. For those that do not know of him, he is an evangelical student of Bible prophecy and has made effort to relate his knowledge to world events for several decades now. I have followed him sporadically through these years and have often found his conclusions to be very insightful.

I was watching his program the other night, which originates in Michigan, and he was alluding to what many consider to be a timetable to man's history written in stone in the Great Pyramid of Giza in Egypt.

Much has been written and studied of this stone monument to man's ancient knowledge and ability to apply it. I personally studied some twenty-five or thirty years ago, the presented, calculated, and, if one would believe, represented prophetic presentations of its physical structure.

Those who claim the correlation allude to mathematical translations of lengths, heights, and directions of passages as associated with years and events in history.

Van Impe made the statement the other night that by one interpretation of these things, the last recorded date of reference in the passages of the pyramid is May 5, 2000, and that is some sixty-two years from the date of November 2, 1937, and possibly well within the lifetime of the person for whom the reading was given.

We know from the Bible that no one, save God, the Father, knows the actual time for Christ to make his saving entry to the madness of man's self-destructive path, but we do know from the continuous fulfillment of end time prophesy that it is near.

I've alluded to this because Cayce, in a reading given July 1, 1932, made considerable comment to the Great Pyramid.

He indicated that the pyramid presents knowledge and represents awareness that sprang from the still existent relationship between the Creator and us, His creatures. It's stated that the Creative Forces are manifest in the material world and that those forces are represented in the pyramid as a readable record. Part of the understanding is that once a much closer relationship existed between those creatures that were and the Creator that brought and allowed their existence.

There is a statement in the Bible that alludes to the morning star as at a point in time being given to the redeemed in Christ. The morning star is called Polaris or the North Star, and it is located in the Big Dipper. The Cayce reading that alludes to the Great Pyramid makes definite reference to this star and claims that at a specific time a line can be drawn from the opening to the pyramid, apparently meaning a line projected from the shaft, to the north star, and definitely states that it is along this course that one's soul takes flight when it has completed its time in this solar system.

Two additional questions were asked in this reading and brought the response that the Great Pyramid was built during the time of Araarat and required one hundred years to complete. The names Hermes and Ra are mentioned, also, and the dates given are from 10,490 to 10,390. The actual time placement is unclear because the reading alludes to a point in time prior to the entry of the "Prince" into Egypt.

Commentary to Edgar Cayce could continue in boundless address, as his readings touched on multitudes of subjects. The intent, however, in this effort is not to intensely examine the content of spiritual communication to depth, but rather to bring light to the continuity of existence of experience by persons of note, so that those of us who are not of such stature to life's recognition might find understanding to one's own experience.

Throughout all this effort, and as it continues, common threads of attachment exist from one individual's psyche, in contact with the spiritual, to the next person's; and it is hoped that this is finding itself known to you. It has taken a great deal of time for me to come to a scattered understanding of such, but of such I am convinced that within these pages a person can attain knowledge that our seen reality is merely an attachment to a far vaster reality, that we are both part of and in travel to.

Cayce's readings did not deal significantly with prophetic statements. You can recall that his desire was to help people, and to this his focus strongly stayed. He did, however, bring forth occasional statements; and one that has importance to me is that during the years spanning 1988 through 1998, big changes would occur in the world, and that the bad that is bade before the biblical prediction of one thousand years of peace is to occur, will see relatable occurrence.

As a notation to the reader, if you were to choose to travel to Virginia Beach to visit the Edgar Cayce Foundation, you might like to be aware that in the midst of the friendly people and presentations, you will find a mixture of those beliefs that are both Christian and metaphysical. It seems to be an unavoidable aspect of presentation, and I have not made the effort to understand it beyond the aspect of Edgar's contact with people of metaphysical knowledge in his life being somehow combined with his devout Christian beliefs.

I have addressed Mr. Edgar Cayce in the manner I think appropriate to those beliefs and will leave you to contemplate the mixture, as am I.

COMBINING BOTH WORLDS OF SPIRIT AND FLESH, ABOVE THE DOOR
TO THE MAIN BUILDING ARE THE WORDS, "THAT WE MAY MAKE
MANIFEST THE LOVE OF GOD AND MAN"

CONSTRUCTED IN VIRGINIA BEACH, VIRGINIA SPECIFICALLY TO
TREAT THE AILMENTS OF THOSE WHO SOUGHT EDGAR CAYCE'S
READINGS, MEDICAL DOCTORS AND NURSES FOLLOWED HIS
RECOMMENDATIONS IN WHAT WAS THEN A NEWLY BUILT HOSPITAL.

IN THE BUILDING TO THE RIGHT OF WHAT WAS A HOSPITAL OF HOPE,
THE A.R.E. PRESS TODAY PUBLISHES BOOKS AND INFORMATION
DEVOTED TO EDGAR CAYCE'S MEMORY.

THE OLD HOSPITAL BUILDING SETS TO THE REAR OF THE MAIN
BUILDING THAT HOUSES CAYCE'S LEGACY.

THE MAIN BUILDING HOUSES A LIBRARY, A BOOKSTORE, ATLANTIC
UNIVERSITY, LECTURE ROOMS, AND A VISITOR CENTER IN
VIRGINIA BEACH, VIRGINIA.

TO THE REAR OF THE BUILDING IS A VERY BEAUTIFUL MEDITATION
GARDEN THAT IS OPEN TO THE PUBLIC.

THE VISITOR TO THE FOUNDATION IS GREETED BY THE MAIN LOBBY
AND BOOKSTORE. THE STAIRS LEAD TO THE LARGEST LIBRARY
COLLECTION OF BOOKS DEALING WITH THE PARA-NORMAL IN
THE WORLD AND TO EDGAR CAYCE'S READINGS, ALL OF WHICH
ARE OPEN TO THE PUBLIC.

THE LIBRARY ON THE SECOND FLOOR OF THE MAIN BUILDING CONTAINS A LARGE VOLUME OF INFORMATION THAT IS EASILY REFERENCED.

USE OF THE EXTENSIVE CARD FILE BROUGHT FORTH A DEPTH OF INFORMATION ABOUT "VICTOR RACE".

**THE SETTING IS PLEASANT AND THE AMAZING VOLUME OF
BOOKS SPAN TIME AND WORLDS.**

**CAYCE'S READING'S ARE OPEN TO THE PUBLIC TO RESEARCH
AND PONDER. IT IS AN INCREDIBLE LEGACY!!**

THE THIRD FLOOR OF THE MAIN BUILDING HAS A MEDITATION ROOM.
THE SIX LIGHTED PANELS ON THE WALL ARE THE PRESENTATION OF
A WOMAN WHOSE ARTISTIC WORKS ARE ON DISPLAY IN THE
NATIONAL MUSEUM OF ART IN WASHINTON, D.C.

IN THE DAYLIGHT THE MEDITATION GARDEN IS A PRINSTINE BEAUTY
THAT OFFERS A QUIET PLACE TO CONTEMPLATE THE ENCOUNTER
OF A VERY UNUSUAL PLACE.

FROM ANY ANGLE THE MEDITATION GARDEN IS A BEAUTIFUL PLACE.

AT NIGHT THE GARDEN BRIGHTENS A SMALL WORLD ALL ITS OWN.

THE HOME OF EDGAR CAYCE'S LEGACY IN VIRGINIA BEACH, VIRGINIA
IS UNIQUE IN ALL THE WORLD. THE PEOPLE I ENCOUNTERED THERE
IN VISITORS, STAFF, AND VOLUNTEERS WERE POLITE,
ACCOMODATING, AND SEEKING A PATH.
WE ARE ALL SEEKING A PATH, THE QUESTION LAYS IN WHAT WE'RE
FINDING. FOR ME CAUTION HAS COME WITH UNDERSTANDING.

THIS PHOTOGRAPH WILL REMAIN SPECIAL TO ME ALWAYS. IT WAS TAKEN SECONDS PRIOR TO THE EXPERIENCE I FELT AND LIVED IN FRONT OF THE HOSPITAL THAT WAS, I'M SURE, AN ENCOUNTER WITH THE PLACE AND LOVE THAT CAN BE KNOWN BEYOND THIS WORLD. TO THE RIGHT OF THE MAIN BUILDING, BETWEEN IT AND THE ATLANTIC OCEAN, IS PROPERTY NOW OWNED BY THE UNITED STATES NAVY. TWO OF THEIR STRUCTURES PROTRUDE THE SKYLINE WITH NUMEROUS OTHER BUIDLINGS OCCUPYING WHAT WAS AT THE TIME THE HOSPITAL WAS BUILT, OPEN TO THE OCEAN.

CHAPTER 7

FRAU FREDERICA HAUFFE

<u>1801 to August 5, 1829</u>

"The Seeress Of Prevorst"

FRAU FREDERICA HAUFFE

1801 to August 5, 1829

"The Seeress Of Prevorst"

You feel the pain of a disease that is bringing you to the point of death. You know the wrenching anguish of the final struggle between the spirit and the flesh and it's draining you further as each moment passes. Finally you've collapsed in wretched submission to the finality of life lost to the attachment and confinement of the body. Death has won.

You see, and know from within, the condition of illness that afflicts pain of the body, feeling the pain or discomfort of the distress.

You feel hurt at the loss of a loved one or relief that someone close is out of danger.

You cry in joy at a movie or cry in pain at the separation of someone who was visiting and close and missed.

In lightness of moment you feel elation at a joy in life. A gift opened in surprise, a hug from someone close, or a kiss that flows through you with a warmth that tingles and pleases as raise of emotion within you fills life's vessels of pleasure.

The proud elation of victory won fills the moment with bursting energy and your whole person is one glowing vestige of brilliance.

You shared a moment in the glowing innocence of a child's joy and felt part of the innocence yourself.

Basking in the moments of innocence lost in the arms of your lover you feel the warmth and passion that two can share and one can give to another, feeling the heat of the pleasured movements, the cascading desires and hearts pulsing rhythm as part and all of your being rises and releases that which brings peace, savored and cherished, or maybe the moment is lost as one is left to turn and toss. Life's rhythm can bring feeling of chasm. All is real and all is felt.

To know these feelings ourselves is normal to life, expected, desired, endured, and feared. Apply the word somnambulist and place sensitive before it, and the feelings of life change for the person whose name is associated with one of life's mysteries.

A sensitive somnambulist is one who can feel in a sleep-waking state the feelings of another. The person can, without voluntary effort, find themselves in the precarious position of knowing and actually experiencing the emotions, pains, and pleasures of another person's being. To know another's feeling is to suffer that person's moments, whether pleasure or propensity.

I have searched a long time for a confirmation of such things, a revealing in written form by a person or persons of consequence to their time, and have found them in the written account of Dr. Justinus Kerner's relationship with one Frau Frederica Hauffe who became commonly called "The Seherin Von Pervorst."

Hidden Shadows

Dr. Kerner, who held the position of "Chief Physician at Weinsburg," was considered to be a religious man of sensible and amiable nature who was also a lyric poet of eminence. Having been well known in Germany, his personal association with Frau Hauffe is still with us to revelation in his written accounts of her terrible life of travail. He described Frederica as being a suffering person whose life was lived on the brink of death.

Frederica was born in 1801 and lived to no more than the twenty-eight years to August 5, 1829. Within the three weeks that preceded her death, she experienced three occasions to second sight that indicated her death was eminent.

The book entitled *The Seeress of Prevorst* by Dr. Justinus Kerner, Chief Physician at Weinsburg, Germany accounts those revealing years.

It is from this book in majority, but not totally, that this commentary is derived, and it is from life's living that revelation is revealed.

Like others that I have addressed in this unusual passage, Frau Hauffe was a simple person, and her formal studies in life were confined to the Bible and the Psalms. From this it could be said that she was a pious person, but she was not hypocritical in nature. Another woman born in this sixteenth century also was a pious person and certainly not hypocritical. She, too, was considered a natural somnambulist. Her name was St. Theresa.

Such people are prone to being in what's called the sleep-waking state, and this state is defined as separation of consciousness to the inner self or spirit.

Frau Hauffe divided the human person into four states of interrelated being, the conscious person or mind; the nerve-spirit, associated with the physical being; the soul, linking both world's physical and spiritual; and the spirit.

Contrasting to her adult life, as a child she was a blooming and joyous child born to the small village of Prevorst, whose population was a mere four hundred people. Pervorst, Germany, was close to Wirtemberg, which lay near to Lowenstein.

She was raised in simplicity and artlessness primarily by her grandparents. Her father had held the position of game keeper or district forester. Her lifetime saw no teaching of language. History, natural history, and geography remained also mere words without depth of understanding. A blooming and joyous child, she saw no teachings in the refinements of feminine aplomb. She was a simple child from a simple town who even in childhood evidenced an inner life.

Sleep-waking can also be defined as having conscious awareness of exposure to presence of the "protector," possibly a guardian angel, by feeling or appearance. Also sleep-waking awareness can be, and usually is, mere flashes of vision or observation that, either in separation to consciousness or superimposed to consciousness, manifest themselves in definite knowing to the person of incident. They are obvious, definable, and usually very vivid. The flash of awareness usually remains strongly known at least for a time. Was the feeling behind me and to my right while standing in front of Edgar Cayce's hospital a feeling of the presence of such an angel or "protector"? I don't know for sure to the answer, but I know the feeling yet.

In her youth, she shared with Cayce the ability to divine water and could also do so with metal.

Dr. Justinus Andreas Christian Kerner

Hidden Shadows

This child that was described as joyous and blooming, at times when walking with her grandfather, would be taken with seriousness and shuddering, and this peculiar condition would also occur in church yards that bore the presence of graves. When within a church that contained the buried remains of people, she could not stand being present anywhere save in the galleries. These events were described as involving the perception or consciousness of spirits.

In a castle in Lowenstein, an old kitchen that had been converted to an apartment also held for her the same distress, and she could not stand to remain in the rooms. Some years later the ghostly figure of a woman was seen in the room by another woman.

Frau Hauffe was all too familiar with the seeing, conversing, and knowing of the presence of apparitions in her adult life, and those close to her came to awareness of this existence by their own perception and experience while in proximity to her.

Frederica's first seeing of an apparition occurred before the age of seventeen and happened in her grandfather's house. To this incident, her grandfather, Johann Schmidgual, can be said to be a party. He, too, had seen the appearance but, fearing ridicule, kept his silence. The child or young woman was not silent.

Recall Rasputin's youth, and you will remember that he had taken it for granted that all could see a stolen object in the hand of the thief and had not been a thief in his youth because of it. In the case of Frau Hauffe, when her father would blame her for loss of an object, upsetting her, the object would appear to her in her dreams, and thus she saw its whereabouts.

Dreams played a distinct role in her childhood, as she would evidence supernatural anticipation or feeling of impending evil in prophetic dreams. This ability was not confined to dreams alone.

Reprove or annoyance that bothered or irritated her mind would bring sleeping reaction. Her nocturnal moments were visited in fashion of instructive, foreboding, or prophetic visions.

Frederica seems to have been a person in many ways doomed to an adult life of inner awareness that started its trek to destiny's end in a childhood that, like others we have seen in this traveling, was wrought with emotional strife. Internal strife is still strife.

It can be said that Frederica's adult inner life began the day of her marriage and followed her to the end, in escalating awareness and suffering to the gift or curse of sensitive somnambulism.

In her early life she had been greatly influenced by a minister of very fine reputation. To tragic misfortune on the day of her marriage, this fine friend died. It was with heavy sorrow that she accompanied his body to its final resting place. The moment did not end with this, as while she mourned at his grave she was overcome with lightness and cheer.

This inner life that was to be hers had awakened, and she became calm, serene, and from this moment forward, indifferent to everything that happened in the world.

Much later, while in a somnambulic state, she alluded to oft encountered events in which the departed minister appeared to her as a form of light, cheering and protecting her from the influence of an evil spirit.

The seeing and conversing with spirit beings of both a light and dark nature became commonplace to her, and she became aware that many levels of spiritual development exist.

Awareness evidenced itself that those spirits she encountered that were dark were often evil, and conversing with them would drain her strength, while they in appearance would grow lighter by her pious words. I did not take this to be that they grew better in being by her words but that they grew possibly stronger as she was giving of herself.

She claimed that she could break off such encounters by a written word used in place of an amulet and that she could free others in like fashion.

Opposite to the beings of darkness were those with a light or bright ountenance that she knew to be of goodness, and conversation with such brought cheer and good feeling and strength with it.

She came to be aware that questions asked of both earthly and heavenly things to both dark and light beings brought evidence of differing ability to answer.

The dark being could answer to earthly questions with ease but not of knowledge and ease of heavenly or spiritual things. Those of a light countenance answered with ease to the opposite circumstance of spiritual knowledge but lacked in ability to address earthly questions.

Edgar Cayce stated that, in his travel to the place of records, first he would encounter dark beckoning beings along his path that tried to talk with him and hold him back. He would ignore these distracting spirits and continue his journey. As he did so, he would encounter lighter less-trying beings and eventually they would be light in appearance; and rather than trying to hold him back or draw him aside, they would bid him onward and be concerned with other things.

I find a definite correlation between the two descriptions, and Frau Hauffe's comments to earthly attachment evidenced by the dark spirits adds impetus to understanding.

Frederica seems to have lived a very caring life that saw her not refuse help to all who asked of her ability to, like Cayce and Victor and Davis, discern physical affliction and suggest treatment; but in her giving, pious nature she seems to have opened herself to that which Cayce resisted.

She, being sensitive in nature and Cayce intuitive, had her whole person come to distress at encounter with the ill. It was her ability or curse to know, feel, assimilate, and suffer the affliction of the person she was addressing who was in physical distress. She could also know the mental state of the person. All this occurred while she was awake. Eventually, she would know this same evidencing of another person's condition from great distance, but not necessarily know whom it was that she was feeling, suffering the feeling just the same.

Hidden Shadows

It was this accentuated feeling that eventually brought her massive travail at the dying of peoples she felt. It was claimed over and over that she experienced the throes of death and the retching illness that might precede it many times over. Her own death was in awareness to what she could suffer, and it brought greatly added travail to her as her struggle ended.

Frau Hauffe could, like Andrew Jackson Davis, know a person's condition by merely touching that person.

Cayce, the intuitive somnambulist, did not suffer such as Frederica, as the conscious mind is set aside to the revelation of awareness in a person of such nature, sparing them the distress. Cayce would, however, be tired when he awoke from his self-imposed trance.

The sensitive somnambulist, according to the Frau, can be found in all of us, but most do not recognize the levels of occurrence. This I believe is quite possibly true, as I know myself to experience things she has described.

She differentiates four distinct levels of somnambulic experience in sensitive nature, and Dr. Justinus Kerner describes them as magnetic degrees:

First:

Her ordinary state was such in that she would appear awake, but actually not be so. Her actual condition was being in the first level or stage of her inner life.

It was the Frau's statement that unsuspecting, many people were in this state, not aware themselves or given to awareness by others.

Second:

Insanity in some she considered to be seen, but in reality it is just a magnetic dream.

Third:

In the third magnetic level, which was half-waking, she would at times write and speak in an inner language that differed totally from her native German and to which she had no conscious awareness of dialect. She claimed this language was used when her spirit was intimate with her soul.

Fourth:

When she was prescribing or clairvoyant, it was considered to be the sleep-waking state.

Between the third and fourth state Dr. Kerner observed what he considered to be an intermediate stage. At this point Frederica would lay cold and torpid and Dr. Kerner called this the cataleptic state.

She believed that in the intermediate waking state, it was the soul that dominated her thought, and that when in the perfect state of clairvoyance, her thought flowed totally from the spirit, and that while in this state, her spirit was freed from the attachment and influence of the nerve-spirit, the mind, and the soul.

Frederica described the magnetic dream as proceeding from the mind, and while in this state *she could not be awakened.* She likened this state to that resembling the sleep-waking state.

Her revealings stated that the sleep-waking state is the life presentation of the inner person and that therein contained is proof of future existence and of reunion after death.

This internal activity in man is in one's normal condition unawakened and is wholly asleep in a person whose life is centered totally in the brain. This state is that of being unconscious to his sympathetic life, not listening to his inner voice. Dr. Wayne Dyer does speak to inner directedness, does he not? He does advocate it, does he not?

Sleep-waking that is produced by magnetic passes is overcoming to this and produces the clairvoyant state in which the inner person is in inspection to the outer.

In a state of clairvoyance, the spirit is free from both body and soul and can travel at will in a flash, just as lightening travels in a flash, and just as Christ is to be seen when He reveals His returned presence to all of mankind in a short time. It is the spirit that quickens the flesh. The flesh counts for nothing.

When Frederica died, this statement was totally proven, for in the account of her death, we find description that suspends thought for a moment, to the physical being we all are for a lifetime.

The account of her death holds sorrow within it, for as Dr. Kerner had said, she knew from the feeling of others, the torment that can be the final struggle of the soul to retain the flesh.

If we set aside the delirium and the moments of lucidity, and her still experienced magnetic interludes, and not speak too loudly to the twice thought moments that death had taken her, only to flutter back at the mention of Kerner's name or the three magnetic passes her mother made to her face that brought lifted eyelids and moved lips, then a great depth of moment can be perceived.

Setting these moments of August 5, 1829, aside and intruding to the finality, we find that at ten o'clock her sister claimed the entrance to the room of a tall bright form. At this instant, Frederica uttered loudly a cry of joy, and her spirit then seemed to be freed. Claimed next is that shortly her soul departed, and it is to this moment that lesson can be learned.

Those present left message that at the departure of the soul, the physical body that had been torment in illness to the Frau became in an instant's time a hulk, a featureless body that bore not a single trace of appearance of Frederica Hauffe. There remained only an unrecognizable husk.

It is from this that it is stated that her countenance during her life was borrowed in total from the spirit within, and it is said further that for this reason no artist was ever successful in painting her image on canvas.

This account is given to us by her friend and physician, Dr. Justinus Kerner, who claimed that in the night subsequent to her death he had, in a dream, seen her in company with two female forms, perfectly restored.

It is the spirit that quickens the flesh. Seven times after her death, her eldest sister claimed appearance to her by the departed Frau. Her sister was considered to be a truthful and upright person.

Hidden Shadows

De Puysequr came to a belief from experiment that all somnambulates possessed the faculty of self-inspection if their depth of sleep was great enough.

This self-inspection by somnambulism is not dependent on abstract knowledge. It is rather in company to an exacted faculty for knowing one's internal sensations and developing this to perceptive presentation.

The clarity of such presentations can reach varying degrees and rise by habit. At first encounter with this somnambulic phenomenon, little is known beyond an awareness of internal feelings of others. With time, it is not infrequent for one to attain the exactness of ability to make anatomical description of great detail. Remember here also that the mental condition can be known along with the emotional. Through pronounced state of emotion, the sensitive somnambulic is brought in touch with the person at issue, though the identity of the person might not always be known.

I spoke previously to the aspect of Frau Hauffe at times while in the third state of magnetic level, being half-waking, speaking in a different language. When revelation came to her in this language and she felt need to translate to her native German, she would have difficulty doing so to total clarity. The language was spoken frequently enough that those who were present to her during those moments began to understand the dialect.

The language was eventually identified as resembling Coptic, Arabic, and Hebrew. Within her sleep-waking state, she stated that it was the language spoken by Jacob of the Bible. She also said that it was the language spoken by ghosts.

Have you ever been in a church gathering and watched and listened to people who, in released emotion that appears to be a total release to some inner self, lose physical control to all manner of movement and speak in that which is called tongues. I have on numerous occasions in the past, and I have made intense effort to listen to one person and another, and it is my firmest belief that I was listening to a distinct language. This often was in repetition to words, one person to another.

Most often, also, those that seemed to be the most prolific in expoundings and zeal were those most simple in nature and life, those who seem to have an inner niceness and purity. The kind of person, one says to himself, "can live next door to me in peace and pleasure," the more worldly, the less prolific.

I also noted that quite often the people were poor and very dependent on strength to life's struggle from faith in God.

As we travel through life, so many things are important to growing in person. If we do not relate that which we learn or see or feel and allow each its place, then we are merely trudging through life wearing the blinders of a draft horse whose burden is not blossoms.

Frau Hauffe said that if one places true in elevation to beautiful, understanding in elevation to *emotion*, the inductive above ideals, and further in like saying to the cares of this world, then the soul's nature is perverted, and comprehension that the intellectual life, which is centered in the brain, is a peripheral or partial power, while the sensitive life is in the epagastric region and is deeper and more an internal power that is central to the organism of the soul, cannot be comprehended in distinction to one another.

Thus spoken, it can be further understood that a soul, given to earthly attention when separated from the body in death, can retain its attachment to the physical level of existence and thus impede its progress or travel to a higher level of promise.

The importance of focus to and acceptance of Jesus Christ is paramount to a fulfillment of spiritual involvement. Without this acceptance and understanding, a person has made difficult his journey in being. Hauffe stated that a worldly-minded sinful man may well advance himself in earthly life by the force of his intellect, but spiritually he is weak, dark, and has not the capability to look within himself to the sensitive life that is life.

In this stead, Dr. George Richie makes reference in his comments to spiritual journey, that he thought or believed that his acceptance of Christ at an early age was having effect on his encounter during the time he was dead. He believed that his act of faith and submission had separated him from the circumstances of distress that he was viewing and that his companion or guide in his journey was in fact Christ.

Richie had experienced an extension of earthly attachment in the first part of what was a journey in two segments in the world of the spirit. His earthly concerns had been totally encompassing at the time of his death, and instant continuing extension of the efforts involved manifested themselves in his spiritual state.

The Frau stated that those baptized in Christ carry with them at death this seed; and even though in earthly life one might not yet have sprouted or grown substantially, the seed still bears fruit in what then becomes its time.

Frederica suffered two massive illnesses in her life, and from these, she grew spiritually from spiritual encounter. Her second illness was such that she never really regained her strength.

During the course of illness, she had given a detailed description of a machine to be constructed to treat her with. The indication from her was that it would affect cure to her ailment. The design of the machine was ignored, and her health continued to fail. Eventually the machine was constructed to the specifications she had given the doctors, and her condition began to improve. Unfortunately, it was too late. The doctors conceded that, had they constructed the device sooner and applied it with intent, Frederica would have recovered. Too late, the effort failed.

During her illness, the Frau was said to have increased in her magnetic abilities, and her extension to the realm of the spirit was definitely pronounced.

The date her first illness started was February 27, 1822, and the second followed beginning December 28 of the same year.

The second illness brought massive travail. Delirium, somnambulic sleep, bleeding gums and the loss of all of her teeth pronounced horror upon a frail life. During this illness, she prescribed her own treatment while somnambulic, and it included magnetic passes for twenty-seven days.

Dr. Kerner described her as being gripped by death but chained by magnetic power to her body. Her soul and her spirit were divided—the soul to the body, the spirit to the world of spirit.

During this time, she experienced a detachment from the body and saw her physical body from a position out of the body. She professed having felt no weight to the spiritual body that she knew at this occurrence.

If you recall when I spoke of Andrew Jackson Davis, I related that the fourth stage of hypnosis or magnetism represented death, and that without the conductor present to sustain the body functions of Davis, he might not have been able to return to physical life.

Recall, also, the same basis commentary as associated with Edgar Cayce. Hauffe, however, makes the expanded statement that sleep-waking is that of the separation of the soul and the body from the spirit and as such bears a great resemblance to death. This state is said to differ from actual death, and she gave this intriguing description of the spiritual activity as death occurs.

She claimed that in the last moments when the spirit quits the body, it becomes weak and helpless, and the soul cannot be drawn with it. The spirit has no choice but to wait. At that point, the dying person is unconscious and awareness to events is not known, the future is hidden, and the person is unable to express himself.

In moments prior to this, if the dying person claims certainty of the existence of the future state, the reason is associated with the soul no longer being directed by the brain, and the recovering of its natural ability of clear-seeing and hope to the future, these things having been obscured prior to this. When the spirit has left the body, the soul then knows it must leave, also, and struggles for freedom. This struggle is identified as the death agony. The Frau claimed that at this moment, also, the spirits of the blest are close by to aid the soul. This struggle in natural deaths is proportional in length, longer or shorter, to the time it takes for the soul to detach itself from earthly things.

This statement regarding the time that the soul remains in the body after what is perceived as death is directly relatable to the reading of Edgar Cayce regarding such matters. Earthly attachment to people, objects, and activities seems to definitely relate to the ability to die in struggle or uplifting release, if one chooses to consider such comments.

The Frau's giving of knowledge as to the treatment that might help her during her illness should be held in the same light to that which Cayce prescribed when struck at the base of the spine, and to Victor when De Puysegur helped effect healing in him.

The words that came from Victor that set the course to the future of hypnosis were, "I have an abscess in the head; it will suffocate me if it falls upon the chest." This simple statement was not scientific and might easily have been ignored, but De Puysegur did not, and from his inquisitive persistence discovered that somnambulistic depth brings forth knowledge from origins that in truth remain a mystery that only death reveals to total truth or deception, maybe!

It is very easy to succumb to the desire to accept too easily the statements from such sources and the caution of the Bible that says to try the spirits to see if good or evil abound in this mystery of life.

In a short while, I'll review and add a little to the mysteries of Frau Frederica Hauffe, but I think it reasonable at this point to look for a moment at two other names in brief comment.

First, to a past noted physician in single reference to him. Medical science owed greatly to advancement from his contribution to the medical knowledge of the time, and it is said of him that much of the knowledge he brought forth was presented to him in his dreams. Society remembers this man as the noted physician Galen.

This man most commonly named "Galen of Pergamum" was a Greek physician born in A.D. 129, who died, possibly in Rome, in the year of 199.

In his seventy-year sojourn in life, he placed an indelible mark upon the medical society of his time by strongly establishing the practices of what may be termed theoretical medicine. This approach strongly contrasted with those who believed that credence could be given only to an empiricist approach which opposed all claims to intuition, imaginative conjecture, authority, and abstract thought. Empiricists promoted the practice of medicine by methods that were only totally known and proven. Some actually viewed Galen's medical theories as being metaphysical. Others termed it therapeutic theory.

He was the son of a very talented architect; and in his years of growth studied Platonism, Aristotelianism, Epicureanism, and Stoicism. He accepted Aristotle's view that "nature does nothing in vain," and he recognized his debt to Hypocrites by following the Hippocratic method.

The "Oath of Hypocrites" has guided medicine for over two thousand years and found its basis in influence established four hundred years before Christ.

"Oath of Hypocrites"

I look upon him who shall have taught me this Art even as one of my parents. I will share my substance with him, and I will supply his necessities, if he be in need. I will regard his offspring even as my own brethren and I will teach them this Art, if they would learn it, without fee or covenant. I will impart this Art by precept, by lecture and by every mode of teaching, not only to my own sons but to the sons of him who has taught me, and to disciples bound by covenant and oath, according to the Law of Medicine.

The regimen I adopt shall be for the benefit of my patients according to my ability and judgment, and not for their hurt or any wrong. I will give no deadly drug to any, though it be asked of me, nor will I counsel such, and especially I will not aid a woman to procure abortion. Whatsoever house I enter, there will I go for the benefit of the sick, refraining from all wrongdoing or corruption, and especially from any act of seduction, of male or female, of bond or free. Whatsoever things I see or hear concerning the life of men, in my attendance on the sick or even apart therefrom, which ought not be noised abroad. I will keep silence thereon, counting such things to be sacred secrets.

Hidden Shadows

Galen's medical studies extended beyond Pergamums boundaries to Smyrna in Asia Minor, Alexandria in Egypt, and Corinth in Greece.

Corinth was given much attention and effort by the Apostle Paul. It was a place of deep debauchery at the time and to be labeled a "Corinthian" was to be considered a person with a very liberal approach to conduct. Paul was called much in question in this city and escaped extremely harsh judgment at the hands of authority by claiming to be presenting the word of the "unknown God." The city had within its boundaries a statue dedicated to such, along with those of many other gods that Paul had happened to see as he entered the city. This explanation of his doctrine was accepted, and he was allowed to preach and remain healthy.

Religious influence had a strong hold over society at this time; and as at the time of Hypocrites, the human body was held sacred; dissection was illegal. This aspect of restriction vastly limited medical progress, and Galen had to restrict his dissection to animals. Not only did this restriction hold to previous history, it extended to the Middle Ages.

Though the *Encyclopedia Britannica* describes Galen as counted with those who were considered "cultured despisers" of Christianity, he is remembered as having, in his writings on philosophy, cited Christians as example to people exerting good behavior even without philosophic ideal.

During this Christian era, Rome found itself the recipient of great numbers of Greek physicians, though Roman society contributed almost nothing to medical knowledge.

In Pergamum, Galen studied theoretical philosophy along with practical medicine, as in that time both were considered to be closely related.

Within the city, a shrine of the healing god, Asclepius, was located; and to this shrine, many of the prominent citizens of Rome would travel in hopes of gaining cures for those afflictions that they might be suffering. It is from the manner of expected response to the pilgrimage that possible relationship might be found with Galen's reputed dream revelations to medical advancement. The cures sought by the pilgrims were said to manifest themselves in their dreams after returning home.

A medical school was attached to this shrine, and it was in this school that Galen gained much of his medical knowledge and met many influential people from Rome. He studied the treatments of diseases as well as wounds while involved with the shrine.

Studying wounds was not difficult, as the high priest associated with the school and the shrine also maintained a troupe of gladiators in association with the higher aspects of his position and calling.

This gave Galen the opportunity to become aware that the blood flowed within the body, but he did not become aware that it circulated. He formulated the hypothesis that it flowed in pulsing to and fro manner originating in the liver and then eventually being formed into muscle in the extremities.

He is credited with making the important demonstration that the vessels in the body carried blood rather than air. It had been taught for four hundred years that the vessels carried air.

Following his studies and travels to Corinth, Smyrna, and Alexandria, he ventured to Rome and, soon after, he was admitted to the Court of the Emperors. At the time there were two, Marcus Aruelius and Lucius Verus.

With this advance, his influence and knowledge became a dominant force in both medical practice and theory. He became literally unchallenged in his domineering, adamant statements. With this dominance, he synthesized and advanced the study of medicine, anatomy, and physiology in the second century A.D. He also is responsible for the origins of the recognition of temperament in an individual and is credited with being the founder of experimental physiology. His contribution led to his being considered one of the most distinguished physicians of antiquity. Eventually, he was appointed to be the chief physician to the heir to the throne, Commodus.

At one point, he had over one hundred and twenty-nine written works to his credit. Through these works, his experiments were repeated and built upon through the fifteenth and sixteenth centuries, making his influence dominate through that time.

During the Middle Ages, medicine passed to the hands of the church and to Arab scholars. From this controlling influence, experimentation was discouraged and disease was regarded as a punishment for sins. Hypocrites had no such regard for thoughts of this nature; and, as you recall, Galen held to the principles he established or purported.

I've said that Rome did not advance medical knowledge through its people but rather assimilated the knowledgeable people it conquered. What I didn't say was that Rome's abilities to organize and build manifested themselves in an archeological excavation in Dussldorf, Germany. It is considered that unearthed there is a hospital of Roman origins that is found to be strangely modern in its design.

Galen's contributions are without question, and also without question is his involvement with the Shrine of Asclepius. Beyond mere speculation, also, is the relationship of dream discovery with both the Shrine and Galen's revelations. The sureness to which Galen asserted himself in his theories and practices, and his ability to exert stringent control and directedness to them, is to me massively revealing to the confidence he held in his own inner perceptions. Without such confidence, you cannot do such things!

Two other men prominent to medicine and our lives also gave deep consideration to dreams and dream interpretation.

Drs. Carl Jung and Sigmund Freud fall squarely within the parentheses of the dream world. So much so that these two men, during the time of their collaboration, actually would sit or dine together and attempt to interpret the meanings in the dreams of one another. They even went to the extent of written communication regarding such activities.

Jung seemed to be the most intense in his pursuits of dream understanding and revelation and applied such in his practice of medicine.

It is strange to me that he would openly pursue the elusive nature of dreams and choose to ignore the possibilities of contact with the potential sources of such through hypnosis and magnetism. It represents a paradox in medical approach, in my estimation, that dilutes the study of the mind leaving a blank space, and promotes the tenets of personal theory.

Galen

Asclepius — Greco - Roman god of Medicine

Another name well known to us is that of Socrates. That which may not be commonly known of him is that he considered himself to be under the guidance of a demon. He believed this demon would warn him of impending danger and that it revealed the future to him and advised him as to how to act.

Socrates, as he grew in age and wisdom, related his thoughts to life's pursuits, and I have long contemplated a certain aspect of his wisdom.

He left us with the remark that the supreme object in living was "learning how to die." This was not meant to be taken in any morbid sense, not focusing, not brooding as to death's moment. He placed the pursuit rather as learning as much as possible about man's place in this mystery of the cosmos. He thought in terms of looking to how we fit, how we fulfill or fail in making the most of our human being and of that which has been given to each individual.

He did not consider such study to be a grim-natured endeavor, but rather an adventure of a joyous nature, connecting psychology with astronomy, with history, and the probes of our origins, problematic destinies, and orbits. He considered the quest never-ending in our brief mortality and the only one worthwhile and for its own sake wholly satisfactory.

He says to us that it is immensely consoling, also. Given that as age advances and our appetites diminish as our senses do, our mind can have sustained vitality and still expand its grasp and vision, and can expire with confidence in having at least pursued and possibly attained some puzzled knowledge of our existence.

In sad warning to the consequences of too late beginning an inquiry to deeper meanings, one can find that, along with the senses, the mind will decay to the disappointment left to clinging to life's diminishing number of escapes.

It is in a way a sad commentary that, if taken to a depth that closes the pleasures of life's escapes from life, can, in my opinion, leave unturned pleasures that should not be missed along life's path. Rasputin comes to mind in his struggle to resolve religious and carnal, the staret with three bathing beauties. It is important not to miss life as life is lived, and depth and pursuit of knowledge can easily place beauty and emotion in subservience to understanding, as the Frau warned.

It's claimed that Frederica was endowed with an intense second sight, and that by recognition of the visions as such, was able to direct knowledge or activity that altered or set aside events that could have been harmful.

A major difference between Cayce and Hauffe lies in the manner of contact to the realm of spirit. Cayce self-initiated the encounters with spirit beings and rejected contact with those of a lower level that were not of benefit to his mission. Recall that his request to the lady with wings was to help children, and to this he seemed protected.

Frederica was not protected, and was not intuitive, and as such and being a willing giver of help to the majority that asked her help, she became subject to contact with spirits that could be labeled troubled, evil, or undesirable to contact.

In this her reality, defense to her person from some was necessary, and she found that she could choose to reject their presence or requests or *commands* by employing the name of Jesus and Scripture at times of need and distress.

Further to this aspect of defense to her person, she, like other sensitive somnambuls, found it absolutely necessary to not be in company with and at times to actually flee from the presence of a person afflicted with epilepsy or syphilis or some such disease that assimilating the condition would bring horrible affliction within. Sensitive somnambulism is both gift *and* curse.

Confirming faith in the name and power of Jesus is overcoming and overwhelming to spirits that are dark and troubling to a person.

In her sleep-waking state, she drew her strength from those in her presence and those present to her often alluded to a loss of strength or energy. She claimed to have no organic strength of her own and received her strength through the eyes and ends of the fingers.

She referenced as part of the human makeup, the nerve spirit, this being or lying between the conscious physical mind or intellect and the soul, and an attachment between the soul and the mind. The nerve spirit, she claimed, is that which imparts to the muscles a greater physical strength than the muscles are capable of exerting by mere physical exertion.

Thus she may well have identified for us, in name and place to spiritual makeup, the strength that we have at times read of that allows a mother to lift an automobile from a child being crushed to death.

The nerve spirit is also identified as being the form that she would see showing the outlined presence of an amputated limb. Just the name she employed in describing this part of a person is relatable to the claims of amputees that they can still feel a lost limb. In this, she claimed also to see that which Kirlian photography is reaching for, and that which Edgar claimed sight to, also.

It is this nerve spirit that she claimed ghosts retain in their existence from physical life and that through this retention, they claim a link to the physical world, reputed to be able by this link to move heavy objects and by link to the air, through it to make sounds audible to human perception.

She claimed, also, that it is this nerve spirit that *can* remain attached to the conscious mind at death and remain with it in passing until the final or general resurrection to God's day of judging all. She claimed to be able to see this nerve projected form in a dead person.

Though no intention is executed to addressing these aspects of the seeress's given experience to these mysteries, as such was avoided with Davis and Swedenborg, speaking to Frau Hauffe leaves little choice, as all is part of one, and much more could be said. She is considered to be the most intensely and validly represented sensitive somnambulist of record, her record being given by a doctor of major prominence to her time.

In finality to life's cautions, we can say that when she assumed a posture in magnetic sleep, it saw her arms and legs crossed. This assumption of posture also manifested itself in her infant son's sleeping position during the first weeks following his birth.

He also was able to see in unhappy circumstance, "Ghost-Seeing!"

Dr. Carl Jung gives us comment to the collective unconscious, which might well relate to Frau Hauffe's encounters with the voluminous spiritual levels that both illuminated and troubled her, in his voluminous *Mysterium Conjunctionis*. He said that attempts to determine the nature that would be revealing to the mystery of the unconscious state find themselves facing difficulties similar to those encountered in atomic physics. Namely, observations in themselves generate alteration to the object to observation. As a consequence to this, he states that presently there is no way of objectively making a determination as to the real nature of the unconscious being.

To the end of statement and consensus, it can be seen why modern psychology is not directed toward revelation through magnetism or hypnosis. Dr. Carl Jung did not understand the phenomenon, could not find continuity to it, and chose to ignore it. Thus, along with Dr. Sigmund Freud's decision to abandon professional pursuit primarily because he was not a proficient hypnotist, we find ourselves enveloped in the theoretical application of objective observation to assumed normality, and the experimental application of medication to help establish the assumed normality of objective observation.

If you should venture to the internal realm of the subjective and then find contact with this social establishment of assumed normality, the possibility of finding friendly recognition to your venture may well find itself faced with the offer of assistance to the assumption of the assumed. "Be careful, they'll call you crazy!"

CHAPTER 8

UPTON SINCLAIR

Born September 20, 1878 - Died November 25, 1968

Author and Social Conscience to a Nation

Upton Beale Sinclair

Mary Craig Sinclair

CHAPTER 8

UPTON SINCLAIR

Born September 20, 1878 - Died November 25, 1968

Author and Social Conscience to a Nation

In a book reprinted by *Time-Life Books* one finds an account of Upton Sinclair and his wife Mary Craig Sinclair's performed experiments in telepathy. Also highlighted are instances of such involvement between Craig and others in mental communication.

Copyrighted in 1930, Upton's book, *Mental Radio,* is one of a list of his more widely known writings. He, being a very well-known writer of social reform in the nineteen twenties and thirties, was cautioned at the time of writing that he might bring suspicion upon himself by addressing aspects of the paranormal. This advice did not dissuade Upton from presenting what he considered to be scientific evidence to telepathic reality. He and Craig spent three years in deliberately-controlled experiments.

Craig was the primary subject and source of information in these efforts, given that since childhood she had evidenced an extrasensory nature about her.

Upton himself had read over one hundred books dealing with the subject of clairvoyance and telepathy. Through their experiments, he completely convinced himself of the validities of occurrence professed by many throughout the histories of printed records.

Craig's childhood, like others I've spoken of, was laced with the unusual. One trait that evidenced itself was the ability to know or sense when her mother was summoning her. She would show up just as her mother was sending a messenger to fetch her, saying she just knew her mother wanted her.

The relationship to her mother also extended itself to dreams of parallel subject in her childhood. On one occasion, both dreamed of a pin being in their bed. Both woke up and both searched their beds. Craig did not find one, but her mother did.

A remorseful moment in history came when the famous author Jack London took his own life. Craig Sinclair had been a close friend of his and in the moments preceding his final desperation, she had sensed and insisted to Upton that he was in a terrible mental distress. Some short time prior to this, another friend had told the Sinclair's of London's troubles, but they knew them to be of long-standing nature and did not take them to serious distress. This notion, however, was intense, and Upton even offered to take her to London's ranch. Craig declined to step into a circumstance that involved a married man unless his wife were to request. It was two days following the announcement of his death that they learned of his suicidal act.

Professor William McDougall of Duke University in North Carolina wrote the introduction to *Mental Radio* in September of 1929. He described Mrs. Sinclair's abilities as being part of rare and sporadic encounter in the mass of people. McDougall comments further that Craig's mental and physical condition during moments of clairvoyant or telepathic encounter parallel those of other persons who experience or have experienced similar activities in their lives.

Spirit revealed in 100 books

Jack London

The experiments that were conducted by Upton and Craig were highly successful and revealed that a state of telepathy can be brought to exist in a person by specific and deliberate attempt. Of extreme importance to deliberate exercise or initiative is a mental state that is focused but passive; the mind must not be engaged in analytical process, and the body must be relaxed. Tension or pain is later stated to be an extension of mind activity, and thus the focus is not eased and natural.

It should be noted that these comments are associated with deliberate intent on the part of the individual and not attached in nature to other manners of encounter I've highlighted in previous chapters.

McDougall describes Upton Sinclair as being very honest, a critical student of society, and a fearless person. I have found that in both viewing and addressing this aspect of life, such qualities are essential on a personal level. You have to be honest with yourself and critical of yourself. Being fearless to what others might say or think is extremely important as well, for it can be a very narrow-minded society at times.   There is an aspect of fear that needs addressing in regard to such directedness in life and that is associated with God. All of this that exists or is allowed to exist is God's work or extension of His will, and the Bible gives no small amount of warning regarding certain pursuits. As you have been reading these pages of revelation and discovery, it should be beginning to manifest itself with you that the realm of the spiritual world is something that man has absolutely no control over, and that without the influence of Christ standing in triumph over the physical and spiritual world, a mere human being is subject to that which he cannot overcome if needs be. Fear has its place!

Mental Radio does not address the realm of the spiritual world but rather lends itself to experiments in telepathy that lead to the word *rapport.*

In the case of hypnosis, *rapport* is that which can develop between hypnotist and hypnotized that affords each the knowledge of the other's thoughts.

In the case of telepathic experiments, *rapport* is the manifestation of image, activity, thought, or feeling being brought to the conscious mind of a seeking individual by means of that person's conscious recognition of subconscious communication.

In the area of hypnosis, a familiar name is Quackenbos, and he is mentioned in Upton's book. Professor Quackenbos of Columbia University is well known for his position regarding the use of hypnotism in therapeutic effort. In the course of his pursuits, he wrote many books on the subject and describes many cases where its application was attempted.

To these efforts is added for us the sharing of his personal experience in the mystery of *rapport,* and it's stated that it is not an infrequent experience for the hypnotist and the person being hypnotized to know the thoughts of the other, and thus suggestion is given and taken without any spoken communication. If you recall, it was Victor Race and De Puysegur who first brought this to light. Professor Quackenbos is in confirmation to their experience.

Another very interesting phenomenon that Upton relates about Quackenbos in his book is that during encounters of hypnotic trancing, it was not an infrequent event for both himself *and* the subject to fall into hypnotic sleep. This would happen to him on an involuntary basis, and at times the nurse present would also fall into a trance with Quackenbos and the subject.

Upton makes it very clear that what Craig experienced was not unique to her at all and that they were repeating textbook experiments. What should be noted is their pronounced success.

Craig developed a *rapport* with a man who was noted in his ability to place himself in a trance and who had done so in many public demonstrations.

Craig's awareness of the thoughts and distant activities of this man actually began to be an embarrassment to him. The detailed descriptions that Craig would relate to him regarding his personal activities were so correct that he began to feel that he had no privacy, and communication between minds was developed to the state that Craig could sit and will movement to the young man's body while he was in a trance. She herself would be in her self-induced state of controlled concentration and relaxation.

It should be noted in regard to *rapport*, which is also called *transference*, that it is not necessary to be in a trance at all for such events of telepathy to occur. Cayce made statement that some are good senders and some good receivers, and some are both. He cited love as being an ingredient to the establishment of the link between minds that Craig called "rapport" and Dr. Carl Jung called "transference." I have encountered one person in life who made strong statement to a deep and running encounter of this nature for many years, and I have experienced it and can attest to its existence as proven to me by living life's encounters. Be careful, they'll call you crazy, when it is really they who are too lazy to venture to mystery's question and follow the crowd. Don't think out loud!

In experiments performed by Pierre Janet in the Saldetriere Hospital in France, that seated the famous school in the teaching of psychology and much clinical study in therapeutic hypnosis, Therapeutic" , where Dr. Sigmund Freud studied. There was found revelation that taste could be transferred from hypnotist to tranced subject, by placing a distinctly tasting substance in the mouth of the hypnotist, and identified by the perceived taste in the subject's mental awareness.

It was revealed in one instance that pain could be felt, in receiving *rapport*, by one individual who was distant from another who was injured. The location of the pain was indicated and proved correct. As the injury involved one of the Janet brothers, J. Janet, and manifested itself in pain felt by a subject of involvement at the time who was with Pierre Janet, its validity might be well taken.

Such can be the circumstances associated with the phenomenon of the *rapport* or *transference*. In Craig's case, she described the process of initiating a telepathic encounter as requiring, during direct effort, the giving of a command.

Craig would, after placing herself in a state of relaxed but focused concentration, give a specific mental command with her conscious mind, to her subconscious mind, to bring to her conscious mind certain information. Her indication was that this activity was similar in nature to one making effort to remember a name that was forgotten.

This deliberate activity could involve receiving information about a person's activities; or in the case of the controlled experiments that she and Upton enveloped themselves in for three years, involved the seeing on the gray screen that is the vision of the closed eye, an image or part of an image drawn on a piece of paper and folded to hide the picture from normal vision.

This manner of experiment was repeated to a large percentage of success in identification or partial identification, *and convinced Upton that telepathy does exist and that it can occur in an induced environment. Through such events as involved Jack London it was also evidenced that spontaneity of occurrence was also possible.* They kept very strict records of their experiments and were very adamant in saying they were not efforts in imagination.

It's very important also to recognize that the "rapport" that was established between Craig and Upton was not of an involvement of hypnosis. Upton was not involved in hypnosis and had seen it performed but a few times.

The "rapport" between Craig and Upton extended itself also to the area of "willed" activity by Craig, directed to Upton, and they stated that she could induce an activity in Upton even when his attention was focused to writing a manuscript. His train of thought would actually be broken.

The "rapport" would work in opposite direction as well. At times Craig would in her dreams comprehend something that did not seem to be anything of significance, but she would write it down on waking. Exploring a little regarding Upton's activities, she would often find the content of the dream to represent something that Upton had been reading or writing at the time of the dream. It is a curiosity to me as to the possible relationship of Dr. Jung's "universal unconscious" to such moments.

The manner of appearance of the vision of the represented item in the folded sketches Craig would try to identify in their controlled experiments would appear as though it were a motion picture in the gray of her eye lids. This most often vague representation of lines would flash with lightening speed and be gone unless deliberate effort would fix it to concentration.

At times the image was so vague that she did not trust it, and in such instances she would clear her mind by the established process she had developed and give an additional command to her subconscious to again produce the image. If the image appeared again and she felt comfortable that it was presented from what she termed the "deep mind," then she accepted it.

Craig cautioned that the subconscious mind cannot be trusted to its own readings. As Craig termed it, she said it was a liar. *Thus imagination is a major factor in induced telepathic communication* and developing the ability to recognize its presence is a necessity in understanding one's own psyche. The conscious mind is said to interface with the subconscious in an effort to bring depiction of sought-after knowledge or information. This information is not connected to the "deep mind" and does not represent anything other than vivid imagination.

A person who experiences spontaneous sensitive somnambulism evidences a more exacting awareness to the depth of information, as the added presence of assimilated sensory input more clearly defines, if definition is possible, the intensities and validities of presented or sought information. The degree to which the somnambulist is sensitive to these things can be the degree to which they are cursed by them; for to know them and feel them is to live them.

Cayce indicated while in intuitive somnambulic trance that the second mind, or the subconscious mind, not only acts as a conveyer in the thought track, but also can interject imaginative thought of its own to the returning information from the super-conscious mind as it conveys it to the conscious mind. It has the ability as well to delay the thought conveyance. You might recall the statement in the chapter addressing Edgar, that the super-conscious mind that rests with the spirit examines thought conveyed to it in mirror to that which *is truth*, and conveys its answer back to the conscious mind through the subconscious mind.

Craig made the statement that as knowledge and experience develops, awareness that the conscious and subconscious minds are really one manifests itself. I believe that Frau Hauffe's statements regarding the first stage of sleep-waking might be associated with Craig's statement. Considering that Hauffe is recognized as having been a well documented spontaneous sensitive somnambul, her revealings carry considerable weight.

Craig considered the subconscious mind to be a storehouse of memories in disheveled composition. Hauffe stated that many were unknowingly in a somnambulic dream state and considered insane. If the subconscious is a storehouse of information that is disheveled but available to the conscious, a person encounters a difficulty if they consider Dr. Carl Jung's identification of a second personality functioning in authoritative, pragmatic influence to a person's conscious statements. There is nothing disheveled about identified secondary personality expoundings, and thus comes thought to Dr. George Richie's experience while dead, that involved the possible entrance to a living person by persons who were dead but clinging to the physical world and attempting pleasured pursuit by such endeavor.

The Bible's warnings that a person is treading dangerous ground in pursuit of such knowledge or contact is continually more evident to me as I come closer to completing this effort.

Within each person of note that we have encountered thus far, there are probable connections, one to the next in evidencing ties to the super-normal. Dr. Carl Jung's noted autobiography places him within the category of self-experienced people as well, and of all of the recorded evidence that I have searched, this personal revealing by him stands to major significance. It is most significant because he would not allow its publication until after his death.

To the book's revealings I'll comment later; but at this point, awareness that its contents tend to the supernatural and that of all places to find compliment to such writing, the *Encyclopedia Britannica* mentions it as one of his best works.

Moving back now from this bit of a deliberate scrambling to future comment, and once again looking to Craig Sinclair, another very significant statement is given to us.

She indicated that when a true telepathic vision evidenced itself, it also brought with it something that she could not really identify, so she called it a hunch.

She described this circumstance as such, that in all occurrences where visions sought and presented to her found consideration, there was always doubt as to correctness until what seemed to be some unidentified intelligence made it known within her that, in fact, it was the correct answer.

Hidden Shadows

She claimed that the subconscious mind always answered questions falsely and that the "deep mind" answers questions correctly. She was able to differentiate between the two sources by the manner the answer was presented.

An answer that was presented from the subconscious mind always came in a quiet manner. One that came from the deep mind was presented with joyousness, inspiration, and conviction.

She claimed the minds to be different from one another, one rambling and lying, the other singing and truthful.

The state of focused relaxation that is necessary to the telepathic state as Craig described it to be, if not sustained by deliberate recognition and relaxed awareness will drift into a sleep that she termed auto-hypnotic sleep.

Craig claimed that once developed to understanding of event, a person can focus a question in the mind while in the relaxed state of telepathic concentration and carry the question into the auto-hypnotic sleep state in search of an answer. This thought that is carried into the subconscious in auto-hypnotic sleep will act in a fashion of one that is given to the subconscious mind by a hypnotist. Once induced, it will dominate the mental activity.

Consider Edison's awareness that answers to questions might surface within the mind at the point of sleep, and one might find relationship to the opening avenue between conscious, subconscious, and super-conscious interaction.

Craig Sinclair, in similarity to Cayce and Hauffe, could and did on occasion demonstrate that it was given to her to be able to see and relate the immediate activities of a subject at great distance.

She once did this in a confirmed encounter involving Upton's secretary. He had misplaced some small parts to his typewriter and was in search of them in their office. From the Sinclair home, and acting in a manner she described as being through Upton, she was able to describe the movements of the secretary in the distant office and relate basic information suggestive to the placement of the parts. When Craig had finished her statements, Upton called the office to find them accurate to the secretary's movements and finding of the parts, which had occurred momentary to the call by Upton.

Craig's activities were not centered to such endeavors, as the experiments with Upton were directed to controlled experiment and not to address of random encounter.

The experiments also required absolute concentration; and if even a slight intrusion to such occurred, it would interfere with the effort. Noise or light could create a disruption that frustrated the efforts.

Within the midst of this delicately balanced activity, Craig recognized the mystery in being able to, while thinking about nothing, having no thought train, remember to give a suggestion and give it as well, and to this recognition she espoused the aspect of the existence of one person having three minds. This premise found backing by the professor who wrote the introduction to *Mental Radio*, Professor William McDougall, whom Upton described as being the "Dean" of psychologists in America. He used the term monads to describe the divisions, there being three monads that interact to their separate existence.

The method that Craig used in her experiments entailed placing the folded paper with an image drawn upon it over her solar plexus. This seemed to help facilitate the telepathic process but was not absolute to it.

Edgar Cayce would not tolerate anything being placed in this region of the body while he was in his self-induced sleep state. This was discovered by someone having moved something inadvertently over him during a reading. He suffered instant travail as a result and instructed that it was not to happen again and that if it did, *he could die!*

There is stated to be a well known psychic phenomenon called "Umbilical Sensory Perception"; and a person named James Fuchs, who was associated with Upton in some manner, called his attention to this. He claimed that Craig was employing a method that had been developed by Dr. Justinus Kerner. This is the doctor who was in close involvement with Frau Frederica Hauffe from 1826 to 1829, and with this we have a tie that dates to the early 1800's. Kerner was born in Ludwigsburg on September 18, 1786, and died in Weinsburg on February 21, 1862. He did not study medicine until after 1799. Frau Hauffe was born at the beginning of the century. Recall that Upton's book was copyrighted in 1930. Dr. Justinus Andreas Christian Kerner studied the works and practice of Franz Anton Mesmer and his theories of magnetism. He published a work on him in 1856. A small article about Dr. Justinus Kerner exists in the *Encyclopedia Britannica*.

The obvious linking of persons and knowledge to hypnosis, magnetism, telepathy, clairvoyance, somnambulic medical diagnosis, and dream involvement trace a path through history that, as I said earlier, shows evidence back through time to early Egyptian representations.

James Fuchs criticized Upton's book, saying that he had presented himself in a naive manner by not speaking to the vast amount of written record to paranormal events. Upton countered that to do so would require vast writing that would fill volumes and that was not the intent in writing his book. His intent was to present the reality of the effort that he and his wife lived.

Upton was influenced by another man of standing, but in an area of society that has a different profile to espoused spiritual events. Ghost seeing was one area that Frau Hauffe claimed distinct involvement, and a Unitarian clergyman claimed both seeing and talking with ghosts. In his belief to events, the Reverend Minot J. Savage of New York took his place in influence to Mr. Upton Sinclair's thirty-five years of interest in the supernatural.

Craig Sinclair was not spiritually minded, as she had experienced numerous bad moments in childhood with evangelical religion.

Another childhood event affected Craig as well. She had an encounter with fire that etched itself on her mind for life, and she was attentive in adult life to anything that related to the hazards of fire. In her experiments with telepathy, she was virtually flawless in her interpretations of anything involving fire. It seems that some enhanced concentration or focus of attention spanned both conscious mind and the minds of the subconscious and deep.

Mary Craig Sinclair grew to what others described as being an extremely understanding and considerate person who bore the concerns and burdens of other people to the extent that her health was broken by the age of forty.

In many ways, she deliberately did bare those burdens, and what came naturally to her paralleled Fredericka Hauffe. Both cared for other people and had a niceness to them. Both she and Hauffe could lay their hands on another person and feel their pain, taking it to themselves. They could feel other people by intuition and, in the same fashion, their actions or circumstance or fear. Dreams also could reveal this to them.

Craig seemed to stay in the first or second state of sleep-waking, and thus was not in an intuitive trance, but rather a sensitive state that allowed her conscious awareness of that which she was seeing, feeling or experiencing. She was able to respond instantly and consciously to that which was going on around her or addressed to her. When she received something, she was able to instantly sit up and draw a sketch if she was involved in a deliberate experiment.

All of this ties her to sensitive somnambulism, but her depth never reached that of Frau Hauffe.

She believed, as did Cayce, that anyone could develop such circumstance with deliberate effort and believed in an existence of a "universal consciousness" or common substratum.

Craig also was party to the psychometry that Andrew Jackson Davis used in his medical practice and to which Hauffe was given voucher to and to which Cayce was aware. Recall that psychometry is presented as the act of touching a person and knowing aspects of the individual. Craig did this to Upton with success.

Craig's passive mental concentration might well be identified with the slowness of Cayce, Rasputin, Victor, and Davis in his early life. She knew that this ability to focus away from conscious evaluating thought was essential. Cayce termed it as being able to completely set aside all aspects of self or self-concern.

To not identify Mary Craig Sinclair as possessing aspects of sensitive somnambulism is to ignore Upton Sinclair's sincere representation of that which he and his wife lived.

Upton Sinclair was born in Baltimore on September 20, 1878, and died on November 25, 1968. He was a graduate of the College of the City of New York in 1897, and he did graduate work at Columbia University.

Upton supported his family by self-initiative in journalistic writing. He became known for his socialist attitudes and wrote to influence society to the relief of the working class of people.

The *Encyclopedia Britannica* credits his book, *The Jungle*, which was written about the meat packing industry in Chicago, as helping bring about package food laws in that industry; it had not been Upton's intent to have this occur. He had been attempting to address the circumstance of the workers.

The Jungle was Upton's first major success and others followed. He wrote *Oil* which based its knowledge on the teapot dome political scandals and *The Fliver King* which found its address to the plight of the auto worker's struggle to gain a livable place in a growing industrial society.

If a person ventures to a major bookstore and inquires to books available that he authored, the computer will present you with a very long, very courageous, and very honestly written list of books to his beliefs and society's betterment. The one that I have lists twenty-six such ventures in life, and I should like to read more than those that I have.

CHAPTER 9

MADAME GULFINA

<u>Presently Alive and Well in Russia</u>

"A Living Proof"

Madame Golfina

CHAPTER 9

MADAME GULFINA

Presently Alive and Well in Russia

"A Living Proof"

We apply the word special to many things in life, and wonder to the mysteries that we hear and read of. In present day Russia, a very special lady is living a great many of the mysteries contained in these pages.

She lives in a city in Siberia named Tyumen, and being in the vibrancy of the middle years in life, is sharing a wonder to hers with many people who are seeking her healing help.

Being precocious or ostentatious is not her nature, but confidence in those powers that are working through her is in no way lacking. She believes and knows that she is somehow in league with the power of God. In this belief, she takes no credit for the healings that are worked by her efforts.

This aspect of Madame Gulfina is identical with that of Rasputin, and she identifies very strongly with him. She claims that his powers of healing far exceeded hers, and recognizes through her experience, the validity of his.

Like others that are written of in this journey of reading you're taking, Madame Gulfina is also in association with the established, practicing, medical profession. The cures that are being worked through her are so well recognized that main stream medical doctors are regularly advising patients with many ailments to seek her help.

She sees eighty people per week in a clinical setting that boasts a very proper waiting room filled with many anxious waiting people, wearing a white medical lab coat; an incredible number of things that are revealed throughout these pages are revealed in her activities.

Madame Gulfina states that voices began to speak to her, inside of her, and they told her and tell her what the ailments are that people are suffering. She states that she can actually see into the person she's treating, seeing the troubled area. Also, she feels the pain and travail of the person within herself.

Relating this to sensitive somnambulism and Frau Hauffe is without question proper, and the transference of travail to her can be unmistakably seen in her face as she addresses her patients.

How other aspects of her actions came to be part of her activity is not clear, but she now also involves a self-induced trance to aid in her perceptions. In this trance, she claims to be in touch with spirit guides that aid the activity.

The list of relatable actions continues with the observance that she makes passes with her hand over the patient. Sometimes they are without touching, staying two or three inches or more away form the body, and others are just lightly touching the surface. At times, she will make a grasping motion with her hand in the area of the pain or distress.

Madame Golfina's healing passes

It's as though she's gripping something and taking it away from the body. She will grasp lightly against the surface or off of the body in what would be the area of the aura.

With all of the actions of passes and gripping, she moves her hand way from the person and shakes her hand and fingers briskly away from the patient and into the air. The actions are as though she's shaking something from her hands, and it is a very deliberate and distinct action. There is no fooling around to this, nothing tentative!

A relationship to the aura is possibly evident, the relationship to magnetic passes is definitely evident, and a relationship to Tantric and Taoist practices is most obvious in this physical movement that somehow is spiritual as well.

Having addressed Tantric and Taoist beliefs and practices in the chapter on Edgar Cayce, I also address them farther in the chapter on Dr. Carl Jung. The relationships are most definite and validate the thoughts of interactive involvement's that manifest themselves.

Aspects of Rosicrucian beliefs and practices that I've addressed, also show evidence in Madame Gulfina's practices.

On a table that looks like a medical stand that sits at her arm as she faces the patient, she has placed a clear glass container about four inches in diameter and about six inches high that's filled with clear water. Also on the table can be herbs in the form of large leafs or parts of them. To the back of these, toward the wall, is a framed, vivid, ornate, color painting about thirteen or fourteen inches high and proportionally wide, that bears the image of the Virgin Mary holding the baby Jesus in her arms. It sits next to a large Bible.

It is very obvious that the power of God is known by her to be the influence working through her. She believes nothing else.

To the water and the herbs, she makes passes with her hand or hands, sometimes pressing or just touching the beaker and the herbs, sometimes not. She also grasps at the top of the water, just as she does by the patient, and will from both the grasping and the passes, at times move her hands away from them and flick or shake them in space.

She does not do the flicking or shaking continuously, as she claims to be transferring healing energy to both the herbs and the water. Once the transfer is completed, she has them consumed by the patient.

This practice of transfer of energy by consumption of water is identical to that described by my Rosicrucian friend.

The action of movement of the hands over or in touch with the beaker and the herbs is not always rapid. It is also slow and intense. Whether rapid or slow, it is always deliberate, concentrated, and intense.

You might recall that Frau Hauffe was said to have drawn strength from those around her, and was also drawn momentarily from death by her mother, who made three passes over her face with her hand when she had apparently died.

Madame Gulfina makes claims to bringing people back to life that have died. She states that she has restarted stopped hearts in people, and that it is possible to speak to the spirit of a person who has died.

Goffina transferring
healing energy to
herbs and water

Frau Hauffe spoke constantly to the departed spirits of people and so did Emanual Swedenborg. Edgar Cayce also is credited with such encounters. It would seem evident that Madame Gulfina is stating that it is the immediate departed spirit that can be spoken to.

If Russia remains open to the rest of the world, I suspect that Madame Gulfina may well become a person of renown and may find people from other countries seeking her out for help.

This woman is very impressive in her seriousness and sincerity. It's very obvious that she is not a charlatan and no charades are involved with what she's doing. She's not employing any mystical props or incantations, and when she prays for the people she is trying to help, it is with concentration and depth.

I do not believe that the medical profession in Russia would involve itself with someone who was not creditable. It would do their reputations harm, and I would think that a doctor's reputation is very important to him in such a setting.

Speaking to the first time that she stopped the bleeding of a person, Madame Gulfina evidenced an awe to the event that has apparently happened many times over. She claims that bleeding can be stopped by her even in cases where a person has experienced an amputation, such as the loss of a hand.

It is an incredible statement, but one that she makes in absolute manner, and she equates it to Rasputin's abilities to help the affliction of the Tsarevich. She has asked many questions regarding Rasputin and his abilities to affect cures to people in distress. She believes absolutely that he could stop bleeding, which was the Tsarevich's affliction, because she, too, can do so, and she states that in the case of Rasputin his abilities were of a far, far greater depth.

I gathered that she feels his influence to effect cures far surpassed hers. If she is right, it full well explains the cadres of people that would gather at the house he stayed in while living in St. Petersburg. Many were said to come seeking his help and generosity.

Rasputin was said to be a very giving person; of himself and money. I wondered where he obtained the money to live on, aside from the generosity of the aristocratic ladies he knew, but with the ability to heal and with multitudes seeking him, he would obviously accept the generosity of those who could pay, but also would share by giving to those in need. He also gave to those people that were close to him.

His wife's tolerance of him might in part be explained by his spending of money to secure the comfort of his family. It's said he built the largest and nicest home in his village for her. It was not a peasant's abode.

Madame Gulfina may well become a living legend, but regardless of whether she does or doesn't, she is now a living reality, and one that spans the activities and knowledge of not just centuries, but millennium, and not just one continent, but many.

I've addressed people, customs, and beliefs from the areas of Asia, Asia Minor, North Africa, Eastern and Western Europe, and North America, and I would not be surprised that if research were to be expanded, the area and numbers of people would expand.

For those who have experienced or studied or both, which now includes you, the reader; Madame Gulfina probably holds a special place in your thoughts. I know she does in mine, and I will be watching and listening to the future and hers.

CHAPTER 10

DR. CARL GUSTAV JUNG

<u>Born July 26, 1875 - Died June 6, 1961</u>

"The Father Of Modern Analytic Psychology"

Dr. Carl Gustav Jung

Sigmond Freud

CHAPTER 10

DR. CARL GUSTAV JUNG

Born July 26, 1875 - Died June 6, 1961

"The Father Of Modern Analytic Psychology"

When Ernest Hemingway set his person to writing, he came to know within himself when he was inspired. Writing was an experience in projection of something that demanded flow and execution of effort to propel his words and ideas to paper and to the minds of generations to follow.

He termed this inspirational writing as "having the juice." He knew when he had it; he knew when he didn't have it. If he didn't have it, he knew that the effort to write would be an endeavor in plodding self-discipline and that it would be determined work that brought forth his rending.

On the other hand, when he would have "the juice," it was a bursting forth of flowing ideas brought to the paper in a manner that keeping up with the torrent would be the activity of necessity, and the keeping up could run for days or weeks on end.

Hemingway recognized that some inner projection required response by his outer person and that by doing so he created his best efforts.

Dr. Carl Jung stated that it was from fateful compulsion that was sourced within him that his writing came. He indicated that he was assailed within himself and that he permitted "the spirit" which moved within him to expound to its intent.

A man named Carl Jung created for himself a world of inner solitude in his youth that he maintained until he was sixty-five years of age. His childhood experiences, beliefs, and formative thoughts were of a nature he considered totally personal. He added them to experiences in the realm of the mind that he encountered in growing up and old and allowed them to be revealed in total depth only after his death at the age of eighty-five on June 6, 1961. The revealing came within the pages of his autobiography which he began writing in 1957 at the age of eighty-one. He had been born on July 26, 1875.

The *Encyclopedia Britannica* makes note of his autobiography as being one of his best works; and its title of *Memories, Dreams, and Reflections* is holding to the truth of his life. The encyclopedia describes him as being a renowned Swiss psychiatrist who is considered to be the founder of modern analytic psychology.

He is credited with having risked condemnation by society for having stated that the content of psychic experience is real and interactive to external life, and considered that had he lived in the Middle Ages, he would have been burned at the stake as a heretic. He in many ways suffered isolation because he addressed things that "normal society" did not understand and believed that his memoirs would be misunderstood.

His life's work could be summed up in the statement that it was a story of the realization by himself of the unconscious, and from this believed that the human experience is a process of psychic nature that is not controlled by us but is possibly partially directed by a person's self.

He believed that the psyche is religious by nature, and initially declared his allegiance to Christianity but fell from a strong belief as his life progressed, just as his father who was a philologist and pastor had done.

He built his life on the premise that only by viewing himself in perspective to his inner happenings could he understand himself.

His early years of rural isolation from other children, save at school where he enjoyed their company initially, helped set his solitary nature and his love of rural settings. Eventually he found that the rustic nature of his schoolmates alienated him from himself, and finally at the age of eleven a change of family environment to one of an upper-class setting brought enhancement to social understanding. Part of that understanding was that in this new setting he realized how poor his family actually was.

His passion for solitude allowed him to find nature full of wonders, and he desired to steep in them throughout his life. He eventually built a very fine home on the shores of a lake near Zurich.

At the age of twelve, he experienced something of an unusual nature that, without self-initiative, changed him, and I wonder that possibly he may have had revealed to him one of Edgar Cayce's presented circumstances to the living of life.

At twelve, he suddenly had a feeling come over him that he was not one person, but two—a schoolboy and a man of high authority. He related the experience to an encounter that he had with an ornate horse-drawn carriage that was from the eighteenth century. It had been restored meticulously and, at its passing, he had the feeling that it belonged to him.

At the point of feeling that he was two people, he claimed that suddenly he became himself; suddenly he had authority, the authority of being. If you recall from the commentary on Cayce, he would see in the aura of a person at times the image of a person who he claimed represented a past life image of the present living person. Recall that the dissertation expounded by the living person would always be adamant to the appearance of the period and person in the aura. Firm or authoritative could be used as a description of the manner of statement. Jung suddenly felt the authority of being.

Jung in his youth thought schoolwork to be a nuisance, hated competitiveness, and found mathematics to be a terror and a torture. To the contrary of such disliked involvement, he immensely enjoyed playing, daydreaming, and strolling in the woods alone as an expansive pleasure.

His pursuit of solitude extended also to the building of his home by the lake. To the rear of it he built for himself a separate small cottage in which to think and study and experience and work, and enjoyed it immensely as well.

In his later life, he believed that his development as a child was a path maker to future events that would occur in his life. To this thinking, his eventual identification of two personalities in a person may well find relevance, for he came to believe that the number two personality lived "in the centuries" and was part of life. It was normal to life, and life was a progressive experience in learning. This experience he considered to be a matter of actual necessity as a teen and disregarded those who were studying Aristotelian intellectualism at St. Thomas, where he attended, as attempting to prove to themselves the validity of belief, because it was a belief. Jung was a person of personal experience from his youth. He did not travel the path of the crowded masses. I think that few who travel such path attain a greatness within or without themselves. They just sort of are.

I think it very unfortunate for both him and those of us whose lives he is influencing that with his personal fortitude to self-observation and self-development in person and in psyche, that he in latter life chose to abandon two aspects of study. Religion, most specifically in Christianity, and hypnosis saw him turn from them, and in doing so, he turned to mythology and alchemy as partial augmentation to his personal studies, experiences, and analyzed conclusions.

It is my now-studied and experienced belief that a study of humanity that excludes these two important aspects of available knowledge, revelation, foundation, and in the area of religion, salvation, ignores keys to a more complete understanding of this lack of understanding that we live. His understanding was that in areas of religious matters only experience mattered or counted.

Jung's father, who was a pastor, struggled with his own belief and eventually fell to a state of rejection. This no doubt influenced Jung in his life's path. It had been considered that Jung would follow in the footsteps of his father, in that relatives of the past from both sides of his family had followed such a course. It was not uncommon during that time for a young man to follow in the footsteps of family that preceded them. Classes had their place. The advent of widely available higher education has in many ways changed that stratification, at least in the upper-lower and middle class levels.

Besides turning to those mentioned areas of revelation, Jung also looked to the observation and study of the mentally ill, and in travel to many different nations of varied cultural and ethnic compositions enhanced his knowledge.

This approach laid basis to his thoughts that "theological religion" was nothing more than believing without hope, and was in contrast to "ridiculous materialism" that psychiatrists espoused.

He considered that both approaches to life and understanding could not withstand or lacked epistemological criticism and experience. This laid the basis for his own approach to understanding.

From this approach, he recognized the separation of knowledge between urban worlds and country worlds. In his love for the countryside, he gravitated toward it and considered urban worlds to be somewhat limited mentally.

Dr. Carl Jung studied formally at two universities—one of Basal from 1895 to 1900 and the other from which he graduated a doctor, Zurich, in 1902. He held position at the Burgholzli Asylum of the University of Zurich in 1900. He was a close collaborator of Sigmund Freud between 1907 and 1912 when they parted ways primarily because of Freud's instance that sexual involvement held sway to virtually all aspects of nervosa. Freud was attempting to establish his theory in concrete by force of person and control of persons around and associated with him. Jung considered that Freud became obsessed with the aspect of sexual dominance in relationship to behavior, and he disagreed with him to the point of separation and publication of different theories. Note that the word theory is dominant here. One man's theory can be another man's passion, and man did not invent passion, but he did invent the assertion of it and its manipulation.

Jung held the position, also, of President of the International Psychoanalytic Society from 1911 until 1914 when he resigned. He also held teaching positions, being Professor of Psychology at the Federal Polytechnic University in Zurich from 1933 to 1941 and Professor of Medical Psychology at the University of Basal in 1943.

Attributed to Dr. Jung as being his first achievement is the presentation of the precept that humanity is divided into two types of persons.

I consider this to be of extreme importance in understanding the acceptance and rejection of those phenomena that are the subject of address in these many pages and am grateful that Dr. Jung recognized the division of man into those that are outward-looking in their personality and manner of living, and those that are inward-looking in theirs.

The first he called or named extroverted people and the second introverted. I believe that our western society is dominated by the aspect of extroverted assertiveness and that eastern cultures are introverted to the search of inner awareness.

Addressing those things that Dr. Jung experienced and studied in an extroverted society was like walking on very thin ice. We find it all too easy to live life in a materialistic rampage, viewing those who choose not to, in lesser and possibly misunderstood light.

Introversion is exactly what Mary Craig Sinclair described as part of her process of introspective revealing, and if you recall, she is said to have borrowed that approach from the good Doctor Kerner of association with Frau Hauffe.

Dr. Wayne Dyer's assertions of inner directedness are more easily understood if one applies the term "introversion" to the desired approach. To a person who is naturally tuned to his inner person, and who has directed his life in response to the awareness of the influence of Dr. Jung's number two personality by natural revelation to its existence, acceptance of the phenomena associated with both sensitive and intuitive somnambulism are quite probably more readily understood, at least to the existence of revelation from sources below the conscious level.

In later effort, Jung gave definition to functions of the mind, identifying four and stating that one or more can be predominant in a person. If one looks at the four stated functions of intuition, feeling, thinking, and sensation, one readily sees that all four are, in fact, associated with the address of the previous paragraph.

Dr. Jung further differentiated the human person by claiming that arch types exist and are instinctive patterns that have a universal character that is expressed in both behavior and images.

Dr. Jung recognized that the mind oscillates between that which makes sense and that which makes no sense, rather than between that which is right and that which is wrong. Thus the address of a materialistic society to the paranormal finds itself examined within the light of an inability to make sense of that which holds no explanation in worldly terms.

The lack of physical explanation is then lent to that which seeks the sensible, and rejection of the spiritual existence results from the inability to prove the existence of both worlds in a worldly objective materialistic presentation of western cultural images. Hence, we have theories.

Freud's attitude as addressing the spirit was that in intellectual representation he considered it to be repressed sexuality. Jung disagreed and considered that Freud had become emotionally involved in sexual theory.

Freud actually approached Jung in written communication asking him to promise that he would never abandon his espoused sexual theory. He stated that he considered it essential to all and that it should be made a dogma and an unshakable bulwark in viewing human motivations and mental travail.

Jung considered that Freud had substituted the dogma of sexuality as replacement to his rejection of religious motivation.

Such opinion should be noted as originating with just that, opinion, and indicates the vulnerability of society to direction by opinion in matters where actual and factual representation can exist to contrary awareness.

It's not inappropriate to say that during the time that Jung was in school, 1898, psychiatry was held in a state of contempt by the medical community.

Jung himself discovered that in his early exposure to psychiatry, the process and objective was to make patient evaluations as cut and dried as possible. They would:

- compile a long list of symptoms

- apply a label

- rubber stamp the diagnosis

- the matter was settled . . .

No consideration was given to the psychology of the person, called patient or subject.

If you have ever followed the course of activity associated with "modern psychiatry" as I have, you know that little differs in some settings to this same approach by some psychiatrists today. Most particularly distressing to this is when court actions become intertwined to the stabilities of a person and the person falls prey to the opinions of the theories of the assumptions and concepts that a materialistic society demands in behavior of its subjects.

In strange contrast to the concepts of encounter and personal directedness of Freud, who was actually a neurologist to begin with, it's found that he was actually the person who introduced psychology into psychiatry. He did this in steps to studies of hysteria and dreams.

Psychology is the study of the phenomenon of the mind in all of its aspects, whereas psychiatry is the study of the illness of the mind in its manifestations. The mixture of both studies, when a person is studied, leaves that studied person suspended in the web that society has created with acceptance of the theories and opinions of the educated opinionated.

Hidden Shadows

Opinion generates confusion, facts create objectivity, but subjective fact can only be experienced, and thus, proving objectivity becomes a pursuit primarily of presented opinion. That is unless, of course, you believe what history has recorded of its past travelers in time.

Jung believed that rationalism was a disease to our society along with doctrinairism. Is this not what society tolerates in psychologists and psychiatrists today?

I commented just previous to this that Dr. Jung's first noted accomplishment was to identify the two segments of extroverted and introverted people. In doing that, I espoused certain views of my own. Commenting now to Dr. Jung's views and beliefs is an interesting venture.

Dr. Jung's comments regarding that basic difference between our western man and the eastern man is to me most appropriate in observation and fact. It represents an observed reality that most of western civilization charges through life without even knowing its occurring; the pace fills the space that for eastern cultures represents a loss of the essence of life.

The quest for opulent materialism has created in us an extroverted society and a people that Jung fully identified.

The eastern quest for inner sanctity has through the centuries created an introverted society that recognizes the inner realms of development while it yet struggles with the savage natures of man.

Dr. Jung considered that our objective extroverted society projects its meanings, considering that those meanings exist in objects.

Our society is hard intended and directed to put objectivity ahead of human life, and in doing so, we are losing ourselves to our own self-blinding to the inner person.

Jung thought that the eastern cultured man, being introverted, seeks to feel the meanings of being within one's self and, as such, radiates a division of both culture and directedness to life's mysterious quest.

Dr. Carl Jung recognizes that meaning is both inside and outside and that the psyche is constantly at work threading and kneading its influence in each person's walk to destiny.

For it is destiny that is to be considered, and surely we have seen through the sharing of life's experience by those that have been addressed in this book. A true mystery exists in man's destiny that even the Bible does not fully reveal.

In the face of such revelation, it takes a massive ego to remain totally objective in thought and inner directedness, and I believe the person who does so is coming up short at the final tolling to life's next step.

Jung was not a religious man, and as such he searched deeper to worldly relationships to subjective occurrence than most. In my opinion, he created for himself and for those who would seek to attempt to follow his line of reasoning, a revealed extroverted western man, struggling with his objectivity in the midst of subjective mysteries that objectivity chooses to attack and denigrate. This left him quite possibly with the thought, "Be careful, they'll call you crazy," and our knowledge that he would not allow publication of his autobiography, that might have labeled him, until after his death, and thus made his ability to escape complete, is testimony to it.

It was his professed belief that a person felt limited if his aims were limited, and that laying importance to false possessions and lowering his sensitivity to essentials lead to a less satisfying life. Thus limited, he felt that jealousy and envy resulted.

He considered this of such an importance that he believed that that which we take with us at death has its basis in sensitivity, not in false possessions.

It is too bad he was not religious; he could have found parallels within the Bible, and with such, expanded his sensitivity.

His depth of disregard for the Bible can be seen in his thought that the prophecies of the Book of Revelation were transparent and that no one believed in them, considering the entire subject to be embarrassing.

In contrast to this, he oddly considered that a psychiatrist was to be a doctor of the soul, and a psychiatrist he was!

Jung's studies of eastern cultures and his personal experiences in life did not bring him to a state of belief in reincarnation. He could not find empirical proof to the occurrence. He did consider the Indian conceptions and thought that if it existed it was an extension of the psyche, without time or without the requirement of space. He never expressly wrote about life after death in this sense, and that which he did say came from memories, images, and thoughts that buffeted him. In his practical pursuits of medicine, he also came to be aware that in distinct honesty some people have no desire for immortality. They feel a disgust for their existence and prefer a cessation of any continuance of life after death.

Next, beyond Jung's identification of introversion and extroversion, we come upon his observation of the existence of two personalities within a person. He labeled these *number one* and *number two*.

His first observation of this occurred in conversational encounters with his mother. He came to realize that apart from her normal everyday person of worldly knowledge and endeavor, she would at times expound intently to a subject or activity at hand. This changing of person within the person was so pronounced that Jung came to recognize it readily in her and subsequently in others. She would be authoritative, exhibit an air of soundness, and expound to significant depth in a manner that evidenced a different source of initiative within her.

Eventually he became aware that his now labeled *number one* personality centered itself to the aspects of science and met its needs within this category of life's pursuit. His *number two* personality was directed to the aspects of studies that touched humanity or historical depths. From this, it can be termed he recognized duality in people.

Expanding to this duality, he considered that the individual is usually unconscious and failing in seeing his potentialities for decision, and that search for evidence in this perplexed condition is wrought with anxiety, as his search centers to external rules and regulations.

He places much blame for this on our educational system that is totally objective in nature, ignoring what he termed secrets associated with a person's private experience. It is just those secrets that he has written about in *Memories, Dreams and Reflections and Reflections"* and which formed the basis for his whole life's work, not his educational experience or his interaction with colleagues. He thought that our educational system teaches ideals that no one could live up to.

In *Memories, Dreams and Reflections and Reflections"* , he quotes a saying that he termed old and fine. The saying is attributed to an old Rabbi and is formed as a question and answer as follows: "'In the olden days there were men who saw the face of God. Why don't they any more?' The Rabbi's learned answer was, 'Because nowadays no one can stoop so low.'"

If Jung was right and we are for the most part walking around in an unconscious state, was this not the state alluded to by Frau Frederica Hauffe when she described a somnambulic dream state in stages one and two of sensitive somnambulism. She claimed that most did not recognize the state or condition and that some were considered insane because of its lack of recognition.

Dr. Carl Jung considered that images that were projected from the unconscious confused the insane but were also a matrix of mythopoeic imagination which no longer exists in a rationalizing society, having been tabooed and dreaded.

He recognized the path to discovery was not popular and was dangerous and ambiguous, but he also recognized that to venture forth was to voyage to what he termed the pole of the other world.

Dr. Jung professed another belief that is also relevant to the address of this effort. He professed and asserted that man's living being is part of a collective unconscious. He defined this as being some aspect of the existence of a mind that is present and functional to all of us on a spiritual level that projects to the conscious level through various avenues.

He considered that each person is part of a collective spirit that's counted in life to centuries of being.

Freud held the view that within the unconscious existed vestiges of the past.

Jung was very careful regarding his statements about aspects of the inner person. He realized that other people could be easily estranged and embarrassed by illusion to such. He realized that when one ventures to the realm of the subjective, one is crossing a line that few even venture to approach, let alone attempt to explore or understand or accept. Freud originally rejected sharply the existence of parapsychology and "occult" phenomenon. He was steeped in materialistic prejudice. It was from a dream that Jung was led to the concept of the existence of the collective unconscious. The dream evidenced levels of human existence by historic reference in the form of varying scenes depicted by floors in a house. Each floor represented a different time frame, and he traveled from level to level in the dream experience.

In his pursuit to understand the unconscious, he claimed to have become aware that the unconscious both produces and undergoes change. Jung, like Hauffe, eventually grew to live on two planes, the conscious and the subconscious, in simultaneous fashion.

He considered that in certain circumstances the conscious tried to comprehend that which was to be projected from the unconscious but could not, and in others the subconscious could relate only through dreams.

Jung came to realize by personal experience that the subconscious could not always relate in its own voice. He experimented with this within himself and established that he could give his voice to the inner perception, and by doing so gained communicative contact. He fully believed this to be a reality of normal human life.

He came to believe or recognize from personal experience once again that internal awareness can manifest itself in manners that are perceived by the external person as being real in physical existence. The opposite he felt was also true in that exterior or worldly conscious things can manifest themselves to the unconscious world as being real in appearance to that realm. He differentiated the two worlds of physical and spiritual and recognized that each has an autonomy. In this same stead, he recognized that the various aspects on the individual makeup have autonomy as well; all part of being one, but parts of one.

Dr. Jung's study by personal experience of unconscious manifestations lasted from 1913 to 1917. At that point the fantasies he was experiencing subsided, and he could once again look objectively at the experience.

He stated very firmly that it was these experiences, which he pursued and allowed to manifest within him, that were formative to him and to his total life. Everything else that he pursued in his life had its basis in the fantasies and revealing of those years.

He believed that denial of the inner images of the unconscious deprives a person of his wholeness and creates or imposes a fragmentary life on the person.

When these inner experiences came upon him, he had been lecturing in a university for some eight years. Finding it virtually impossible to allow manifestations of that which was being trust upon him from auras of the unconscious unknown, and continue to lecture objectively, he actually resigned his position at the university and allowed himself to sink into the reaches of the psyche in dreams and fantasy. He had actually experienced a cession of intellectual activity which forced him to make a choice. He had been at the university from 1905 to 1913.

His truthful claim was that that which was brought to light literally had stricken him dumb and forced his withdrawal from the public. He could neither understand the occurrence or give it form. It just was.

It is important to understand that statements that became public regarding these three years of his life were not made until fifty years after their occurrence and were presented after his death in his book, *Memories, Dreams, and Reflections.* Throughout his lifetime, he did not like having his personal life brought to public view. It is little wonder considering the secrets he held within himself, regarding yourself.

Relating this time in his life to another person I've commented to, we might recall that Emanual Swedenborg also withdrew from public view to bring forth those revelations that are attributed to him. Note very strongly here that Dr. Carl Jung read seven volumes of Swedenborg in his pursuits of inner understanding. Recall that Swedenborg claimed contact with angels for that which spanned the final twenty-six years of his life and wrote a new Christian doctrine that was attacked by the established Lutheran Church.

Jung struggled with what he termed *his experiences into the unconscious world of fantasy* and clung to the real world by maintaining within himself a duality of focus.

He was able to hold to the tangibles of family and medical practice in an effort to mentally sustain himself. He believed that without that anchor in conscious reality, he would not have been able to sustain himself.

At one point during his experiments, his family began to experience a haunting of the house and their lives, seeing ghostly images. If you choose now to recall, Frau Hauffe's relatives came to know and live with the same occurrences, seeing spirits in the house, around Frederica, and traveling to and fro from her. She came to accept their presence and conversed with them without difficulty in somnambulic state.

At every step of Jung's experimentation, he encountered the same psychic material that is associated with psychosis and the insane!!

Did not Hauffe state that many who are considered insane are in a somnambulic state but that it is not known that they are? The individual's maintaining of awareness to their state of consciousness is apparently crucial to the retention of stability.

Jung considered that the final analysis should lie with the conscious mind which can differentiate circumstance, recognizing that communication from the unconscious can have a subjective meaning that does not relate to conscious events and that at times definition is a difficult thing, considering that he felt our world lacked a psychic connection.

Jung contradicted himself somewhat in this regard by saying something that may well relate to our present world. *You see, he stated that from within and without comes mass degeneration, and that the collective unconscious contributes. It cannot contribute without connection.*

He contradicted himself further by recognizing that the unconscious communicates things that are unknown to the person within their normal consciousness. He alluded to:

- premonitions
- dreams that manifest to reality
- synchronistic phenomena.

Without a connection at all, there could be no basis for his espoused belief that the collective unconscious is common to all and that the ancients called it the *"Sympathy of All Things."*

Without an exposure to spirit, none of those things which Jung espoused could have been related with conviction, and as we have so far touched on the:

- introversion and extroversion of people
- number one and number two personalities
- subconscious
- universal unconscious

Comment to Jung's early exposure to spirit is next, and in thinking to it one must keep in mind that at the time of Jung's three-year struggle with the unconscious realm, he could not see the interaction of both worlds. He saw only contradiction between both worlds. It was later that he saw or developed to believe in an interactive state.

In 1898, Carl Jung's family and he encountered the realm of the séance, table taping, and table turning. Every Saturday night brought effort with a fifteen-and-a-half-year-old medium, a young woman who was said to produce somnambulistic states and other phenomena of a spiritualistic nature.

In the two-year span of time that this practice occurred, Jung's family were present to hear a solid oak table split for what was said to be no reason. A solid steel knife broke into several pieces with no faults in the metal and no explanation. It just broke in pieces.

These two events occurred not during a séance but before Jung joined the group. During his involvement in the group, they experienced communication and tapping sounds from within the wall and the table. The table moved of its own volition but not without contact of questionable nature by the medium.

Jung formed his thesis for a doctorate from these encounters, which he broke off when he caught the medium attempting to fake some activities.

He claimed that by some means through this spiritualist exposure he came to know how a number two personality is formed, how it enters a child's consciousness and then becomes integrated into itself. Whatever that means!!

He considered this to be one great experience that erased all of his earlier philosophy, making it possible to develop a psychological point of view.

He had discovered objective facts relevant to the human psyche. However, because of the nature of such experience he found himself again unable to speak of it.

If you felt the ground shake from these minor revelations, know that I have not. It was a very spurious basis, to say the least, upon which to begin formation of opinion and theory that would help shape this world we live in.

Since I have now addressed his early spiritual encounter and now add it to the list, it brings with it circumstance relatable to all, for dreams are considered to be had by all, and Drs. Jung and Freud are to be given credit for making theirs come to focus in all of our lives.

To my wonderment, the degree to which importance was placed upon dreams, and interpretation of those dreams, by men who were supposed to be objective, casts looming shadows to consider.

Both Jung and Freud actually would spend time together and make effort to interpret the dreams of the other. Jung claims that Freud had the lesser ability of the two and did not do well with relating the meanings of those that he had. It actually came to be that Jung considered that a latent psychosis within a person could reveal itself in a person's dreams and be addressed before it manifested itself.

In my readings of Jung's works, his emphasis on dreams astounded me. His attempts to objectively apply reasoning to such abstract subjective occurrence lends itself to groping the caves of the mind with a flashlight that has dead batteries in it. Certainly it's accepted that dreams can manifest themselves to reality and that they can carry communication from beyond this physical world. To deny this is to deny the Bible, as it is overflowing with examples, but to apply abstract speculation to the depths of a person's being is surely an inappropriate intrusion to the privacy of a doctor's patients' integrities. This abstract speculation was actually done initially by Jung with his patients. Eventually he abandoned this practice and avoided trying to apply rules and theories to the interpretation of dreams had by his patients. In abandoning this approach, he took up the task of merely trying to help his patients to understand their dream images by themselves.

I am grateful that I never had to stand in a grocery store check-out line behind Jung and Freud. The frozen chicken would have completely thawed before we would have made it past the dream books to the question of paper or plastic, in both compensation and cartage.

One reason that Jung believed that dreams held a practical importance in psychiatry, and to understand them as important, stemmed from the fact that he relied heavily on his inner perceptions and dreams in forming his philosophy. Thus, to a great extent the psychology that influences modern society is based in conscious interpretation of subjective encounter. He definitely believed that dreams bore a direct relationship to events of conscious revelation to inner being, and that both the number one and number two personalities were included to this consortium of being that we are.

As Jung experienced life, his perceptions of the inner person expanded, and he came to believe that, existent within each man and woman, there co-resided a counterpart being. In the man, it is a female. In the woman, it is a male.

To these counterpart beings he gave names. Labels and titles are important in the area of psychiatry; without them, labeling is difficult. To the male part of a woman he gave the title of *animus*. To the female part of a man it is *anima*, and he thought these to be the "soul" of a person.

He believed this integrated yet autonomous being that dwells within is the personification of the unconscious and that it dates to prehistory, embodying the past. He considered them to be all previous life, that is, still alive. Jung thought himself to be a barbarian in comparison to his anima.

In this line of thinking, if one considers that a being or person of another gender is within him, and that from this source, influence to the conscious manifests itself, then the self is really more than the duality of number one and number two personalities, more than the added unconscious and the also added universal unconscious. It is:

- the conscious, thinking, worldly being - the mind
- the dual personalities that couple the ordinary to the profound - the ?
- the unconscious that continuously tries to surface, to influence, to express - the ?
- the universal unconscious that is in all one, and of one, and that links knowledge and past with present and future - the ?
- the anima or animus that knows its purpose within the man or woman who knows not their's - the ?

Drs. Jung and Freud interpreting dreams

Jung thought the anima and animus to be of deep cunning, and that its purpose was to totally take over and control the person it is part of, and that it is the spokesperson of the unconscious. He believed that, if listened to, it would destroy a person.

Jung communicated with his anima, and he believed that it produced images from the unconscious. He would request help or awareness to inner emotional feelings that he would be experiencing and the images would help resolve the feelings.

Dr. Jung's presentation of anima and animus may well have been drawn from an Eastern cultural basis.

In Tantra and Taoism the recognized and centered-to belief in the energy forces of *yin* and *yang*, feminine and masculine, permeate the relationship of the person with and within themselves. The coming together of a man and a woman in attraction and affection, both given and received, is possibly centered within this duality of being, within the being.

A person whose primary energy is Yin, feminine, is said to contain a small amount of yang, masculine. Conversely, a person who is dominant to yang is said to contain a small about of yin.

Jung referred to people as being anima or animus dominated, and he is given credit with having identified these two traits in people. Anima is feminine, and animus is masculine—the same traits, just different names and different times, times separated by some seven thousand years or so.

Dr. Jung's idea is obviously not original in nature, and since he studied Eastern cultures and came to an understanding of yin and yang, I can easily speak to the relationship in exotic massage and love making.

Dr. Jung liked to use the term "instincts," and if they exist, then his statement that "sexuality is the spokesperson for the instincts" may well find basis within the existence of yin and yang.

In Tantra, sexuality is not in opposition to spirituality, and it is actually considered that sex is a sacred art. Because of this and other factors, many Hindu temples are covered with both pictures and statues of couples engaging in a wide variety of sexual acts. It is not considered to be pornography, but is rather an aspect of worship.

Rasputin certainly would have had little difficulty in being part of this Eastern culture had he been born in a different place.

The Chinese beliefs of yin and yang are depicted in the symbols of a circle that is segmented into halves. Each half represents either yin or yang, with the dark half being yin and the light half yang. Each half has within it a small circle or dot that is of the opposite color, and thus energy.

Each half is to itself and yet imparted with characteristics of its opposite. Both halves make up the whole of being, and thus we find a goal in the loving union of a man and a woman.

The goal is for each to experience that part that is opposite to the primary energy of either yin or yang, while at the same time becoming one person with the person with whom they are in loving embrace.

It is a beautiful goal and one of a loving intent that brings peace to and with those who can share it. Within this approach can be found a love affair that is a journey of discovery.

The philosophy of Taoism is to find a balance between opposites. It does not condemn physical pleasures in a puritanical manner; neither does it indulge them. It seeks through these pleasures a celebration of mind, body, and soul.

The Chinese believe that yin and yang are not separate, but are rather interdependent.

A sage from ancient Greece named Plato suggested that each soul had been divided into halves, female and male, and that to be whole, people have to find their other half, their soulmates.

Whether true or not is a matter for speculation, but it is a certainty that both men and women seek partners in life and love that complement their own qualities. Recall that the auras of people actually show attraction and repulsion.

A principle of yin and yang also involves breath. The ancient Eastern teaching states that the breath is a life-energy. The Chinese call it *Chi*. The Indians call it *Prana*. Our word "spirit" is derived from a word that means breath.

This life-energy is important in acupuncture, as it is believed that Chi is the energy that flows through the channels or meridians, and thus around the aura, which is described as being the energy-body that surrounds the physical body.

Massage is believed to both relax the physical body and invigorate the energy body. A power point lies just below the navel and is part of this energy system. It's called the *Tan Tien* by the Chinese and the Indians give it the name *Hara Chakra*. There is an erotic massage intended to invigorate the energy of the body and focus it in the Tan Tien. Many manuals of lovemaking speak to this area as being one of great sensuousness, but few talk of this energy. Western society is very mechanical in almost everything.

Joy in kissing is certainly a joy to cherish, and I've spoken of sparks literally flying on film when the right two people share its joy. Revealed in the Eastern knowledge of energy flow within the body is something virtually never spoken of in Western circles of love's embrace.

A major channel for the flow of energy is said to exist between the upper lip of the mouth and the genitals. Have you ever wondered why kissing is so erotic?

In Tantric and Taoist practices of sharing love, love's embraces are very open to imagination and impulse. With the knowledge of this erotic channel of energy, the upper energies and the lower energies can be mingled in various ways to bring stimulation to both partners as inhibitions are lost to the desires of love.

In Taoist and Tantric practices, openness, harmony, lose of inhibition, sharing, balance, and mutual caring are all considered important to the balance of energies within the body, and life.

Keep in mind that Dr. Jung is the man who founded "modern" analytic psychology. He is a man who became convinced that value lay in oriental knowledge and expressed belief that crippling and injury prejudice the phenomenon of the psychic life, stating that he knew little of psychic life, and yet he is a man who professed that what he termed "hypnagogic" images appeared to him regularly and once saw Christ in the color of green at the foot of his bed. He is a man who in childhood from seven to nine played with fires that without explanation he considered sacred and living in nature, and thought that fires of other children were profane. Along with this, he kept in a secret place a small carved figure, a rock, and a small scroll in a small pencil box, and all of this was of a ritual that he knew not. There were the fire of seven to nine and the pencil box at age ten, but the ritual unknown, and each scroll added to the box, of a character solemn. These things were done in childhood, in secret, and then forgotten until the years past until around his thirty-fifth.

He was studying for a book he intended to write and stumbled on a cache of "soul stones." He read of a find of such stones near a place called "Arlesheim" and in Australia found those called Churingas.

The stones were oblong, as was his in the box of childhood ritual, blackish, and divided into two painted halves. To this revealing came also the small box and represented with this, the mannequin.

As things revealed themselves more, it became evident that the little mannequin of discovery was a cloaked God from antiquity. The name Telesporos named the mannequin god, which stands on the Asklepios monuments and from there reads from a scroll.

It was at this point in his life that he formed the hypothesis, which for him was a conviction, that there exist archaic psychic components. He considered that these components enter, without a direct line of tradition, the individual psyche.

These events that spanned decades in life were undeniable evidence to him, and believable evidence to me that that which we are in conscious being and physical action is a momentary presence in what we call time.

Have you ever done anything that you didn't know how to do and wondered at the occurrence? I have and too many times to remember!

It is so easy to cling in naïve denial of inner direction that doing so seems normal. If a person allows attention to them, then awareness to a far grander scheme of things can become normal as well.

Years later in life, Jung saw the ritual performed in Africa by natives. He claimed that they did this act without awareness to their activity and that only when completed and long afterward would they reflect on their activity.

Dr. Carl Jung (Great Grandfather)" was a man of secrets, and this was another one. He kept them until he couldn't be hurt by them, but between him and Freud, they established patterns in psychology and psychiatry that can hurt others today. It is an ill-informed populace that is allowing the rampant practices of individual medical authority to promenade the theories, opinions, dreams and psychic events of powerful men within it, and to hold a deep and at times defaming hand over those they choose to point a finger at or are asked to point a finger at.

The tragedy to this is that the sincere reserved, and "Hippocratic" doctors in the midst of this, are just that, in the midst!

The fact that Jung himself recognized that within his experiences, he walked in the same realm of psychic auras that are associated with psychosis and insanity should give all of us over to the thought that if one's business and directedness to life is to deal with insanity and psychosis, where first is a person liable to be labeled? Psychic or psycho?

"Be careful, they'll call you crazy!"

Alchemy can be defined as medieval chemistry. An alchemist is a medieval chemist. One of the major endeavors of early alchemy was to develop a means to turn base metals into gold. However, those who had a deeper understanding knew that their real purpose was to produce the uncommon gold, a philosophical gold. They centered their thoughts and activities to the concern of spiritual values and those things associated with psychic transformations, or so believed Carl Jung.

Within these nondescript borders of alchemy lay the name of Michael Maier, a name associated with the Rosicrucians. He lived from 1568 to 1622 and was a founder of the hermetic or alchemical-based philosophy that I have made mention of, if you recall.

He was well known and younger than the lesser known Gerardus Dorneus. Dorneus had written a treatises in 1602 that was of note.

Frankfort, Germany, seemed to be a city of alchemical philosophy at the time that both lived there. It was during this time that Michael Maier was of some local notoriety, as he was Count Palatine and Court Physician to Rudolph II.

Carl Jung considered that his great grandfather, Dr. Carl Jung (Great Grandfather)", who lived close to Mainz, was familiar with the writings of both men, and laid speculation to his interest in that which had preceded in his family involvement. He felt very strongly that he was under an influence of questions and things that had gone unanswered or were left incomplete by both his parents and grandparents, along with more distant ancestors. *He thought that possibly an impersonal karma existed within their family that passed from generation to generation.*

Jung felt compelled to answer questions left by his ancestors and possibly that it was his to address things which previous ages left unfinished.

He questioned whether these things were of a personal nature or of a collective one and leaned to the collective.

He considered that the collective problem would always manifest itself to the individual as personal unless recognized as such, and in such cases where recognition did not take place. Then the individual oft was considered to have a difficulty in the psyche personal. He stated the personal sphere to be disturbed but that the disturbance needn't be primary, but secondary to the person, and cause for the travail should be looked for in the collective situation.

Jung recognized the collective nature of life, while also living the duality that he recognized within his own person.

Duality of basis to his analytical psychology was thought to exist by him within the bounds of both alchemy and myth. With such being the case, he studied mythology as well, and his writings are laced with all three influences. His book, *Mysterium Conjunctionis*, is a vivid example of the combining of his personal experiences with both alchemy and myth, and it records his knowledge deeply within its pages.

Another way to say this is that he considered that analytical psychology had its counterpart in history in alchemy; he thought it coincided with it. He considered also that his psychology of the unconscious found its counterpart in alchemy, also.

Alchemy may well be the tailing end of the knowledge of the ancients that lost itself to a regressive nature in man, as some have held the thought to be.

Jung believed also that alchemy lent a corresponding knowledge to the multiplicity of occurrences that was "labeled" the transference. He also called it the "conjunctio," and he wrote two books about it. One is titled the *Psychology of the Transference* and the other *Mysterium Conjunctionis.*

Drs. Carl Jung and Sigmund Freud both recognized and gave credence to this phenomenon. Both agreed and considered it to be the most distinct problem in psychotherapy. Both considered it to be the absolute in importance to the same, and both called the transference an unconscious identification between patient and doctor which can lead to Para-psychological phenomena. As you learn of the transference, I believe you will agree that if the transference is not Para-psychological phenomena, then nothing is.

Jung frequently encountered it in his practice. Before Jung split with Freud, over Freud's announced intent to identify theory and method and make them a dogma, the cohesive bind of recognition that the transference lay at the very heart of psychotherapeutic address was paramount to intent's direction, and fear's recognition. Feared, because of the depth and intensity it can attain and the permanency it can establish, it can be both revealing and destructive, truth and fantasy, and regardless of which or all, *it is real*!

Dr. Carl Jung said that the transference is:

1. without uniformity or order
2. important to the individualization process that is life's traveling
3. transcending from the individual personality to the collective social sphere
4. considered to be at the crux of, or the critical experience of, analysis, tethered between objective and subjective and lost to the sight of both.

In Freudian technique, the transference is fought off by the doctor, sometimes at the expense of the doctor's mental health.

The transference can occur beyond the perimeters of therapy or analysis *and is considered to be a frequent natural experience*, according to Freud!

He claimed that where any relationship involving even a small amount of intimacy exists, the transference will occur to some extent, virtually all the time!

Edgar Cayce said that love had a great deal to do with his description of the natural phenomena.

Some have written and termed the transference to be a neurosis. Freud said that the aspect of relationship between neurosis and transference *is not* one of the transference creating the neurosis, but that a previously existing neurosis is merely combined with the new phenomenon of the transference.

Dr. Freud placed enormous importance on the transference and evidenced it on occasion of his first meeting with Dr. Jung in 1907. During this meeting he told Jung that it was the alpha and the omega associated with the process of analysis and considered it the most important aspect. Jung's concurrence with him enhanced their initial encounter.

Freud recognized that spontaneity exists in the transference as well as progressive development, and the word love, that Cayce used as well, can play a part in the aspect of occurrence.

A firmly stated precept to encountering this natural occurrence can be centered to high activity in two areas. First, and probably to Freud's delight, the erotic and the sexual are manifest in their feeling and knowing to experience of each to the other.

A person can know and feel, and in the eye of the mind or separation of somnambulic state, see the activity of another person. Time and distance mean nothing to the binding of the inner person to the subconscious of another.

The feelings are open moments of being with, or being part of, the other person. The flames of another's passions become the flames of your own, and becoming one flesh becomes a known reality to the person experiencing the transference. The erotic moments are as real as holding one close and as real as being the other person. The other person's physical and emotional feelings are felt by the person enveloped in the throes of love's embrace, by the grasp of the inner person.

To this knowing can be added the joy of sharing with one close, or the hurt of knowing the distance between and the direction of affection. It is a dangerous ground to tread, and in ways spotted with dread.

The other centered area is pronounced to power and will. Surging efforts of control or influence can manifest themselves and struggle within to the influence of another's intensities to life's struggle and can be known and be part of the conscious awareness to the unconscious.

The struggles that can ensue between the two, the sexual and erotic, and the power and the will, can become a paralyzing conflict that overwhelms the strength of the conscious and fatigues life's path.

This living event, this transference of being, one to another, was considered by Dr. Jung to be instinctive in part. He stated it is almost impossible to differentiate between that which is spiritual and that which is instinctive, and I would like someone to explain to me how he thinks he knows the difference, if there is one!

When the transference seats itself between two people, be it doctor and patient, passioned lovers, or those enveloped in life's intensities of power and will, the relationship becomes locked and the foundation seats itself in the unconscious mutual conjunction of the participants or victims of this mystery in life's travel.

Dr. Jung knew of cases where the doctor assimilated evident conditions of mental illness for short periods of time while being involved with such people as had lost the firmity of what we call sane. During these episodes, the doctor would feel distressed and the patient would feel better.

This transfer of being and strength from one to the other was the fate of Frau Frederica Hauffe, if you recall. Remember that it was revealed that a person who is a sensitive somnambul flees from such people who are disturbed or afflicted with terrible illness in self-defense to his own well being.

These things are not secrets to the well read and well informed in society and in the medical profession, but they are too much denied by objective smoke screens of unnecessary prejudice.

To be a psychiatrist is to be in many ways a courageous person. The personal risks to travail are a matter of statistical reality. I once read, while sitting in the waiting room of a doctor's office, a medical journal that had made an analysis of white collar professions. They studied the incidence of divorce, alcoholism, mental illness, and suicide. The compiled data showed overwhelmingly that psychiatrists were massively ahead percentage-wise to the group in all four categories.

Our society is listening to a professional segment of the medical profession in courtrooms and law enforcement investigations, in domestically travailed settings, and in communities where mental health care is a sincere area of concern; that is a concern in itself. Objectivity is a state of mind and subjective denials distort and manipulate all too easily the lives of real people. If you have ever seen a picture or a painting of a psychiatrist's office with the doctor sitting behind the patient who is stretched out on the infamous couch, then you have seen the effort of the doctor to, by seating himself in such manner, fend off the establishment of the transference. Eye contact and personal closeness was avoided intensely. I am speaking here of reality. These things are not turned on and off like a television. One can't just throw the switch and go to bed to avoid this reality—this hidden reality!

Were it not hidden, the statistics might possibly be different, and a doctor like Jung might not feel obligated to concealment of reality to his or her grave.

Freud and Jung disagreed on the basis of the transference. Freud considered it to be personal—one on one. Jung considered it collective or archetypal. From all of these pages of thought and revealing, do you not think it is of both? I do.

Dr. Jung brought forth further thought that at the onset and during the presence of the transference, both parties are led to, through alteration of psychological stature, direct confrontation with demoniac forces that he claimed to be continually lurking.

Dr. Jung also revealed that dreams always were had in conjunction with or preceding the transference. This would seem to evidence a definite effort by the total of a person to be not only involved with itself but also with the total of the person with whom this linking is occurring. Linking is a better word than transference.

In this linking, a person can endure intense suffering at its presence, but illness is not a necessary development from the experience. It is just suffering, and in this thinking of Dr. Jung, one sees, coinciding with Dr. Freud, the belief that the transference is not in and of itself a neurosis, but rather its own mysterious self.

Jung's revealings further relate to us that the anima and animus of a man and woman can be involved in their own little mischief within us. They, too, can transfer one to the other; and if enough intensity occurs or if the conscious does not recognize and control the event and influences, then the traits of the other's anima or animus, male or female being, can be taken on by the person. The word disaster can easily become associated with this, for if you'll recall, the intent and impetus of activity of the anima and animus is identified as being directly trying to take over a person's being.

Further to such activities as should be considered of a psychic nature, Jung observed that in circumstances where an increase in psychic activity manifests itself, a loss of conscious energy or initiative can occur that is associated with an ability to, on a psychic level, be everywhere. Recall that time and distance mean nothing to the psyche, only to the conscious and physical is it associated. In primitive peoples this loss of conscious and physical energy was given a name. To name something, one would think it to be recognized in reality, or fantasy, or imagination. They called it "loss of the soul." The phenomenon is recognized as occurring in civilized man as well and involves an increase in psychic potency and a decrease in conscious potency. As this occurs it is not necessarily known on a conscious level, and a duality can exist that is troubling and exciting. Troubling in that this lowering of energy can precede psychosis and exciting in that it can also precede the bringing forth of creative work.

As I stated, Jung himself experienced the transference many times over, and he did share occasions with us.

One such event occurred when he was treating a woman patient who was deeply psychotic. Her transference to him was quite strong and from it, while not in her presence, her voice was manifested within his conscious awareness just as though she were present with him.

This can definitely occur within a person, and the awareness of the voice to the receiving person is recognized in personage and in clarity. The voice is not heard in the ears; it is heard in the conscious, just as Jung related. It can be a projection of another person's thoughts while in his presence that emanates from his direction, or it can be a sudden filling of the head with the person's voice that instantly occurs without direction. It happens in the person's voice that is being heard. It is not heard in the voice of the hearing person and is thus recognizable. Immediate presence is not necessary, as time and distance are not blockages to such activity. The occurrence is easily recognized by the receiving person as being of a nature different than normal voice-to-ear communication.

Dr. Jung related a very poignant example of the transference in relation to the collective unconscious in his *Memories, Dreams, and Reflections.* He tells of an evening in which he had given a lecture, and throughout that evening, his feelings were of an uneasy nature and somewhat nervous. These feelings were contrary to his normal ones.

After the lecture, he returned to his hotel at close to midnight; but before retiring for the evening, he sat and talked with some friends. When he did retire, he did not fall asleep until about 2:00 a.m.

Awaking with a start, he felt that someone had entered his room but saw no one, and even got out of bed and checked to see if someone was in the hall. He felt sure that someone's presence had existed.

Attempting to recall exactly what had happened brought recollection that he had been awakened by a dull pain felt in the front of his head, and then to the back of his skull, also.

Hidden Shadows

A telegram arrived the next day telling him that a patient he had a deep relationship with committed suicide by shooting himself in the head.

Dr. Jung considered it to be a synchronistic phenomenon connected with an archetypal situation, that in this case was death. I call it a tragedy.

The transference can be things other than this and can involve imagination and involvements of objects. It can become total nonsense; and if a person's conscious mind is not diligent to the involvement, perspective can be totally lost. Identities can transfer and reality can become a distortion. Playing with the transference is playing with fire, so to speak, and Jung did play with fire, both physically real and subjectively real.

In *Memories, Dreams, and Reflections,* he relates a story that has me intrigued. The reason for the intrigue is that the personal incident he relates possibly has combined within it involvements associated with Cayce and Hauffe, along with himself and others I've addressed, as you might choose to identify.

The story relates to Cayce in that the aspect of a universally available knowledge of the lives, and life's activities, are considered available to a person with the spiritual flexibility to gain access to them, as Cayce did or claimed to, as one chooses to believe.

The relationship to Frau Hauffe is such that in the incident he would seem to have become subject to some stage of sensitive somnambulism.

In relation to himself, he may well have fallen prey to his own transference theory.

As the incident was related, Dr. Jung had been dining in a public setting with people he was not well acquainted with, and he engaged in conversation with them. He was addressing a specific man, and during the telling of a distressing story, this man to whom Jung was speaking had a changed expression that set Jung back. The others also withdrew in silence to his actions. The dinner was almost complete to the moment that Jung realized something was wrong, and finishing, he withdrew to some distance and contemplation.

After he withdrew from the quandaried circumstance to ponder it, a person in participation by presence approached and rebuked him for that which he had done.

Jung responded by saying that he had fabricated the story he told at the dining table and was astonished to learn that, in making up a story about a nondescript person to illustrate a point, he had actually told the story of a real life involvement of the person he was directly addressing in conversation.

At the ending of the conversation with the person who rebuked him, Jung became aware that what was considered at the time a terrible indiscretion on his part, was no longer remembered as to the words he used, and the lack of recollection occurred at the ending of the telling of the story. To the remainder of his life, he could never recall them.

Contained within this real life revealing, Dr. Jung had actually experienced a duality of represented self. If you recall, Frederica Hauffe said that a person could function in a somnambulic state while fully conscious and not be consciously aware that the state existed. In this case, there seems to be a mixture of conscious and unconscious and universal unconscious all *playing* together with Jung as the perpetrator, participant, puppet.

When viewed step by step in the light of known knowledge to Para-psychological occurrence, intrigue is stealing about. Jung described what he called the "natural mind" as being a ruthless being that was absolute in its straightness. To the definition, he associated its projected nature to the number two personality of some. The story was apparently ruthless in its straightness, and he definitely knew things that he could not know.

Another story that ties Jung to Hauffe has its basis in a garden party that was part of a dream. The dream followed a course that saw Jung at the party, and while there he saw two people that were dead in attendance, along with those he knew to be living. As the evening progressed, he eventually saw his departed sister, who had been the first of the two departed that he saw, walking with a living lady well known to him.

In the dream he had concluded that the woman was marked for death. When he awoke from the dream he could not recall who the woman was, but several weeks later recalled her well to his acquaintance and the dream when he was informed that she died.

Jung had other dreams that revealed the death of someone as pending.

On one occasion, he awoke at three in the morning to arouse his wife with the travail and to verify the time. At seven in the morning he was roused to the news his wife's sister had died at 3:00 a.m.

On another occasion while riding on a train, he had an overwhelming image of a person drowning take his consciousness. When he arrived home, he found news that one of his second daughter's children had nearly drowned at exactly the time he had been taken by the image on the train.

Dr. Jung believed that the unconscious communicates things to the conscious level in an effort to help; and as some think it true, it can be in the form of second sight where action at the time will change the perceived occurrence. It can be premonitions and dreams that are either figurative or direct in revelation. Synchronistic phenomena is another term we've heard. All is a melding of two worlds that are strangely intertwined, but little understood.

Dr. Jung, like Cayce, like Hauffe, also could sense the presence of spirit beings and claimed on one occasion to feel the presence of a great many. He, like Cayce, like Hauffe, communicated with them, and in this particular instance asked of the reason for their presence. In explanation and chorus, he claimed they answered him and said they had been to Jerusalem but had not found what they were searching for.

Before you read on, contemplate that statement. Think of the biblical descriptions of New Jerusalem and who may enter and who may not. Think of those spirits of low nature that visited and plagued Frederica, think of those also that beckoned Cayce in his travel to the place of records. Contemplate, also, Dr. George Richie's experience and the scene in the barroom by the navy base, and consider that Dr. Carl Jung's name is in the *Encyclopedia Britannica*.

Dr. Jung knew the reality of Ernest Hemingway's "The Juice" and had in three evenings-time flow from him *Septem Sermones* and considered it to be a Para-psychological-natured phenomena because it happened that the presence of the ghostly group that had returned from Jerusalem vanished from his presence when he took up pen to write its entirety!

He considered that the intellect would have liked to write the experience off, as it violated the rules of physical knowledge, but recognized that rules are sometimes broken.

Dr. Jung stated that his subjective views relating to his own person were not the result of rational thinking, but rather the product of experience. He believed that anyone who deliberately strikes out to find an understanding of subjective realities will do so by viewing with a lessor consciousness the events that present themselves to the conscious. Impressions that are taken in distinct rational perspective are left to the conscious motivations and thus lost to what is termed the ancestral psyche's understanding of the present.

He believed that inner peace and contentment were dependent on a harmony of understanding and acceptance of the short-lived conditions that comprise the present conscious encounter by the past psyche, which is present and active, with the conscious person.

He believed that our unconscious is a product of past being and that it responds to present happening, but without an inner perception by the individual the circumstance of acceptance or rejection, understanding or confusion, guidance or repulsion, remain unknown to the individual, and awareness to the influence of the psyche to this objective life is not seen or known. The individual remains in a state of ignorance to the response of the psyche to his conscious activities and exposures.

The rules of life's existence were changed for him when in 1944 he broke his foot and then suffered a heart attack and then experienced visions and deliriums that he believed occurred while he walked to the edge of death's pathway.

The nurse who was in attendance to him said that he had been surrounded by a bright glow and told him she had seen it before in the presence of the dying.

The experience that he describes might well be classified as being a near-death encounter with the hereafter, or maybe better stated near after, for though the encounter encompassed distance, distance does not mean a great deal to the revelations of such encounter.

Finality of the understanding attained by him was that from such, a person can become what he termed "one self." They become a person changed in their understanding of objectivity, removed from the bindings of emotion and valuations. Objectivity exists, but it has undergone a transformation by the realization that that which is, before the experience, taken to be subjective in being and understanding has become and is objective to the reality of the real person.

A person can encounter grave difficulty once this metamorphosis has occurred. What becomes a very normal state of acceptance of subjective reality for the person freed of the bindings of "accepted normal" and "normal objectivity" becomes at the least a curiosity to the objective masses still trapped in the emotion of being, and with this it's very easy to be called crazy.

It is without question that Dr. Jung realized this and protected himself from the labels and the labelers by silence and sequestering, but it is also without question that he was right in his understanding.

Once attained, trying to walk a balanced line in life is more of a trapeze act than a high-wire delicacy. The wrong words to the wrong people in the wrong place and, presto, you will have at least one label; but label or not, you will still have Dr. Jung's understanding that subjective is objective and real!

Dr. Jung experienced several things in his visions and deliriums that might be equated to a near-death encounter:

- He experienced a weightlessness.

- He was a great distance above the earth.

- Thoughts occurred that he was approaching the revealing of understanding to unanswered questions.

- He believed he was about to encounter other people that he belonged with.

- His journey was stopped short of reaching fulfillment and he had to return.

- He considered his return a captivity.

- He was on a journey.

- Aspects of his earthly experiences and beliefs manifested themselves in his journey.

- He felt that he was being required to leave behind the attachments of this life and could take with him only his self.

- He recognized that he was on the point of departing from earth.

- He floated in space.

- When he returned, he had difficulty deciding if he would live.

This last of listed items is most significant of all, for another man's life hung in the balance of Jung's decision, that is, if you would choose to believe his story told.

For in Dr. Jung's journey above the earth in distant space (one hundred thousand miles by his calculation when he returned) he claimed that it was his doctor who influenced his return to earth. His doctor did not function in and from an earthly place but followed Jung into deep space.

He told Jung that a protest was mounted on earth to him that his departure was not right, that he had no right to die. It was actually at that moment of protest that Dr. Jung's vision ended, and he was deeply disappointed.

Jung considered that they were both in what he termed their primal form, and according to Jung, this meant that they should have to die.

Dr. Jung thought that his doctor, whom he had observed floating up to him in space from what he perceived to be Europe, was a special person.

In his coming to Dr. Jung, his floating form was enveloped by a golden chain or possibly a laurel wreath that was golden, also. Seeing this, Jung related at once from his knowledge of myth and antiquity that the doctor was a Basileus of Kos, a King of Kos. He then thought him to be an avatar representing the Basileus in his life.

Kos was a place famous in antiquity, being the temple site of Asklepios. This is considered to be the birthplace of Hypocrites.

Dr. Carl Jung returned to his objective reality knowing the objectivity of subjectivity and did not make up his mind to live for three weeks time. At the end of this three weeks, he sat up on the edge of his bed. On the same day that Dr. Jung did this, the avatar of Kos that had courageously followed him on extremity's journey took to his bed.

Dr. Jung had been impatient and angry with the doctor's nonchalance. To the urgent matter of pending death and his ignoring of Jung's statements to his being a Basilus of Kos, Jung thought that he was pretending not to know.

Jung had felt a violent resistance to the doctor upon his return. He didn't want to come back, but at the same time he was in fear for the doctor.

Somehow it was believed by Jung that if one attains the primal form that it is necessary for that person to die. The reason stated is that once attainment occurs, one becomes part of what he termed the "greater company."

With realization enveloping him, Jung came to the thought that possibly the Doctor was going to die in his place.

The doctor refused to speak with Jung about all that had occurred in his vision, and this angered the doctor who was in concern for the avatar's well being and safety.

The doctor was stubborn in his refusal to address the subject with Doctor Jung, and ultimately when Dr. Jung sat on the edge of his bed some three weeks after the vision and much ado with the Basileus, the avatar took to his bed on the same day and never rose from it again.

It was April 4, 1944. The avatar was struck with intermittent fevers and died of septicemia.

Dr. Carl Jung thought him a good doctor with aspects of genius to him.

CHAPTER 11

"FINALITY"
The Pathway to Eternity

CHAPTER 11

"FINALITY"

The Pathway to Eternity

In life's experience we walk many paths but for each of us all those paths lead to the doorway of eternity. It is because I stepped twice through that doorway that this book was written. The wonder and mystery of that event set me on the course of seeking understanding of that which lies beyond this physical existence.

The Bible describes this life as a vapor that passes all too swiftly, and I know how swiftly the truth of that statement can occur.

I'm writing this final chapter as an absolute. For me, it is—for you it is a matter of choice. My step into eternity came at a moment when I was alone. No one can confirm or deny that which follows. With that in mind, I leave it to you to accept or reject that which I'm going to share with you.

That is all this is—it is a sharing, an offering to you to consider the experience and contemplate the future.

Edgar Cayce stated that at times during his travel between this world and the world of spiritual revelation, he recognized and crossed a border, an evident separation between life and death.

In my searching, when I read that, understanding leaped from the pages.

When I read in Dr. George Richie's book the account of the open plain filled with people struggling and trapped in angry, vehement, and lustful activity, I gave to consider once again.

Encountering Dr. Jung's statements of movement and weightlessness in his journey above the earth and his feeling of fatigue and decision to live upon return, I stopped cold in understanding.

I shared with you my experience while taking pictures in front of the hospital that Edgar Cayce gave readings in connection with and mentioned the feeling of presence behind me. It was the same presence that stood hidden behind me once before, beyond the border that this chapter, "Finality," shares.

In the chapter "Rasputin," I shared the presence of four occasions of visitation to me by what I considered to be a spiritual being associated with death and presented the relationship between those visits and either death or distress. I believe the last of those visits may well be associated with my experience.

For in the same room where I had lain upon the couch and the presence moved down the hall to stand behind me, I—less than a year later—knew that I died.

Hidden Shadows

My circumstance had totally changed as divorce had completely overwhelmed me; and its ravaging tentacles that slithered into every aspect of my life, to strangle and destroy, had destroyed and were destroying a lifetime of effort and hope.

The house was up for sale, the majority of furniture and belongings had seen the gavel of the auctioneer fall in finality, and pension and income were in process of being cleaved in a cleavage of passion whose climax froze instead of flamed.

To this setting of a few remaining sticks of furniture and an odd pot or pan that occasionally clanked in sorry memory to delicacies past, I sank into a recliner in the empty room at around midday.

The siege had lifted from things physical to do. My wife was gone to another state, and our daughter stayed mostly with friends. I was alone, devastated, and in absolute and total physical and mental exhaustion. There was nothing left of me or in me. Twenty-two years of experience in life and marriage were ending, and I believe had I chosen, so would my sojourn in this life with it.

As I sank into the lonely chair that in no way supported a lazy boy, I realized that I could let down the guarded barrier that had been battered relentlessly. I sank to a release of tension and worry and reaction to the unimaginable. I let go, knowing that, at least for that moment, I could actually breathe for a moment without assault.

I did not expect or anticipate what happened at that moment of release. It was midday or so and the sun was bright, and in that brightness, I very slowly felt strange for an instant, a few seconds. Every feeling was very subtle as it occurred. Nothing was sharp or abrupt in nature. It was sort of a transition that I was aware of but almost uninvolved with. A very subtle difference in the feel of physical had occurred. There was a distinct yet disregarded transition to being without any physical sensation. There was no physical tension, no feeling of weight, and no feeling of bodily presence or containment.

Suddenly but softly, I was in a different place and though my consciousness was crystal clear, it was different. I had felt no sense of movement, I had not seen the change or travel from one place to another. I was just suddenly but rather gently somewhere else and somehow else.

All aspects of visual awareness were totally clear, as was that of mental awareness. What oddly didn't dawn on me until later was that at that moment I was seeing my person and knowing my consciousness from a place distant from the visual body that I didn't feel but was still part of. I had a duality of consciousness that was one with the other but separate.

The body that I saw was not the body that was physical. The body that I saw seemed to have no legs below about the knees but was still me and was clothed in the same clothing that I was wearing when I sank into the chair.

The aspect of duality hadn't really dawned on me yet, and everything seemed a totally normal aspect of being, but somehow from within I knew that the totally normal aspect of being was totally different.

At about that point I became aware, or was already part of the awareness, that my consciousness that was observing my changed non-physical body with my other consciousness which was together with that consciousness but separate from it, was now watching the bodily movements and knowing the aspects of thought and mental feeling that I began to experience. I was one self but somehow two separate selves.

I knew that I was myself in all aspects, but I knew I was not my physical self in any aspect. I watched as the aspect of mental discernment began to take total command of the situation in total clarity of discernment and decision. There was absolutely nothing fuzzy to the awareness of being. There was a super clarity to this as I watched and at the same time, felt and knew.

I first saw from within and without that I was on a road or path, and I saw that I was totally alone. Looking and turning, I saw that the road or path was straight and flat, stretching a great distance in one direction but not too far in another. As one is in a total environment but not always aware of the totality, I next saw that the road had a border of shoulder on each side that sort of fell just slightly away as it stretched from the road.

Mental perception of feeling next crept in; it was uneasiness, a bad feeling, and I focused direction to it. It was not uneasiness or bad feeling within me; it was from somewhere, and as I looked in the direction the road traveled a great distance, I knew the feeling was coming from that direction and thought, "What is that?"

Looking back in the other direction, now in question was what, if not where. My person on the road looked and my person to the side watched me look, and then looked and saw that the first had just seen that a border or line existed that contributed to the shortness or caused the shortness of the road in that direction and wondered, "What is that?" but seemed to know what it was; and as attention turned again to distance in the other direction, my awareness opened fully to the place that was there all along but just now was being focused to.

All this happened and I don't have any idea that might depict the time to event; and in the total duration of the experience there was no sense of time. Time did not exist and eventually in clinging to something known, I invented time by forcing the thought that time had and was passing, that time might be short and decisions should be made quickly. Time, however, was not there. Physical was not there and there was no feeling of atmosphere or breathing. Neither was there any feeling of hot or cold.

The road stretched a great distance, and in the distance toward but not to what should have been a horizon but was not, there stood what looked like a city or structure of great size, but from that direction the bad feeling came, and now with the feeling came fear to me, intense fear.

The directional feeling was very real to whatever it was, and my fear immediately took on the aspect of massive concern that insanity was to be feared.

My world here had become a world of insanity to happening, but not to my person. I still had and knew I had my sanity, but this feeling there brought massive fear that traveling in the direction of the structure and the bad feeling could bring insanity with it.

In subsequent study to near-death experiences, I have learned that taking the concerns of this life to the experience that is considered potentially death, is not uncommon.

Hidden Shadows

The revealings of psychic experience as given to us by some of those I've talked about, reveals that concern to this world can not only be carried to the spiritual side but can actually bind or hold a person to this sphere.

I took the concern of losing my sanity with me and focused to it; and as I further share with you, I believe you'll see that it is the probable reason I am here writing this, instead of there being dead, but alive.

Opening along with the perception of the distant structure was realization that the road and the border or shoulder was contained. There was what I first took to be a line of trees running parallel to the road on both sides of the road. They seemed very high, and I wondered why they did not extend back over the clearing. Looking closer, and in later realization to what I was seeing, and what my circumstance was, it became evident that only three choices were given to the moment: (1) I could just stay where I was; (2) I could return to the border; or (3) I could move toward the structure.

The road was actually contained, not tree-lined, and to describe the actual place, one can say that the road was about fifteen or twenty feet wide—that's about the length of a full-size car. The borders were about two or three feet in width and the distance to the edge of the walls was about thirty-five or forty feet from the edge of the border.

The road was flat in width and length and dark in color. It was not gravel, and the borders or shoulders were greenish or brownish in color. The area from the edge of the shoulder to the base of the wall was clear and flat but possibly slightly lower than the surface of the road. Its color was either green or brown, and one might have called it short-cut grass.

The walls extend up at about sixty degrees from the base and went at least as high as very tall trees. The sides of the walls were covered with a very thick stemmed flowering bush whose density would have prevented any attempt to climb. The wall extended to the border, but I could not tell for sure if it extended beyond. In the other direction, it was evident that it went a very long way, but the distance was great enough that the end could not be seen.

The sky above, if it was a sky, was cloudless, and the entire place on that side of the border was brightly lit.

A very deep oddity existed in this place regarding light. I did not realize it until some time after my return; but in sitting in recollection and contemplation, I realized that though the light was bright and intense, it was totally even in dispersion. There were no dark places and *no shadows*!

A biblical verse from the King James Bible reads as follows:

> Yea though I walk through the valley of the shadow of death, I will fear no evil; for thou art with me; thy rod and thy staff they comfort me.

> Psalm 23:4

A shadow cannot cast a shadow and everything associated with God is of light. There did not seem to be a source of light. It just was.

In being in this valley, I knew fear and the fear was of a terrible evil to life. I did not have God's words in mind and heart as the Bible tells one to keep. I believe that keeping that instruction in life and in death is value without price, because the price has already been paid.

Curious and wanting to go farther toward the distant city or structure, but in a growing fear that doing so was taking me to possible travail to insanity, I struggled inside, but had the thought that I would like to go there.

With that thought, it is appropriate to talk about movement, for next came a new revelation, and possibly relating from my notes is best to clarify that which I experienced.

The aspect of movement was definitely not to be associated with what I know it to be in this physical world.

Whether movement was initiated by thought or the result of thought is at question. It just seemed to happen and there was no feeling of steps whatsoever.

The only aspect of movement that was *felt* throughout the encounter was sensed just prior to realizing that I was back in the chair again when I returned.

Movement on the path or road was not ever seen from the duality of my consciousness that was outside the body on the road, but happened to realization as looking from within my consciousness on the road by seen perspective of relationship of distance to the border or line, or the aspect of movement of the head and the changing perspective to scene to attention, inside and out.

The position outside of the body from which observation was taking place by my duality of consciousness, was about at where the base of the wall was, and from that vantage point the evidence of movement of the body on the road was seen by that consciousness as a now new fixed position on the road, evident by seeing, through observation of the diminished line or border by that consciousness. The perception of observation of the border was the same within the body and without, but both were yet separate.

While moving on the path toward the distant place and looking back and forth from the border to the structure, the thought occurred in question of what to do. Movement continued but was not known at all until looking back toward the border. Perceiving that the line had grown more distant and fearing less perceptible to return, the perceptionless movement only stopped when fear and concern to return and concern to madness mounted in intensity.

There was absolutely no feeling of movement, but my mind generated for itself the presence of it, like it was supposed to be there, but it wasn't.

The knowledge of perception to place of consciousness was absolute, and the vision of person from outside was absolute. There was a duality to the consciousness that was totally unique to existence as we know it. I was outside the body, seeing and perceiving total circumstance, distant place, fear, vision of the border, seeing of the body, surroundings, knowing of mental feeling within the body from without, conscious of observation, aware of travail to decision, observing of the movement of my head, and all seemed normal and appropriate to the moment.

The aspect of movement and time, the perception of movement and time, the existence of movement and time was relative *only* to the conscious mind of what is on this side of the border or line. It seemed that the mind wanted or maybe needed to create both for reference. They had to be consciously made known from within.

It was evident that some form of the body and more than one aspect of the consciousness exist on both sides of the border, but the sensation of or perceived event of movement and passage or existence of time did not.

Movements just happened and consciousness was not limited to the perceived body on the path but could be in both places at once, *but* once the duality of consciousness combined in the body on the path, the duality of thought or perception ended and all was one.

When the combining occurred, all was seen and felt within, *but* feeling was *not* bodily but mentally, and the aspect of being in the body was not confining in and of itself.

The speed of movement was immeasurable to normal perception. It was almost instantaneous when placed in perspective to our normal movement.

Edgar Cayce was able to travel in spiritual being to make contact with the physical and spiritual being of another person in almost instantaneous movement. His movement was not limited by distance. If he knew the location of the person to be in Europe, he had merely to travel to the exact place to seek and find the body. It was virtually instantaneous.

Andrew Jackson Davis, when diagnosing a person, would travel to and fro in the same instantaneous manner between his body and the body of the subject. He could not relate from a spiritual form to the physical form as Cayce did, but rather had to make a move to the physical body to, while in a magnetized state, speak in physical manner of the person's ailments. This occurred with about every sentence.

Later in life, he seemed to develop to being both sensitive and intuitive in somnambulism and developed to the use of, or experience of, psychometry—The touching of a person to know the person.

With the awareness and instant apprehension that I had because of the distancing from the border, I thought I should stop and did. I became deeply afraid that the border would disappear, and I would have no choice but to stay, and kept looking from one place to the other in haste.

I kept thinking, "If I go to that place, will I become insane?" and then, "If I go there and become insane, will I have to stay there and be insane, or will I have to go back to the other side and be insane there?" The fear in me was mounting, and the emanating bad feelings from the distance were as intense as ever. There had been no change, no explanation, and no way to make a determination, nothing. I had total choice. My mind was incredibly clear, and I was in a state of absolute intensity.

The awareness at this point of the expenditure of energy in this mental struggle became a background to the main events, and it is very important to describe because when I returned, I was changed.

Relating this so very important aspect of this happening, I think, can be best conveyed by sharing the notes that I made following the event by some several months. I wrote them in a fashion that I could easily relate to and recall and relate to others. They are not written as an entertainment or frivolity. That which followed my return regarding energy was neither.

Energy:

Energy is a key word, but the word does not come close to the description of expenditure of energy during the happening or afterward (and very nearly to date).

I was aware that the usage of energy within me was at a tremendous level, but there was no lack of it. It was a superficially knowing that a floodgate was wide open and being used to the drop, but yet there was no feeling of the level lowering.

I think an analogy could be framed around our favorite star ship, if one would picture our favorite captain on the bridge, with the ship at warp seven racing to a rendezvous to and with the unknown, and the captain calling the chief engineer and asking, "How long can you maintain power?" With him replying in his serious contemplative voice, "The warp drive is holding, sir, but the dilithium crystals could begin to overload at any time. All that'll be left will be impulse power if we lose the warp drive."

That's what existed; the energy flow was constant, intense, but expected and secondary to the mission, to the happening. The aspect of the energy running out was not thought, but the knowledge that it was being used was an undercurrent to what was happening.

Once back in the chair and when full awareness came to be again, only the impulse power remained. (From then until just recently, it's pulsing was not very much.)

What I would term normal energy availability has been felt on only the briefest of occasions and then for only an hour or two, and then gone. I feel like the crystals melted, like the mission was aborted and like I'm in the neutral zone trying to figure out what was supposed to happen, what did happen, how to fix the ship, or if to try to fix the ship, and hoping the enemy doesn't attack in force.

Such were the notes I made, and for over two years that which is described dominated my person, and then physical illness made it worse, or possibly offered some explanation for its lingering so long after its *instant appearance* when I gained awareness that I was back in the chair.

When the perception of movement and distancing to the border became mentally evident, and a moment of decision seemed imminent, I suddenly but gently, and with some very small awareness of instant travel, found that my duality of consciousness had combined with itself on the road. That which had been two in being one became one, and with it awareness of the event became more background to what was happening.

I did not feel any entry to the body; I was just there and one, in an environment of the absolute that silence is. There were no sounds of any nature in this place.

Awareness that the fear was very real was paramount to everything now, and knowing that no one knows what insanity really is, but knowing that it is all too real, hastened decision to return.

It was very clear that choice existed, but answers to a background of mental questions of circumstance did not. Everything was decision from perception, and perception was totally clear.

Being in total awareness that I was not insane and absolute in resolve that I did not want to be so, I decided the chance was too great. In an environment where there was no sound coming from anywhere, apprehension focused to the thought of not being able to return to the border, and that not doing so quickly could bring a loss of ability to do so. As decisions were made, the fear did not lessen.

My curiosity to the structure in the distance had not lessened, but the road was not of yellow bricks. Though the man on the road had succumbed to being made of straw, and his heart had been broken and courage was waning in this world, his perception noted very clearly this new reality.

The structure itself was not foreboding in any way. It was merely the feeling from that direction that was so. In appearance it was light in color and irregular to what could be called a horizon, but the distance to the horizon was about two thirds of that which is normal to perception; and the structure, which looking closely now might be termed the outline of a city, was not all the way to the horizon. It was about three quarters of that distance.

It was an off-white color that tended toward aging ivory or a very light cream, and in description to outline it appeared to be something similar to a grouping of inverted laboratory glass test tubes. They were of varying heights and setting close together as though, all combined, they were attached and made one structure. The feeling was such that one thought it to be a homogenous environment within, yet with a separation to each tube, and it was definitely thought that the place which was within was somehow its own place. There was no preception of windows or doors and no movement evident.

The thought in curiosity that existed when attention had intently focused while in duality of consciousness was still the same, "What is that place?"

In the other direction, the border was of great concern to fear of its disappearance. In appearance, it had no form to it, no solidity whatsoever. There was awareness that it was straight and absolute. There was no fence or wall or curtain or mist. No change in the appearance of the atmosphere was evident, if there was an atmosphere, from one side to the other.

The confining walls extended to this division between worlds, but I don't know that they extended beyond.

I was distinctly aware that a difference existed on the other side, this side. I knew that the other side was this physical world; somehow I knew that.

There were no objects to be seen on the distant side of the border. The ground was a continuance of the same flat surface with the same road or path, but I can't say for sure that the walls extended to the far side of the border.

The colors were different. They were less vivid, not as nice, and there was a haze or cloud that was like a wall of fog that ran parallel to the border but about forty or fifty yards beyond it. I can't say how high it was but it was at least as high as the walls on the other side.

The road definitely ran in a straight line from the distant structure to the border, to the grayish cloud.

I was standing in a sensory void where sight and mental emotion were the only offerings to decision's input, no heat, no cold, smell, taste, sound, or physical feeling aided the moment.

The Return:

The return from where I was to wherever this place is presents another aspect of this encounter with the unknown. It combines both places to awareness and thus differentiates best between both.

The thought or, better put, decision to go back, "I better go back, I better not take the chance, the risk is too great!!" triggered the end of perception of being on the road.

I was looking at the border at that moment and was going to initiate conscious effort to movement in that direction. I was very scared but confident that I could yet return. No movement was felt and everything went blank, but I knew I was returning.

There was no awareness of crossing the border or anything else.

Just prior to becoming aware of being in the physical body in the chair, I felt a very slight but very distinct, slightly physical sensation of movement, and I knew that it was towards the body. I couldn't see anything and I felt no entry to the body.

After re-entering the body I recall sort of very slowly coming to a state of consciousness. It was like nothing I have ever experienced. The awakening was physical and mental and sensory. It was a sort of slow dawning that reached just barely a state of understanding to where I was, but no thought to where I'd been.

I immediately drifted back into sort of a stupor, and I felt tired or drained, and I remained drained and dazed for an extended period of time. I don't know how long it was before I regained mental intentions.

I do know it was daylight when it began, and it was daylight when I became attentively aware again. I felt weakened inside, not just tired, weakened both physically and mentally. Drive, ambition, desire, goals, concern to events past and present lessened. Some curiosity as to what had happened grew within me, but not sharp. I just sort of wondered about what had and was happening.

I was on impulse power in the neutral zone! The crystals *had melted*, the mission had been aborted, and I was beginning to wonder what was supposed to happen, wonder what did happen, and wonder what had happened to the ship. I knew the ship was broken, but I didn't know how to fix it or if to try to fix it, and I was hoping the enemy wouldn't attack in force!!

I was on impulse power in the neutral zone!!??

The Remains:

I had written aftermath and thought it too stark, so I decided on remains because for two years that's all I could make claim to from a life of continuous striving. Remains is vividly correct in description to my person and my material life.

Gauging the depth of destruction and change within me was impossible. Dr. Carl Jung spent three weeks deciding if he wanted to, or was to, live following his experience that neared death. I spent two years wondering, wandering, analyzing, and experiencing in mind, the abyss and the revelation that had befallen me.

My energy level remained in its ravaged condition for that time and then became worse as physical illness struck its unwieldy hand into matters as well.

Mentally I became a different person. My values changed and concerns to material things diminished to a subsistence level. Most of this I took to be from dealing with the divorce, but there is something deeper to it as well.

I became, in part, a subjective person rather than a fully focused materialist American. Normal life became enhanced and plagued by a massively expanded perception of the interactive conglomeration of spirit and flesh.

Were it just my spirit, then dealing with myself, within myself, would have been a matter of separation by adherence to the normal requiem of work and scheduled behavior, just as Dr. Jung did during the time following his withdrawal from the university to subjective encounter and experiment.

This, however, was not the case. The case is that revelation to the intensity of knowing and feeling and interacting with the spirits of other people became ordinary to life. The intensity now has lessened, but it still exists and is still vividly real.

At the inception of this definite change in person to now what I believe to be the "one self" that Dr. Jung identifies in his writings, I was puzzled by the vivid realities of subjective interaction to "normal" life, and I began to seek answers.

Most all of us have awareness to the words psychic and clairvoyant and telepathic, and those were all that I had at the time. Now, four years later, I have a far greater vocabulary that I have shared with you in this book.

The amazing part of the vocabulary is that the words are not just real words; they are at times and in some ways, real experiences.

My number two personality was at times loud, authoritative, and assertive, and it had surfaced many times in many public places; and when in the depths of this spiritual wonder, sometimes I would rather it not. I knew its presence before, but did not have a "label." I now recognize my whole self, and harmony has evolved.

The medically hidden terminology of the transference holds tight not only to Jung and Freud, but also to Edgar Cayce's insertion of love.

For I fell deeply in love during this time and eventually came to fear the medical professions professing that the transference can be permanent. A permanent state of knowing at times the depths of another person, and other persons, is a wonder to itself.

I've found that knowing one person—myself—is enough to cope with. The adding of knowing the thoughts, physical feelings, activities, and depths of emotion of others can be almost oppressive. Some form of collective unconscious does exist and is more a part of our lives than we perceive.

What Drs. Jung and Freud identified is all too real, and fearing is all too appropriate. They are correct in knowing that this unexplainable phenomena in objective terms is to be feared.

In reading Dr. Justinus Kerner's accounts of Frau Hauffe, I found explanation and understanding not only to the recent encounters with myself, but importantly to a lifetime of living the sensitive somnambulism that she said most or all live, but don't recognize it. I now recognize it and suspect that you will, in yourselves, recognize aspects of it as well. Do you ever stare blindly, with your mind in what seems to be detachment from your physical body and surroundings?

We seem to be living in a information void regarding the spiritual person that we all are and coming to understanding is possibly good and bad. The Bible warns us deeply to not learn or practice the black arts that may well be touched on within these pages. I know now from both study and experience that there are circumstances and "things, living spiritual things," to be feared.

In this journey to some small understanding, I have learned that there is virtually no defense against the onslaught of spiritual encounter that can come upon a person and not all is good. Without the acceptance and presence of Christ, I fully believe that a person can be totally overwhelmed by that which is not seen in physical terms. Christ is the only one who overcame this physical and spiritual world, and those in knowledge in the medical profession and others who have studied to some depth the available documentation, know full well that spirit is real and acting with and on us.

Edgar Cayce and Frau Hauffe present a paradox of sorts. I believe Edgar was protected to his request to address a specific aspect of life through spiritual awareness. Frau Hauffe on the other hand seemed to be wide open in personal acceptance to encounters of multiple natures, and with it she suffered tremendously.

Cayce told us that, when one ventures into spiritual avenues of thought and activity, the objective aspects of life will have a strangeness as a person returns to them, and vice versa, if a person is exposed to spiritual depth from an objective base, the spiritual will seem strange.

I can say that such is totally true to my experience and that maintaining a balance to life's effort required a disciplined application of conscious thought.

I could write a book as large as this with no difficulty that would present the experiences that concentrated to the two years that followed my journey from and to the easy chair in the living room. That, however, is not the purpose of this effort, and my relating personal experiences through this effort is merely a sharing with you of that which became real to my life.

In ending this chapter, I think it appropriate to relate possibly the most important part of the experience on the road.

That lies hidden in feeling, a subtle feeling. It was one that I didn't really recognize until sometime later, at least not to acceptance that it was real.

The feeling now relates to two distinct events in my life. Both are totally clear to me in their reality.

While on the road in duality of being as the events were unfolding, I thought myself alone. I saw no one else in the entire event. There was, however, a slight strangeness to the feeling of being the being that was to the side of the road watching my body and other consciousness in its quandary of perception and decision.

As a person can sometimes feel or sense the presence of another person present with them, I felt but did not acknowledge or attempt to look to such a feeling that was with me.

It was to my right and behind me, but just slightly. The presence was very close and it was evident that its attention was directed to me; and as I sit now and return in thought to the moment, I can still feel a sort of gentle, friendly companionship.

Companion is the best word. There was no feeling of forcefulness or directedness. It was a pleasant presence that ended when the consciousness combined.

In that which I described to you in the chapter that reveals a part of Edgar Cayce, I related the encounter of surprise in front of the old hospital.

The feelings were like in nature. They seemed to be on the same basic involvement as touching the presence that in both places was felt to the right and rear.

In front of the hospital, it was deliberate and stronger, but of the same nature.

To consider that we walk this path alone in life is, in my opinion, being in denial to ourselves, and for me argument or reason to the contrary by those who feel differently is their entitlement. The Bible states that the path of life is a choice, a decision placed upon another and another, and as this effort is both a sharing of person and a comparative analysis of those it touches. Hopefully, decision and perception for you has been given to influence and revelation.

THE CONCLUSION

THE CONCLUSION

In conclusion, and I'm sure you've drawn more than a few by now, I find myself in a state of person I consider equitable to that which Dr. Jung called being "one self."

It has not been a voyage in life that I care to repeat, but without it this book would never have been written, and it is not an impossibility that the existence of the book is part of the reason for the voyage. Speculation perhaps, but why not speculate and contemplate.

I would hope that, as we have now traveled this winding path through an unclear facet of life together, you have drawn some conclusions similar to mine. Naturally the possibilities to difference are relevant as well, and in any case one should wear his own face.

To write my conclusions forward or backward to illustrate point is something I'm now pondering. To write them backward, I reveal immediately my final conclusion and maybe lose you to personal depth of reaction too soon. To write them forward, I risk you following without regarding your own assent to reasons knowing, and it is not at all my purpose to impose or afflict thought upon you.

So with this quandary, maybe I'll just begin somewhere and let you sort of sort it out.

I seem to have grown to an understanding that some form of continuity and relationship exists between the very evident realm of the spirit and the surrealistic world of living life with mere glimpses of life's total. It sort of makes me feel that life is like eating from a box of raisin bran, that in fact is shredded wheat, and not recognizing that being fruit loops might really be the reality.

We may think we have our raisins evenly distributed in the bran of thought, but the evidence would seem to assert that really all we have are shreds of understanding, and with those shreds we have a society that too easily does loops with each fruit that comes along.

I don't think I had to die to figure that out, but I know it helped. Interestingly, as I finished writing that sentence, I felt a little lighter inside. I wonder why?

We each are walking our own path to destiny, and each step once taken can't be retaken; only a new step is possible. So each step you take from this moment forward will be new and influenced by what you've just read, and so will mine at having written it.

The deepest influence that has settled upon me as I ventured through this effort finds itself seated in a growing fear of God. The depth to that fear has compounded itself many times over from that which existed within me at the onset of expanding my understanding of both myself and this world we live in and on.

Learning of the plight that was Frau Hauffe's life struck me to such depth that at times I quaked a little inside in consideration of the personal tragedies that evidenced themselves in her life, and in spirits that she encountered, and those that actually sought her out. The revelations that Dr. Kerner recorded brought strong the realization that walking through this life without the protection of the recognition and acceptance of the overcoming sacrifice of Jesus Christ is not just foolhardy, it is living in denial to the frailty of our total existence and the visible finality that is wrought to physical life.

Acceptance that the physical and spiritual being are both separate yet mingled to one should quicken the awareness that we have almost none. The conception that spiritual perception can within be brought to the conscious level, and in consciousness mingle both spiritual and physical realms in continuous perceived interaction is, I believe, being "one self," a new self, wiser, deeper, and more detached from those who are not.

Detachment is another conclusion to be reached. Left in the wallowing mass of momentum that society is, the individual's needs are lost to the value of eternity and the promise that it offers.

Considering that only one man, Jesus Christ, was ever able to walk a physical path that did not deny Him the promise of the Father, and thus gave each accepting person the promise as well should stay the conscious mind to seek the truth of the unconscious world within the projecting pages of the Bible and the quickening of spirit that faith brings. That is the conclusion that I have reached. It is the reality that belief should be lived. Inner perception brings with it both revelation and danger.

Danger is an appropriate word. If looked at just in the area of Dr. Jung's transference, a person can readily become aware that what begins as legitimate inner perception can readily evolve into an unbalanced fantasy land of imagination, and when such happens, both the conscious physical being and the unconscious spiritual being become a confusion of the confusion that Frau Hauffe revealed to exist in the lower spiritual realm.

It is a dangerous path and both Dr. Sigmund Freud and Dr. Carl Jung recognized it. If they lived their lives in the midst of the physical-spiritual void of mental deficiencies and knew the reality of the danger, then we should readily know the reality of the existence, persistence, and prominence of spiritual influence, both good and bad, in our daily lives.

Another conclusion that I have come to evolves around the prescription of varying Christian doctrines that daily moments be devoted to thoughts and prayers to God. The world of the spirit is a continuous existence, and the influences within the existence are both good and bad at our level of being, with each person being under the good and bad spiritual influences as they mingle with the physical. The devotion to God, I believe, affords a protection to person in both physical and spiritual being.

Protection is a correctness of description. For to accept the revealed realities of spiritual existence is to become aware that "prison camp earth" is the cell of Satan and his fallen angelic host.

We live in the prison with them, and what we perceive to be the courtyard of that prison is really just part of the prison cell. It is a crowded place, and contact is frequent with the others housed here.

God's angelic host might be described as the guards and staffs that hold tight to the staff of life, and throughout our fleshly struggle assert influence, protection, and guidance to our physical and spiritual being. I believe that daily moments spent in inner projection to God strengthens the bond to the good beings of spirit and helps separate the other inmates to their own path to eternity with their spiritual leader, Satan.

The spiritual world does not seem to be a homogenous one, as was evidenced by Cayce and Richie. We appear to be living on this earth in a very low state of spiritual existence but do not see it within the egotism and pride of life. The sojourn to eternity that the passions of physical life represent are merely a part of the parcel of existence.

The Bible says that man perishes for lack of knowledge, and offers knowledge, and is a refuge for the seeking soul. The knowledge of inner perception and influence to the inner being is something the Bible recognizes as a desired pursuit of growth to being. There is a passage within it that says very distinctly that a man who rules his spirit is of a great price. You cannot rule your spirit without an inner perception that it exists, and to this passage one might allude in thought to Frau Hauffe's comments to the stages of sensitive somnambulic being.

Somnambulic is an inner spiritual involvement which Hauffe claimed to be normal and continuous to our daily moments, and recognition of our own conscious placement and interaction to that spiritual existence is quite possibly part of the process necessary to ruling one's spirit. Mary Craig Sinclair could be alluded to as possibly ruling her spirit. She talked of communicating with the subconscious and actually instructing it to do the bidding of the conscious mind.

The combinations of all of these things should expand the understandings we have of ourselves and help us to realize that we are not alone in this flight through life. That we are flying on instruments in a clearly clouded spiritual reality is very clear to me, and with that clarity the awareness that one's future in God's creation is both a guided and chosen place makes it important to wear one's own face, in the face of the mass of momentum that society is.

Cayce chose to reject depth of contact in the lower spiritual realm and in so doing gave us an example of ruling a part of spiritual encounter as well.

God seems to have created in us at least a semi-autonomous being that will come to him as a matter of choice. Hopefully that which I have shared with you will help you, and thus all of us, as we seem to be part of some form of collective unconscious, discern a little better your own person. I believe that if you allow its influence upon you, your choices to inner perception will guide you to a path in life that will be an enhancement to yours.

I seem to have reached the beginning, or the end, or the middle of those conclusions that I mentioned.

EPILOGUE

EPILOGUE

Rhode Island U.S. Senator Clairborne Pell, twenty million dollars, the Central Intelligence Agency, and the University of California at Davis have something in common. Also linked with them are U.S. Senators Daniel Inouye and Robert Byrd, along with a five hundred thousand dollar a year budget for a program at Fort Meade in Maryland. The names Defense Intelligence Agency and the Pentagon find themselves in the same interesting parade of responsible parties. Soviet submarine construction and tunnels in North Korea come together also in this plot of unfolding folds.

From where do these names find airing in common? From *Time Magazine's* December 11, 1995, issue, and from an article in this issue, a name is attached to the twenty million dollars of U.S. taxpayer's money. It is "Star Gate," and it is a code name for a program whose ten-year duration searched the realm of the psyche in search of knowledge that would benefit the objective efforts of our armed forces and government agencies.

The senators named are those whose support helped sustain the interest in the psychic effort. Senator Pell is thoroughly convinced that the research should continue.

An investigation conducted by the American Institute for Research, on contract by the Central Intelligence Agency, found that the Pentagon's "Star Gate" psychic predictions program achieved approximately a twenty-five percent accuracy achievement. This predictive success was, however, often permeated with large amounts of irrelevant information. Congress had commissioned the C.I.A. to take over the program and do the study. The University of California at Davis contributed as well to the study and stated that, though unpredictable as to when they will occur, predictions had proven to be correct but often was less than explicit in description.

The C.I.A. conducted its own experiment with the unknown between the years of 1972 and 1977. They spent a disclosed amount of seven hundred fifty thousand dollars on the project and found it to be of no value.

The Pentagon's efforts involved the employment of three "psychics" on a full-time basis at Fort Meade.

The military's psychic efforts included attempts to locate Soviet submarine construction sites and twenty tunnels near the demilitarized zone in North Korea. Both involvements were said to be successful. Efforts also extended to trying to locate a kidnapped U.S. Army officer in Italy.

Whether the United States Senate, or the military, or the Central Intelligence Agency are to be thought errant in their pursuits, or correct to the realities of both the subjective and objective worlds we live in, is for you to contemplate as the project is said to be ending, and you are paying for their contemplation and being careful that they don't call you crazy!

The End

PARTIAL INDEX

—A—

—B—

—E—

—F—

—G—

—H—

—I—

—J—

—K—

—L—

—M—

—N—

—O—

—P—

—R—

—S—

—T—

—U—

ABOUT THE AUTHOR AND THE BOOK

Leonard A. Sharkey is a published nonfiction author. His new work, *Hidden Shadows – An Opening to the Windows of the Mind* evidences an expansive journey into realities of life that focus to the inner person's presence in the total of life.

Over seven years of effort in researching, experiencing, and writing has produced an unparalleled presentation of revelation in human understanding that links the unseen world of our spiritual existence with the physical being of our persons' within this place we call our world.

Clamoring within us is our desire to know and understand the complexities that daily affect us. *Hidden Shadows* reveals that prominent to our continuing existence, society has continually evidenced and recorded the lives and events of well known people who have, through their living and sharing, made known the pronounced absolute link between spiritual influence to individuals and mankind's continuing advancement.

Evidenced as intertwined realities that are constantly in conscript to the spiritual nature of being; religious, medical, physical, sensual, and spiritual aspects of our presence are presented in a reader and writer harmony that allows the writer's confidence of subjects and circumstances to envelop the venturing person.

In the extensive effort to bring this work to fruition, Leonard conducted research at the Edgar Cayce Foundation in Virginia Beach, Virginia, using the largest library reference collection on the paranormal in the world, attended lectures there, and spoke directly with people involved at the foundation.

Leonard further researched material regarding Andrew Jackson Davis that was in part provided by "The Duchess County Historical Society" in Poughkeepsie, NY.

University and local libraries and the Detroit Public Library also provided materials in establishing and expanding a personal deepening basis for the work.

He also used biographical material he obtained by haunting used archival book stores in the university campus communities of Ann Arbor and Lansing, Michigan, where the University of Michigan and Michigan State Universities are seated.

He searched both secular and religious encyclopedias and aged works from eastern cultures that evidenced knowledge spanning centuries of man's existence. Coupling this with documented presentations provided a wellspring of knowledge that spills over in abundant reading and revelation about the prominence of societies, persons, and organizations.

In the work, Leonard holds nothing back in an effort to allow the readers to relate to their own inner person by relating to those prominently presented in open exposition, and a new "normal" is established by revealing that it has always been. This frees the reader to expansions in understanding that otherwise would not be possible.

Hidden Shadows

This book contains photographs, sketches, and portraits that join with and provide visual enhancement to the scenes of life that are the book.

The effort to precision and flow in the text have been held to an exactness of factual presentation that does not fail in drawing and holding the reader's interest and focus.

Leonard's experiences in life have included deep exposures to persons suffering from mental and physical illness, contact with people whose Christian ministry is focused to demonic influences, and self-pursued reading of biographical first-person materials written on the subjects of spiritual and demonic influence by bona fide doctors and priests. The depths of this brought extensive exposures to doctors and hospitals and the medical system. Also inclusive to this that has been in part a trial in life, was extensive exposure to the medical insurance systems that both provide to and leach upon society.

These exposures, activities, and sufferings accomplished infusion of maturity of perception in fashions that manifest themselves in *Hidden Shadows* from beginning to end.

From this that has been, Leonard has come to the conclusion that the term "normal" as applied to the human condition is a misnomered conception that is as varied as is the perception of what God is perceived as being and intending.

With the multitude of varied things being constant to life in influencing life's directions, important to Leonard is to consider himself accomplished in the chaos of life, experienced to understanding society, and most importantly to be continuously growing in awareness to what he considers to be the universal, but special needs to being part of the sensual creation of God's work, and fulfilling and enjoying the desires, aspirations, and passions that are a major part of life's journey to destiny's beginnings.

Leonard was born on May 21, 1946, in the state of Michigan and has lived his lifetime there in both rural and metropolitan settings of the state that is as diverse in culture, industry, tourism, recreation, education, and agriculture as exists anywhere in the United States.

In his professional life he is a published nonfiction author, having written *Split Decision*, a powerful first-person journey into the jarring realities of abortion's travail that holds truth of being as a foundation to validity.

He has produced photographic work for use in his books and being a long-term Tool and Diemaker Leader with Ford Motor Company, where he also devoted several years of fulltime effort teaching Industrial Energy Control and Power Lock-out and in presenting the hazardous chemical and substance information mandated by Congress in the "Hazardous Communication Standard" to Ford employees, now looks toward retirement.

In his personal life, Leonard is a self-motivated advocate to the public's health and safety, and an opponent of the expansion of, and continued use of, nuclear energy for global non-military power production. He has studied biblical prophesy; is a Dale Carnegie graduate; holds a private pilot's certificate; has studied customs, knowledge, and teachings of eastern cultures, focusing to the self-awareness that the sharing of male and female intimacies of mind, person, and energy are the essence and essentials that are life.

Leonard belongs to the National Geographic Society, the Michigan United Conservation Clubs, the Drummond Island Sportsman's Club, the National Rifle Association, and Boat U.S.

He helped raise two children one of whom is a stepchild; was married twenty-two years and finally divorced after the ravages of mental illness had their sway in wasting two lives, which has now for his wife become God's domain in life's inevitable, and hopefully, peace.

In writing *Hidden Shadows*, Leonard has given of himself in fashions that evidence an insight to life that has helped gain much valued inclusion in the prestigious Marquis *Who's Who* publications of:

Who's Who in the Midwest

Who's Who in Business and Finance

Who's Who in America

and

Who's Who in the World

www.ingramcontent.com/pod-product-compliance
Lightning Source LLC
Chambersburg PA
CBHW041455280526
45792CB00004B/1024

9781419669088